# COMPLETE
## *Book of*
# HERBS

### *Using Herbs to Enrich*
### *Your Garden, Home, and Health*

With the American Herb Association
and Kathi Keville, Director

Contributing Writer: Jeffrey Laign

Publications International, Ltd.

Louis Weber, C.E.O.
Publications International, Ltd.
7373 North Cicero Avenue
Lincolnwood, Illinois 60646

The American Herb Association is an educational and research organization dedicated to expanding the public's knowledge about herbs and promoting the increased use of herbs and herbal products.

**Kathi Keville** (Consultant and Contributing Writer) is the director of the American Herb Association and editor of the *American Herb Association Newsletter*. She has been a writer, consultant, and teacher in the herb industry for more than 25 years.

**Jeffrey Laign** (Contributing Writer) is a writer and editor with a special interest in herbs. An author of many books and magazine articles as a freelance writer, he has also been managing editor for Health Communications, Inc.

**Illustrations:** Virge Kask, Bev Benner, Marlene Hill-Donnelly, Sandra L.Williams

**Craft designs:** Norma Coney is a floral designer whose work has appeared in a number of books on gardening, crafts, and cosmetics. She cultivates herbs and other plants in her commercial nursery, Tanglewood Gardens.

**Crafts photography:**    Peter Dean Ross Photographs, photography
Danita Wiecek, stylist
Theresa Lesniak/Royal Model Management, model
Karen Stolzenberg, technical advisor

**Additional photography:** Sam Griffith Photography; Sacco Productions Limited.

**Additional contributions:** Carol Landa Christensen is a writer specializing in gardening topics. She has been a contributing writer for various CONSUMER GUIDE® publications, including *Herbs: A Guide to Growing, Cooking & Decorating*.

# Contents

# INTRODUCTION

Of the millions of plants that grace our world, herbs, by far, are the most useful and intriguing. For millennia, we have used herbs to flavor our foods, perfume our bodies and homes, decorate our environments, and cure our ills.

Their usefulness to human beings elevates even the most common roadside herbs to hallowed status. Take the dandelion, for instance—that ubiquitous invader of manicured lawns. How can we call this vital herb a weed when it provides us with nutritious salad greens, a delectable coffee substitute, a skin cleanser, and remedies for myriad ailments?

Herbs possess a natural grace and alluring beauty that set them apart from other decorative garden plants. Our ancient ancestors recognized the value of herbs for their survival, using them as food, medicine, and even poison. Early in the Eastern world, physicians wrote tomes on herbal remedies, some prized to this day as authoritative medical sources. Druids revered the oak and mistletoe, both rich in medicinal attributes. Later, the Greeks and Romans cultivated herbs for medicinal and culinary uses as well. Hippocrates, considered the father of Western medicine, prescribed scores of curative herbs and taught his students how to use them. In the Middle Ages, monks grew herbs in monastery gardens throughout Europe.

But knowledge of these miraculous plants has carried with it danger, too. During the Inquisition, millions of wise women and other village herbal healers were branded as witches and put to death.

Nonetheless, our fascination with herbs continued to flourish. It was the search for precious herbs and spices that led Europeans to the New World. There they found scores of new plants which they brought back with them to the courts of England, Spain, and France. By the early 18th century, herb gardens were common throughout the continent. Colonists venturing to America brought herbs and seeds with them to cultivate in their new home.

The advent of the Industrial Revolution, however, spurred an exodus of people from rural to urban areas, and herbs gradually lost their mystique as science captured the imaginations of an increasingly sophisticated populace. Urban dwellers, with limited access to gardens, began to buy their medicines and foods instead of growing and preparing them at home.

But in recent years, herbs have enjoyed a renaissance as our technology-laden culture has looked back to the benefits and charms of more natural times. Today, herb gardening and cultivation is an industry for some and a satisfying hobby for many others. As countless people are discovering, the use of herbs is as varied and intriguing as the breadth of their scents and foliage.

What exactly is an herb? No group of plants is more difficult to define. In general, an herb is a seed-producing plant that dies down at the end of the growing season and is noted for its aromatic and/or medicinal qualities. How did we decide which plants to include in this book? We chose those herbs that we judged the easiest to grow and the most useful for creating savory meals, aromatics, cosmetics, decorations, and herbal medicines.

Sooner or later, most herbal enthusiasts decide to try their hands at growing a few of their favorite herbs. We may start out with a single basil plant in a terra-cotta pot or window box. But once we start, we often find we cannot stop. That pot becomes a backyard garden, and that window box venture springboards into a lush, landscaped collection of fennel, garlic, chives, and southernwood.

Most herbs thrive with very little care. These rugged, hardy plants survive and even flourish in poor soil and with wide temperature fluctuations that would prove disastrous for other cultivated species. A large part of herbs' appeal is their ability to respond well to their surroundings without excessive care.

Herbs fit beautifully into any landscape. Ground-hugging thyme is a perfect choice for planting between cracks in a flagstone walk. Tall clumps of angelica or rue provide attractive, dramatic accents in flower borders. Nasturtium, calendula, chives, and lavender add vibrant color to a garden and make handsome decorations as well.

This book provides the basics on how to grow, propagate, harvest, and store the most popular herbs. It also includes advice on how to use herbs in your home and garden. Lists of herbs best suited for certain uses such as potted plants, potpourri ingredients, and fresh arrangements provide quick reference. The encyclopedia section features an illustration of each herb along with notes on its culture, hardiness, harvest and storage techniques, and uses.

Cooks will find that an herb garden provides a tremendous opportunity for experimenting in the kitchen. The addition of just a teaspoon or two of a particular herb can transform an ordinary recipe into a gourmet feast. A detailed chart in this book lists a variety of food categories and corresponding herbs whose flavors best complement specific dishes. Also included are recipes for appetizers, soups, sauces, entrées, vegetables, and desserts that make use of commonly grown herbs.

Whether you want to grow a few herbs in your kitchen window as a source of fresh flavoring for your meals, or you wish to design and plant an elaborate formal herb garden, you'll find here the basic information you need to get started. As you become more familiar with herbs, you'll probably find yourself increasing the amount and varieties you grow. *Complete Book of Herbs* will help you along the way.

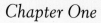 

# Chapter One

# Growing Herbs

Attila never endured a more barbaric day. Your hard drive crashed. Your boss's peptic ulcer gave everybody at work a pain. The freeway was as packed as a rock concert. And you barely have the strength to untie your shoes.

But instead of reaching for the aspirin bottle, you head for the backyard and your little piece of Eden. You spread out on your garden bench and inhale the pungent aromas of basil and fennel. You savor a sprig of mint and understand what gardeners the world over have known for ages: Nothing is quite as rewarding as growing your own herbs.

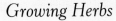
Herbs are among nature's greatest gifts. A cook's best friends. A decorator's dream. A cure for countless ills. What's more, herbs are fun to grow. And cultivating them is a lot less expensive than buying them at the supermarket or health food store.

If you're like most beginning gardeners, you may be put off by the prospect of growing these magical plants. Herbs, like children, do require care and attention. But once you understand the basics of herb gardening, you'll soon be enjoying the delectable fruits of your labor.

## How Do I Start?

Begin by asking yourself how you plan to use your herbs. Do you like to cook? Then consider growing culinary standards such as parsley, rosemary, sage, and thyme. Will you make teas? Then plant mint, which comes in scores of varieties, including lemon, orange, and pineapple, or chamomile, which makes a delicious, apple-scented brew. If you intend to put your produce to cosmetic purposes, think of aloe, a wonderful skin refresher, or calendula, one of nature's most potent topical healers. For ornamental purposes, how about lavender or nasturium? Perhaps you'd like to

*Lavender and creeping thyme provide attractive edging along a stone path.*

*Consider the topography of your garden and the presence of trees as the owners of this hillside herbal garden did. These factors will influence the amount of light and water your plants receive.*

try your hand at varied herbal crafts. Plant yarrow, hyssop, or santolina. Of course, you don't need one purpose to grow herbs—it's perfectly all right to mix and match. All you need to do is get started.

## Are Herbs Easy to Grow?

Herbs are wonderfully versatile, and many are among the plant kingdom's hardiest specimens. Although some herbs have specific gardening requirements, others—including many popular varieties—will sprout up just about anywhere. To grow herbs, you really need just three ingredients: soil, light, and water.

The key to success in growing an easy-care herb garden is to choose plants that thrive in the type of soil, water, and light available in your area. If you live in a part of the country with rich, moist soil and sunlight only part of the day, consider planting rue, sweet woodruff, peppermint, and spearmint. If your soil is dry, rocky, or sandy, grow sage, thyme, chamomile, and oregano, which

thrive in those conditions. It's possible to live just about anywhere and produce an herb garden to enrich your senses and your pantry.

Of course, you're not restricted by your environment. If your area does not have the right conditions to support a particular herb, you can manipulate the soil, water, and nutrients to accommodate its needs.

One of the simplest methods of growing herbs unsuited to your area is to plant them in containers. Another method is to fill a planting bed with the type of soil your plants require. To do this, remove the existing soil in the bed to a depth of 8 to 10 inches. Then replace the soil with a mix you've bought or prepared yourself. Because the level of your soil will be shallow, it's best to choose herbs that do not produce deep tap roots.

*Rosemary, an evergreen perennial that spreads as it grows, spills over the side of a raised bed.*

## Soil Mix Recipes

These three basic soil mixes work well for most herbs. Note that these recipes are general guidelines. You may vary them somewhat without suffering disastrous results.

### Sandy, well-drained mix
2 parts medium to coarse sand
1 part perlite
1 part potting soil or garden loam

### Average soil mix
1 part potting soil or garden loam
1 part moistened peat moss or compost
1 part sand or perlite

### Rich, moist mix
1 part potting soil or garden loam
1 part moistened peat moss or compost

Note: Do not use beach sand, which contains salt. Get sand from a sand pit or builders' supply store. Also, peat moss is acidic, so avoid using large amounts when growing plants that need an alkaline environment.

An alternative method is to construct a raised bed of the same depth. This works well if your plants require good drainage, or if the added height from a raised bed will give your herbs better visibility. You may enrich the soil of your beds by adding compost, lime, sand, or peat moss, depending on the particular needs of the herbs you choose.

Although light conditions are more difficult to control than soil conditions, you can adjust them to some extent. If you live in a sunny, hot area, look for ways to shade your plants. Perhaps you could construct a fence or simple arbor to provide a quick source of shade. For a long-term solution, plant leafy trees or hedges where you plan to grow herbs.

If you don't get enough light, thin adjacent trees and shrubs to let in more. Or plant your herbs in containers and shuttle them in and out of the sun. Most potted plants need to spend at least half a day in a sunny location; keep your containers small enough to rest on a wheeled base so you can move the herbs quickly and easily.

If you wish to grow herbs indoors, set plants under an artificial light source to ensure that they prosper. With grow lamps—available at most garden supply stores—you can augment or replace existing natural light.

Beginning herb gardeners, eager to nurture their plants, often make the mistake of watering their gardens every day. Don't do this. Under normal conditions, herbs need only about 1 inch of water a week. If your area gets very hot in the summer, if you have sandy soil, or if winds tend to dry out your garden, then you may need to water more often. But resist the urge to overwater. Not only does overwatering cause herbs to lose their flavor and fragrance, excess moisture may lead to fatal fungal diseases in plants.

Light, frequent watering also encourages plants to develop shallow roots. Thus, if it gets too hot or if you leave home to visit Aunt Betty for a few days, your poorly rooted plants may not survive. A good deep watering once a week encourages plants to sink roots deep into the ground.

How much is a good deep watering? You could buy a rain gauge and install it in your garden. But why work any harder or spend more money than you have to? Here's a simple gauge that lets you know when it's time to turn off the tap. Place an empty coffee can halfway between your sprinkler and the farthest point it reaches. Then time how long it takes for 1 inch of water to accumulate in the can. Next time you water your garden, run the hose for that amount of time.

In general, overhead watering with a hose or watering can is perfectly acceptable. This method, in fact, cools plants and washes

*This medieval knot garden, planted with lavender and green santolina, has a formal appearance.*

dirt off their leaves. If any of your herbs develop leaf spot or mildew disease, water in the morning so the plants are not wet during the night.

If you live in an area where water use is restricted, try this simple trick. For herbs that prefer moist soil, mix a quantity of organic matter, such as compost, into the planting bed, and mulch around the plants with additional organic matter. This helps your thirsty plants retain what precious water you can give them.

## Planning Your Garden

You wouldn't try to build a house without blueprints. Neither should you attempt to cultivate a garden without a plan. Once you've decided on the herbs you want to grow, take a moment to sketch a layout. You needn't be Matisse to do this. A simple sketch will do.

Herbs are often planted in formal designs, but doing so is by no means a requirement for success in growing them. Herbs may be integrated with other plantings. Many brightly colored herbs dramatically accent simple flower beds, and herbs lend flair to gardens when planted as borders. Low-spreading varieties make fine ground covers, and some herbs are excellent for creating low hedges.

The only herbs you have to watch out for are invasive ones, such as mint. These plants will take over your garden if you don't take steps to curb them. (See Invasive Herbs, page 14.) Unless you want a quick ground cover, invasive herbs are best planted in containers or in separate beds, where you can control their spread. You can even sink containers of herbs into the garden bed itself.

Containers look great on a deck or patio, too. (See Herbs Suited for Container Growth, page 16.) And pots are practical: Growing culinary herbs in containers outside your kitchen door makes for easy access when you're cooking.

If you do decide to plant a garden, you can choose from many layouts. You can plant your herbs in a formal design—a medieval knot garden perhaps—or allow them to spring up as they will for a wild, natural look. When you make your choice, you'll have a garden that is uniquely yours. And adding your "signature" to a garden design is half the satisfaction of gardening.

*Strive for contrast in color, height, and texture. Herbs with colorful flowers accent plain green varieties.*

*This herb garden is a lovely mixture of formal and informal styles. It also blends herbs of different colors, textures, and heights.*

When planning a garden that includes herbs, follow the same basic rules of design you would employ in decorating a room. Place tall plants at the rear of beds, plants of intermediate height in the middle, and low-growing plants at the front. In central beds meant to be viewed from all sides, place the tallest plants in the center, the shortest around the outer edges, and the intermediate heights between the two. That way, all your herbs will be visible, and each plant will receive an adequate share of light.

Many herbs have small inconspicuous flowers, so color and texture are your most important design factors. Strive for contrast. Herbs with silver-gray, blue-gray, or purple foliage dramatically accent plain green plants. Herbs with fine, fernlike leaves lend a soft, airy look when placed next to plants with large, rough leaves. Round-leafed nasturtium and grasslike tufts of chives provide interesting variety among more common leaf forms.

Although you'll want to take all of these factors into consideration when designing your garden, don't let yourself become over-whelmed by details. Don't fret that your design must be "perfect." Unlike building a house, it's fairly simple to change a garden layout. In many cases, you can simply dig up your plants and move them to a new location. Lay out your garden to the best of your ability—and then plant it.

## Invasive Herbs

| | |
|---|---|
| | Chives | Motherwort |
| | Comfrey | Peppermint* |
| | Costmary* | Raspberry |
| | Dandelion | Red Clover |
| | Feverfew | Shepherd's Purse |
| | Garlic Chives | Spearmint* |
| Catnip | Horseradish* | Tansy* |
| Chamomile | Lemon Balm | Yellow Dock |

*Worst offenders that require containment; others can be more easily kept in bounds by frequent removal of excess growth.

The best way to begin a garden is to make a list of the plants you'd like to grow. Then note their soil, light, and water needs; height and spread; and any special details, such as foliage, flower color, or unusual growth habits (consult the Herb Growing Chart on pages 22–24 and the individual herb profiles in Chapter 4 for this information). Make a secondary list of plants you might enjoy growing if you have room left in your garden.

Sketch the garden area to scale (for example, 1 inch on the sketch represents 1 foot on the ground), decide on the size and shape of the planting beds, and determine where in the beds you will place each plant. Once you have filled in all your favorite plant varieties, choose from your secondary list to fill any empty spots. If you have planted perennials and are waiting for them to fill in the garden, you can plant annuals in the spaces the first year or two.

Be sure to consider the natural features of your garden, including its topography and the presence of trees or shrubs. These factors influence the amount of light and water available to your herbs.

Small hills and valleys, for example, may interfere with sunlight and water runoff. Do not place delicate herbs or dry-soil plants such as rosemary in a valley where they will receive too much water; water-loving herbs, such as peppermint and spearmint, on the other hand, prosper in moist, soggy soil.

If you plant on a hill, consider the placement of taller plants in relation to smaller ones. Smaller plants will be stunted if larger ones prevent them from receiving enough sunlight.

## Classic Herb Garden Designs

Classic designs are typical of gardens favored by European aristocrats of centuries past. Formal gardens usually revolve around a structure, such as a fountain, sundial, garden seat, statue, unusual plant, or birdbath. The goal is to draw the eye to this feature. Try a brick-paved pathway leading to a simple wooden bench. Or place a sundial in the center of your garden, with paths fanning outward.

*Classic designs include an herb-laden stone path leading to a bench and an herb garden arranged around a clay vessel centerpiece. Both designs have a focal point.*

## Gardening with Raised Beds

Raised beds are a good choice if the soil in your garden is sparse or of poor quality. Lined with pressure-treated wood, reinforced concrete, or mortared brick, stone, or blocks, your raised beds may be any length, but the soil should reach a depth of at least 6 inches. For easy maintenance, lay out beds no wider than 4 feet. By filling some beds with a rich loam mixture and others with a sandy, well-drained mix, it's possible to provide the ideal soil requirements for a wide range of plants.

## Informal Herb Garden Designs

Perhaps your tastes are more eclectic. In that case, simply sow and grow. Some of the most beautiful herb gardens are random and wild, reflecting nature at its most glorious. Consider planting your backyard with a ground-covering herb such as chamomile instead of grass. Imagine running barefoot through your own fragrant field of low-growing mint. The choice, again, is yours.

## Growing Herbs Indoors

Of course, you don't need a backyard or even a patio to grow herbs. You can cultivate your garden indoors. Indoor gardens, in fact, have some advantages over outdoor gardens. Herbs in pretty containers enhance any decor and often create dramatic design effects when used as centerpieces or bookends.

What better place for culinary herbs than a kitchen countertop? Fragrant herbs in the living room or bedroom serve as wonderful potpourri. And nothing brightens a rainy day like a thriving indoor plant, providing you with a link to the great outdoors.

While herbs grown indoors may not be as vigorous as those grown in a garden, it's quite possible to produce a more-than-adequate

tabletop crop. And caring for indoor plants is not nearly as difficult as you might imagine.

To flourish, herbs prefer at least four or five hours of strong sunlight every day. If it's not possible to provide sunlight, give your herbs eight to ten hours of artificial light daily. Try to maintain a constant temperature in the room that houses your plants. Like people, herbs dislike extreme changes in temperature. Herbs also need good air circulation to minimize incidence of pests and disease. And give them plenty of space.

Your indoor herbs also need adequate drainage. Use clay or plastic pots with holes covered with pebbles or newspaper. To complement your decor, place the containers in a trough or tray of ceramic, wicker, or tin. If you plant herbs in a decorative jar that has no water holes, place a layer of gravel or pebbles on the bottom, followed by a thin layer of broken charcoal to "sweeten" the soil, or keep it clean of pests and disease. Following these procedures allows soil to drain and prevents waterlogging.

In any case, don't use soil from your yard. It may contain disease organisms and pests that could flourish in a warmer indoor envi-

## Indoor Air Circulation

Outdoors, plants are exposed to air currents. Indoor plants need air movement, too. Circulation helps to ventilate a plant's waste gases, remove excess heat, and prevent diseases that can develop in closed spaces. Often, air circulation is adequate near large windows. If your home is not well ventilated, run a small fan now and then to keep the air in motion. Under plant lights, you are creating an artificial growing situation, so you may need to run a fan continuously to mimic the outdoors. Don't direct the fan on the plants—just having it in the same room provides the needed circulation.

## Herbs Suited for Container Growth

| | | |
|---|---|---|
| | Calendula | Oregano |
| | Catnip | Nasturtium |
| | Cayenne Pepper | Parsley |
| | Chives | Peppermint |
| | Geranium, Scented | Rosemary |
| | Ginger | Rue |
| | Horsetail | Sage |
| | Lavender | Savory, Summer |
| Aloe | Lemon Balm | Spearmint |
| Basil | Marjoram | Thyme |

ronment. Instead, buy a soil mix, or make one of sterilized loam combined with sand. Compost—either purchased or made from scratch—works well, too. Many of the most common garden herbs found in this book prefer a neutral soil. A pH between 6 and 7.5 is optimum, but most will adjust from a pH of 5 to 8. (A pH of 7 is neutral. A higher number indicates alkaline soil and a lower number designates acidic soil.) Compost alone helps adjust the soil's pH. If your soil tends to be acidic, you can make it more neutral by adding lime to the soil mix or compost. To make soil more acidic, add peat moss. You can find all of these products at a nursery. Your local nursery should also have specific suggestions on how to improve the soil conditions where you live.

Most herbs do not require much in the way of fertilizer. In fact, if you feed them too much, they may look extra lush, but they can lose much of their flavor and even their medicinal properties. Your best bet is to mix compost into the ground and, if your soil is very poor, use some fish emulsion and/or seaweed to fertilize it. Perennial herbs also appreciate a fish emulsion spray at least a few times a year.

Water indoor herbs only when the top inch or so of soil has dried out. Your watering needs will vary according to the tem-perature and humidity of your room. If your house is centrally heated and kept at a fairly high temperature, you may need to water every other day.

Because indoor herbs are not as prolific as those grown out-of-doors, harvest your herbs with restraint. Pluck leaves from side shoots instead of cutting from the main stem. This encourages your herbs to produce over a longer period.

## Where Do I Get My Plants?

New plants come into being in five ways. A simple—and the least expensive—source is seeds. The best way to propagate most annuals is from seed.

The second source of new plants is rooting cuttings from perennials. Many plant stems generate their own roots if you cut them from a parent plant and insert them into a growing mixture.

A third method of getting new plants is through layering. Most perennial herbs with sprawling stems layer well. Press a stem into the ground and mound dirt over it. When a root has formed, cut the stem from the mother plant and repot it.

Another easy and inexpensive way to acquire new plants is through division. You simply pull apart the roots of a large perennial plant to create several smaller ones. Choose plants with roots that sprout from the base and have more than one stalk.

Finally, you can buy plants from a nursery or garden shop. If you're not on a budget, this is the quickest and easiest way to obtain an established herb planting. You can also purchase plants by mail order—this may be the best source for a wide variety of plants. Unless you have a friend who will share clippings from his or her plants, it may be necessary to purchase—initially at least—one plant of rosemary, oregano, lavender, and specialty varieties of thyme and other herbs. Once established, you can make cuttings or layerings from these herbs. French tarragon, horseradish, and many scented geraniums do not produce seeds, so they must be purchased or divided.

## Starting from Seed

You can start plants from seed in two ways: Sow the seeds directly in their garden bed, or start them in containers and transplant them later. How you start your seeds depends on the type of herb you wish to grow. Some herbs—especially annuals—grow quickly from seed, so they can be sown easily in their permanent locations. These include basil, calendula, chamomile, chives, and nasturtium. Other herbs don't like to be transplanted. For that reason, they, too, are easier to grow directly in beds. These include angelica, anise, borage, caraway, chervil, coriander, and dill.

Still other herbs—lavender, marjoram, rosemary, rue, and wormwood, for example—are slow starters or difficult to germinate. Thus, it is wise to start them indoors in containers and transplant them later.

Another reason to start seeds indoors is to get a jump on the planting season. Sow seeds in containers during the last few weeks of winter, then transplant the seedlings in beds after your soil is warm enough to accommodate them.

Either way, be sure to label your rows. Don't fool yourself into thinking you'll remember what's what. It's easy to forget by the time annuals come up—in about two weeks; perennials take two weeks or longer.

## Starting Plants from Cuttings

The best time to take cuttings is during the middle of the growing season, usually in late spring or early summer, before the herbs have flowered.

Fill a container with a moist rooting medium. Your cuttings will live in this medium until they develop roots. At one time, coarse sand was the standard medium for rooting cuttings. Sand still works fine, but better alternatives are now available, such as equal amounts of perlite mixed with peat moss and vermiculite. Or you can combine one part polymer soil additive (which has been expanded with water) and two parts peat moss.

With a sharp knife, cut a stem 3 to 6 inches long from the parent plant. Cut just below where the leaf attaches to the stem. Be careful not to crush the cutting. Carefully remove all leaves and shoots from the bottom one-half to two-thirds of the cutting: A tear in the stem can become a site for rot.

### Herbs Suited for Seeding

| | | |
|---|---|---|
| Angelica | Dill | Meadowsweet |
| Anise | Echinacea | Motherwort |
| Arnica | Elecampane | Mullein |
| Basil | Fennel | Nasturtium |
| Borage | Feverfew | Oats |
| Burdock | Gotu Kola | Parsley |
| Burnet | Hops | Passion Flower |
| Calendula | Horehound | Plantain |
| Caraway | Hyssop | Red Clover |
| Catnip | Lavender | Rosemary |
| Chamomile | Lemon Balm | Rue |
| Chives | Lovage | Sage |
| Coriander | Marjoram | St. John's Wort |
| Dandelion | Marshmallow | Santolina |
| | | Savory, Summer |
| | | Shepherd's Purse |
| | | Sweet Woodruff |
| | | Thyme |
| | | Wormwood |
| | | Yellow Dock |

## Herbs Suited for Cuttings

| | | |
|---|---|---|
| Butcher's Broom | Hyssop | Rosemary |
| Chaste Tree | Lavender | Rue |
| Costmary | Lemon Balm | Sage |
| Feverfew | Lemon Verbena | Tarragon |
| Geraniums, Scented | Marjoram | Thyme |
| Hops | Meadowsweet | Witch Hazel |
| Horehound | Motherwort | Wormwood |
| | Passion Flower | |

Next, if you wish, you may dip the base of the cutting into a hormone rooting powder. In most cases, this isn't necessary. But with some difficult-to-root herbs—lavender and rosemary, for example—using rooting powder is a good idea.

Try to transplant your cuttings within 15 to 20 minutes. If that's not possible, place cuttings in water and replant as soon as you can.

Poke a hole in your potting medium and insert the cuttings. Don't  crowd them or you'll inhibit air circulation, which could encourage fungal growth. Water the cuttings immediately, but don't get water on the leaves. Keep the soil damp continuously. Place the cuttings in a spot that receives a generous amount of light, but don't put them in direct sunlight.

After a week to ten days, check to see whether any roots have appeared. Do this by gently inserting a knife blade under the cutting and lifting it out. If you don't see any roots, reinsert the cutting and check it again in another week to ten days. Some plants take six or more weeks to root.

Once the roots are a quarter-inch long, plant the cutting in a small pot filled with commercial potting mix or one you've made. Water from above, and use a drip tray. Don't allow plants to stand in water for more than two hours. Keep the potted cutting out of direct sunlight for a week to avoid wilting the plant. Grow the cutting as a potted plant for a couple of months before transplanting it to the garden.

## Starting Plants Through Layering

Layering is suitable for many perennials with strong stems. Select an outer stem from the base of the plant and push it to the earth. Mound a pile of dirt on top of the stem, leaving at least 5 inches of the stem end uncovered. Pack soil tightly and water the mound well. Keep the plant well watered for several weeks. Then check for the appearance of roots. When they are well established, make a quick clean cut through the stem, using a trowel or shovel to separate the layered herb from the original plant.

## Herbs Suited for Layering

| | | |
|---|---|---|
| Catnip | Motherwort | Savory, Winter |
| Costmary | Oregano | Skullcap |
| Hyssop | Peppermint | Sweet Woodruff |
| Lavender | Rosemary | Tarragon |
| Lemon Balm | Rue | Thyme |
| Marjoram | Sage | Wormwood |
| | Santolina | |

Repot the new plant—take care not to disturb the roots. Keep the potted herb in a bright area away from direct sunlight. In a couple of months, you should notice leaves developing. Once they are well established, transplant the new plant.

## Starting Plants Through Division

Most perennial herbs may be divided successfully, except those with deep tap roots. The best time to divide plants is early to mid-spring when growth starts or in early fall, about six weeks before the first full frost.

Carefully dig up the plant. Try not to damage the root system. Keep as much dirt on the root ball as possible. Gently pull apart the roots to create two plants. If the roots are too strong to pull apart by hand, use a trowel or knife to divide them. Replant divided plants before they dry out.

If you divide herbs in the fall, cut the tops back by about one half when dividing. Treat new plants as you would seedlings. Water them immediately, then daily for about a week. If tops wilt, cover with a plastic pot or move the plants to a shady location.

## Purchasing Plants

Buy plants close to the time you want to set them in their beds or containers. If this is not possible, you may need to water the plants every day to keep them from drying out. Look for healthy plants that show no sign of insects or disease, are not too tall or spindly, and show signs of new growth. When you purchase herbs for cooking, smell the leaves. If you order plants from a mail-order supply house, water the plants as soon as they are delivered and keep them out of the sun until they revive. If your plants don't survive transplanting, the company may supply replacements.

### Herbs Suited for Division

| | | |
|---|---|---|
| Catnip | Lovage | Tansy |
| Chamomile, Roman | Marjoram | Tarragon |
| Chives | Motherwort | Thyme |
| Comfrey | Nettle | Uva Ursi |
| Costmary | Oregano | Valerian |
| Echinacea | Pennyroyal | Watercress |
| Elecampane | Peppermint | Wormwood |
| Feverfew | Rosemary | Yarrow |
| Gentian | Rue | |
| Gotu Kola | St. John's Wort | |
| Horsetail | Santolina | |
| Hyssop | Savory, Winter | |
| Lemon Balm | Spearmint | |
| Licorice | Sweet Woodruff | |

*The popularity of herb gardening means an increasing number of herbs are available for purchase.*

# Plant Hardiness Zone Map

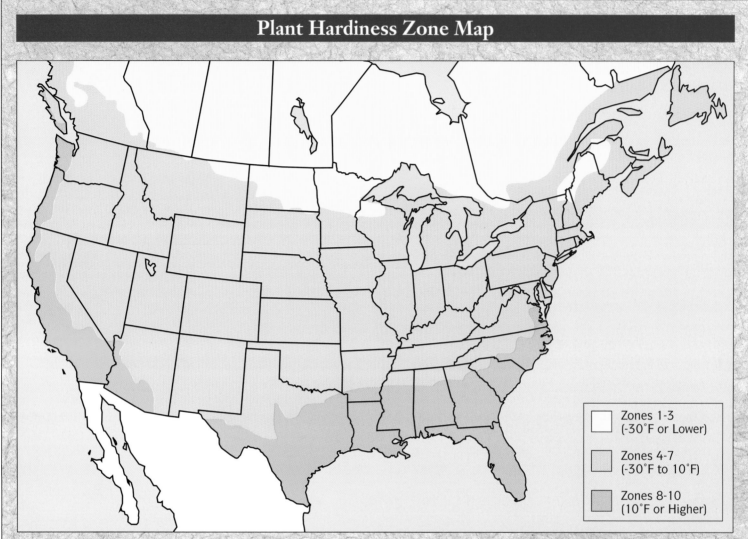

| Zones 1-3 (-30°F or Lower) |
| Zones 4-7 (-30°F to 10°F) |
| Zones 8-10 (10°F or Higher) |

*Our Hardiness Zone Map links temperatures and frost dates with regions. Based on the U.S. Department of Agriculture Plant Hardiness Zone Map, our map collapses the ten zones of the UDSA map into three large areas. Zones 1 through 3 in yellow represent the coldest areas; Zones 4 through 7 in green represent moderate temperatures; Zones 8 through 10 in orange represent the warmest zones. The USDA Plant Hardiness Zone Map is a more thorough approach to depicting temperature zones, but even that map is not perfect. Both maps offer only a guideline to temperatures and frost dates. Use this map to help you determine which plants will survive in your garden. But note that plants recommended for one zone might do well in the southern part of the adjoining colder zone as well as in the neighboring warmer zone. Factors such as altitude, exposure to wind, and amount of available sunlight also contribute to a plant's winter hardiness. Also, the indicated temperature are average minimums--some winters will be colder, others warmer. See page 21 for a list of herbs and the zones they can tolerate.*

# Hardiness Zones

Plant hardiness zones reflect the average annual winter temperatures a plant is able to endure. Bear in mind that the zones, determined by the U.S. Department of Agriculture, are general, not specific. Zone 6, for example, runs from Maine to Nevada. Even if a plant is not considered suitable for your area, try growing it anyway. Perhaps you can manipulate conditions to increase your chances of success. Zones are not listed for annuals since they grow in the summer months.

| Herb | Zone | Herb | Zone | Herb | Zone |
|---|---|---|---|---|---|
| Aloe | 10 | Feverfew | 5 | Nettle | 2 |
| Angelica | 3–4 | Garlic | 3 | Oats | Annual |
| Anise | 3 | Gentian | 3 | Oregon Grape | 3 |
| Arnica | 6 | Geranium, Scented | 10 | Parsley | 9 |
| Basil | Annual | Ginger | 9 | Passion Flower | 7 |
| Bilberry | 5 | Ginkgo | 5 | Peppermint | 3 |
| Black Cohosh | 3 | Ginseng | 9–10 | Plantain | 3 |
| Blue Cohosh | 3 | Goldenseal | 4–5 | Raspberry | 6 |
| Borage | Annual | Gotu Kola | 10 | Red Clover | 3 |
| Burdock | 3 | Hawthorn | 4 | Rosemary | 6 |
| Burnet | 3 | Hops | 5 | Rue | 4–5 |
| Butcher's Broom | 3 | Horehound | 4 | Sage | 4–5 |
| Calendula | 7 | Horseradish | 4 | St. John's Wort | 3 |
| Caraway | 3–4 | Horsetail | 2 | Santolina | 6 |
| Catnip | 3–4 | Hydrangea | 5 | Savory, Summer | Annual |
| Cayenne Pepper | 10 | Hyssop | 3–4 | Saw Palmetto | 10 |
| Chamomile | Annual | Juniper | 1 | Shiitake Mushroom | Annual |
| Chaste Tree | 6 | Lavender | 5 | Shepherd's Purse | 3 |
| Chives | 3 | Lemon Balm | 5 | Skullcap | 4–5 |
| Comfrey | 3 | Licorice | 9 | Slippery Elm | 5 |
| Coriander | Annual | Lovage | 5 | Sweet Woodruff | 3 |
| Costmary | 4 | Marjoram | 9–10 | Tarragon, French | 4 |
| Cramp Bark | 3 | Meadowsweet | 2–3 | Thyme | 5–9 |
| Dandelion | 3 | Marshmallow | 5 | Uva Ursi | 1 |
| Dill | Annual | Milk Thistle | 4 | Valerian | 4 |
| Echinacea | 3 | Motherwort | 3 | Willow | 1 |
| Elderberry | 5 | Mullein | 3 | Witch Hazel | 3 |
| Elecampane | 3 | Mustard | Annual | Wormwood | 4 |
| Evening Primrose | 4 | Nasturtium | 9 | Yarrow | 2 |
| Fennel | 6 | | | Yellow Dock | 3 |

## Herb Growing Chart

| Name | Plant | Light | Soil | Height | Spread | Culture |
|---|---|---|---|---|---|---|
| Aloe | P | PS,S | A | 1–5 ft. | 1–3 ft. | E |
| Angelica | B | FS,PS | A,M | 5–6 ft. | 3 ft. | E |
| Anise | A | FS | A | 1½–2 ft. | 8 in. | M |
| Arnica | P | FS | S | 1–2 ft. | 10 in. | M |
| Astragalus | P | FS | A | 4 ft. | 1½ ft. | M |
| Basil | A | FS | R,M | 1½ ft. | 10 in. | E |
| Bilberry | P | FS,PS | A–S | 1–2 ft. | 3–4 ft. | M |
| Black Cohosh | P | S | R,M,H | 3–6 ft. | 2 ft. | M |
| Blue Cohosh | P | S | R,M,H | 1–3 ft. | 1½ ft. | M |
| Borage | A,B | FS | P–A | 2–2½ ft. | 1½ ft. | E |
| Burdock | B | FS | A | to 6 ft. | to 3 ft. | E |
| Burnet | P | FS | A | 1½ ft. | 1 ft. | E |
| Butcher's Broom | P | FS | A | 4 ft. | to 3 ft. | E |
| Calendula | A | FS | A–R | 1–2 ft. | 1 ft. | E |
| Caraway | B | FS | A | 2 ft. | 8 in. | M |
| Catnip | P | FS,PS | A–S | 3–4 ft. | 2 ft. | E,R |
| Cayenne Pepper | P | FS | R | 1–3 ft. | 1 ft. | E |
| Chamomile | A | FS | A–P | 2 ft. | 4–6 in. | M,R |
| Chaste Tree | P | FS | A–S | to 20 ft. | 6 ft. | E |
| Chives | P | FS,PS | A–R | 8–12 in. | 8 in. | E,R |
| Comfrey | P | FS,PS | A–R,M | 3 ft. | 1 ft. | E,R |
| Coriander | A | FS | A | 2–3 ft. | 6 in. | E |
| Costmary | P | FS,PS | A | 2½–3 ft. | 2 ft. | E,R |
| Cramp Bark | P | FS | A–R,M | to 13 ft. | 6 ft. | M |
| Dandelion | P | FS,PS | P–A | 6–12 in. | 1 ft. | E,R |
| Dill | A | FS | A–S,M | 2–3 ft. | 6–12 in. | E |
| Echinacea | P | FS,PS | A | to 4 ft. | 2 ft. | E |
| Elderberry | P | FS,PS | A–R,M | 12–50 ft. | to 20 ft. | E |
| Elecampane | P | FS,PS | A–R,M | 4–6 ft. | 2 ft. | E |
| Evening Primrose | B | FS | A–R | 3–6 ft. | 1½ ft. | E |

**KEY:**

**PLANT:** A = Annual  B = Biennial  P = Perennial

**LIGHT:** FS = Full Sun  PS = Partial Shade  S = Shade

**SOIL:** P = Poor  A = Average  H = Humusy  R = Rich  S = Sandy  M = Moist

**CULTURE:** E = Easy to Grow  M = Moderate  D = Difficult  R = Rampant grower; keep restricted

## Herb Growing Chart

| Name | Plant | Light | Soil | Height | Spread | Culture |
|------|-------|-------|------|--------|--------|---------|
| Fennel | P | FS,PS | A–R | 4–7 ft. | 3 ft. | E |
| Feverfew | P | FS,PS | A | to 2 ft. | 1–2 ft. | E,R |
| Garlic | P,B | FS | R | to 2 ft. | 6 in. | E |
| Gentian | P | PS | A–R,M | to 3 ft. | 1 ft. | M |
| Geranium, Scented | P | S | A–R | 2 ft. | 1 ft. | M |
| Ginger | P | FS,PS | R,M | 1–4 ft. | 1½ ft. | E |
| Ginkgo | P | FS,PS | A | to 100 ft. | to 20 ft. | E |
| Ginseng | P | S | R,H | 1½ ft. | to 1 ft. | D |
| Goldenseal | P | S | R,H | 1 ft. | 1 ft. | D |
| Gotu Kola | P | PS | A–R,M | 6 in. | 6 in. | M |
| Hawthorn | P | FS | A–R | to 25 ft. | to 10 ft. | E |
| Hops | P | FS | A–R,H | 20–40 ft. | vine | E |
| Horehound | P | FS | P,S | 1–2 ft. | 8–12 in. | E |
| Horseradish | P | FS | A | 4–5 ft. | 2 ft. | E,R |
| Horsetail | P | PS | H,M | to 1½ ft. | 6 in. | E |
| Hydrangea | P | FS,PS | R,M | to 9 ft. | to 6 ft. | E |
| Hyssop | P | FS | A–S | 1½–2 ft. | 1 ft. | E |
| Juniper | P | FS | A | 2–20 ft. | from 4 ft. | E |
| Lavender | P | FS | S–A | 2–4 ft. | 2–3 ft. | E |
| Lemon Balm | P | FS,PS | A–S,M | 3 ft. | 1–2 ft. | E,R |
| Licorice | P | FS,PS | S,M | to 3 ft. | 2 ft. | M |
| Lovage | P | FS,PS | R,M | 4–6 ft. | 2 ft. | E |
| Marjoram | P | FS | A–S | 1 ft. | 8 in. | E |
| Meadowsweet | P | PS | A–R,M | to 6 ft. | 2 ft. | E |
| Marshmallow | P | FS,PS | A–R,M | 4 ft. | 2 ft. | E |
| Milk Thistle | A or B | FS | P–A | to 3 ft. | to 3 ft. | E |
| Motherwort | P | FS | A | 4 ft. | 1 ft. | E,R |
| Mullein | B | FS | P | to 7 ft. | 2–3 ft. | E |
| Mustard | A | FS | P–A | to 2 ft. | 1 ft. | E |
| Nasturtium | A | FS,PS | A,M | 1 ft., bush; 5–10 ft., vines | 1½ ft., bush | E |

**KEY:**

| | | | | |
|---|---|---|---|---|
| **PLANT:** | **A** = Annual | **B** = Biennial | **P** = Perennial | |
| **LIGHT:** | **FS** = Full Sun | **PS** = Partial Shade | **S** = Shade | |
| **SOIL:** | **P** = Poor | **A** = Average | **H** = Humusy | **R** = Rich   **S** = Sandy   **M** = Moist |
| **CULTURE:** | **E** = Easy to Grow | **M** = Moderate | **D** = Difficult | **R** = Rampant grower; keep restricted |

## Herb Growing Chart

| Name | Plant | Light | Soil | Height | Spread | Culture |
|------|-------|-------|------|--------|--------|---------|
| Nettle | P | FS,PS | A–R,M | 3–6 ft. | 1–2 ft. | E |
| Oats | A | FS | P–A | 2–4 ft. | 1 in. | E |
| Oregon Grape | P | FS | A,H | 3–6 ft. | to 4 ft. | E |
| Parsley | B | FS,PS | R,M | 2–3 ft. | 8 in. | E |
| Passion Flower | P | PS | R,M | 25–30 ft. | vine | M |
| Peppermint | P | FS,PS | A,M | 2–2½ ft. | 1 ft. | E,R |
| Plantain | P | FS,PS | P–A | ½–1½ ft. | to 7 in. | E |
| Raspberry | P | FS | R | 4 ft. | 3 ft. | E,R |
| Red Clover | P | FS | P–A,M | to 2 ft. | 8 in. | E,R |
| Rosemary | P | FS | A–S | 4–6 ft. | 2–4 ft. | M |
| Rue | P | FS | A–S | 3 ft. | 2 ft. | E |
| Sage | P | FS | A–S | 3 ft. | 2 ft. | E |
| St. John's Wort | P | FS | A–P | 3 ft. | 1 ft. | E |
| Santolina | P | FS | S–A | 1–2 ft. | 1 ft. | E |
| Savory, Summer | A | FS | A–S | 1–1½ ft. | 8–12 in. | E |
| Saw Palmetto | P | FS | A,M | to 6 ft. | sprawls | M |
| Shepherd's Purse | A or B | FS,PS | P–A,S | 1 ft. | 6 in. | E,R |
| Shiitake Mushroom | A | S | R,M | to 6 in. | to 6 in. | M |
| Skullcap | P | PS | A,M | 1–2 ft. | 8 in. | M |
| Slippery Elm | P | FS | A,M | to 60 ft. | 25 ft. | M |
| Sweet Woodruff | P | PS | A,M | 6 in. | 6–8 in. | E |
| Tarragon, French | P | FS,PS | A–S | 2 ft. | 1 ft. | M |
| Thyme | P | FS | A–S | 10–12 in. | 1–1½ ft. | E |
| Uva Ursi | P | FS | A | 6 in. | 3 in. | E |
| Valerian | P | FS,PS | A–R,M,H | 3–5 ft. | 1 ft. | E |
| Willow | P | FS | A,M | 35–75 ft. | to 5 ft. | M |
| Witch Hazel | P | FS,PS | R,M | 8–15 ft. | 15 ft. | M |
| Wormwood | P | FS | A–S | 3–4 ft. | 2 ft. | E |
| Yarrow | P | FS | A | to 3 ft. | to 1 ft. | E |
| Yellow Dock | P | FS | P–A | to 3 ft. | 1 ft. | E,R |

| KEY: | | | | | |
|------|------|------|------|------|------|
| **PLANT:** | **A** = Annual | **B** = Biennial | **P** = Perennial | | |
| **LIGHT:** | **FS** = Full Sun | **PS** = Partial Shade | **S** = Shade | | |
| **SOIL:** | **P** = Poor | **A** = Average | **H** = Humusy | **R** = Rich | **S** = Sandy | **M** = Moist |
| **CULTURE:** | **E** = Easy to Grow | **M** = Moderate | **D** = Difficult | **R** = Rampant grower; keep restricted | |

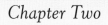

# Chapter Two

# Harvesting, Preserving, and Storing Herbs

**A**ncient cultures regarded the harvest season as sacred, a time to reap the fruits of a year's hard labor and rejoice in the Earth's abundance. Harvest your herb garden with no less reverence. Collecting a bounteous crop of plants you've cultivated yourself gives you a tremendous sense of satisfaction—not to mention herbs you can put to myriad uses.

But to ensure that you have herbs to use throughout the rest of the year, you must properly preserve and store them.

As a rule, herbs are at their flavor peak just before they bloom. Thus, plan to gather your crop at this time. Various methods of preservation influence the aromatic and textural characteristics of your harvest, so consider how you want to use your herbs before you attempt to preserve them. The herb profiles in chapter 4 contain instructions on the best time to harvest each herb listed, as well as the best methods of preservation.

Herbal preservation methods include drying, freezing, candying, salting, and pressing. Each method captures different attributes of a plant. In every case, it's important to pick herbs at their peak, process them, and properly store them as quickly as possible. That way you obtain the best possible quality of herbal product.

Note that some herbs don't retain as much flavor when preserved; these are best used fresh. You can extend an herb's producing season by growing the plant in a container indoors during winter.

Not only will you have fresh herbs on hand for cooking or decorating, you will also have a fragrant reminder of what awaits at winter's conclusion when you begin next year's garden.

## Harvesting Your Herbs

You may harvest herbs for fresh use throughout the growing season. Pick herbs early in the morning. Don't pick diseased or insect-infested portions of plants. If you must wash dirt and dust from leaves, try to do this the day before you plan to harvest to give the plant time to dry. Washed herbs have a tendency to lose more of their flavor and medicinal properties. For the same reason, avoid picking wet herbs right after a rain shower or after you have watered them.

Chances are you will collect most of your herbs from your garden, but if you pick herbs growing wild—a practice called "wildcrafting"—be certain you've identified them properly. Some poisonous herbs resemble harmless ones or grow alongside them. When you venture into the wild to harvest, choose areas where the herbs are clean and free of pesticides or other pollutants. Avoid herbs that grow near roads, since gas fumes leave residues on the plants for many yards off the road. If you must collect herbs that have dust on them, rinse them off very quickly and immediately shake or pat them dry.

Do not harvest rare or endangered plants from the wild. Many plant species are threatened through both overharvesting and loss of habitat; therefore, wildcrafting is becoming less and less acceptable for some species. Echinacea, ginseng, and goldenseal species, for example, are all declining. Certainly we still have some dandelion and red clover to spare, but it is now preferable to cultivate many medicinals rather than pull them from their native habitats. Be especially conservative about digging up roots in the wild since doing this usually means destroying the entire plant.

The best time to dig up roots, such as those of angelica, ginger, and horseradish, is in the fall.

*Harvest herbs in the morning hours to ensure peak freshness.*

Allow most perennials at least two growing seasons to ensure the roots are large enough before you harvest them.

Harvesting seeds can be tricky. You must allow seeds to ripen, but catch them before they fall off the plant. One way to accomplish this is to check your plants every day and harvest the seeds as soon as you notice they've begun to dry. Carefully snap off seed heads over a large paper bag, allowing the seeds to fall into it. Then leave the seeds in the bag until they've dried completely. Remember to gather seeds you may want to use in cooking, such as caraway, coriander, dill, and fennel.

To harvest seeds from large herbs, you can also wait until the herb has flowered and green seeds appear. Enclose each seed head in a small paper bag. Then, after the heads dry, the bag will capture any seeds that fall. Once you notice that seeds are falling off, snip off the heads, bag and all, and dry them indoors.

After harvesting your herbs, follow the preservation instructions on the following pages. Again, try to anticipate how you'll use your herbs so you can employ the appropriate preservation method.

## Drying Herbs

To dry fresh herbs, as well as flowers that you may want to use in arrangements, gather the individual flowers or buds, or harvest stems with leaves and flowers intact. With larger plants, shrubs, or trees, collect the part to be used: individual leaves, flowers, or buds. Lay buds and flowers on a screen; if you have large enough screens, you can also place the stems on these to dry. Or tie the stems at their base with string (or rubber bands for a quick job) and hang them upside down in a place that is relatively dark, with no direct sunlight.

It's best to dry herbs in a place that is hot, well ventilated, and free of moisture: An attic, barn, loft, breezeway, and covered porch are good choices. Under these conditions, moisture evaporates quickly from plants, but aromatic essential oils remain in the leaves. You can also dry herb leaves, stems, or flowers in a conventional oven with just the pilot light on and the oven door open.

*Drying herbs is an effective method of preserving their flavor and aroma.*

## Drying Methods

**Method 1:** Bind herb and flower branches with string or a rubber band and hang them upside down in a hot, dry place that receives little or no light. Ensure that your drying area has good air circulation to prevent molds from developing on the plants. Keep bunches small if your area has high humidity.

**Method 2:** Remove petals from flowers and leaves from stems, and spread herbs thinly on a tray made with a clean screen, which allows air to reach them from bottom and top. Leave space between herb pieces to ensure adequate circulation. Place the screen tray out of the wind, but in a hot, dry place that receives little light.

**Method 3:** Spread petals and leaves on a layer of paper towels. Place the herbs in a microwave oven. Set on low for one minute at a time; check often to determine how well the plants are drying. Remove them from the oven before they are fully dry and allow them to air-dry for a few days.

**Method 4:** To dry seeds, hang bundles of plants as in Method 1, but place each bundle inside a large brown paper bag to catch the seeds. Or hang bunches from poles laid across an open cardboard box lined with a sheet of paper.

**Method 5:** To dry roots, scrub them thoroughly and split thick ones lengthwise. Slice roots in ¼-inch-thick pieces. Air-dry as in Method 2, or spread roots on cookie sheets and dry them in a conventional oven at the lowest setting or with just the pilot light.

Depending on weather conditions, leaf and stem thickness, and other variables, it can take anywhere from a day to a week to dry most herbs. Check every day to see how the drying is progressing. Bear in mind there is a delicate balance between drying herbs too quickly and not quickly enough. If herbs are dried at a temperature that is too high, moisture and aromatic essential oils may be drawn out of leaves or stems, and your herbs will come out tasting pretty much like sawdust. If dried too slowly, essential oils may evaporate.

As soon as leaves are completely dry, but before they become brittle, strip them from stems and immediately store them in airtight containers to preserve as much flavor and aroma as possible. Label the containers to indicate their contents.

## Storing Herbs

Careful storage of herbs is just as important as preservation and preparation. If you don't follow proper storage methods, oxygen will break down the herbs, and they will lose essential oils—the source of an herb's flavor and perfume. Once you've fully dried your herbs, don't delay in storing them in airtight containers. Simply crumble the herbs before storing. Avoid grinding and powdering herbs because they won't retain their flavor as long.

Glass jars with tight-sealing lids or glass stoppers are ideal for storing dried herbs. You may also use porcelain canisters that close tightly, plastic pill holders with tight covers, and sealable plastic bags, buckets, or barrels for large pieces. Store frozen herbs in tightly sealed plastic or glass containers.

Store herbs in a dark place to preserve their color and flavor. If you must store your herbs in a lighted place, keep them in dark-colored jars that block out most of the light. The worst place to keep herbs is in a spice rack over the stove. Heat from cooking will cause your herbs to lose their flavor quickly.

## Storing Herbs

**1.** Gather several sealable jars, pill bottles, and plastic bags in a variety of sizes. Thoroughly wash, rinse, and dry containers and lids so no odors from previous contents remain.

**2.** As soon as they are dry, but before they crumble when touched, remove leaves, flowers, or seeds and put them in a bowl. Leave herbs whole or crumble them with your fingers or a mortar and pestle. But don't grind or powder them. Powdered herbs lose their flavor more rapidly. Powder them when you're ready to use them.

**3.** Roll a clean sheet of paper into a funnel, and pour prepared herbs into containers.

**4.** Be sure to clean and dry the bowl, mortar, and pestle before processing the next type of herb. Label containers clearly with the name of the herb and year of harvest. Without labels you'll soon find it difficult to keep your inventories straight.

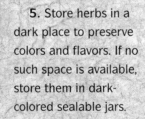

**5.** Store herbs in a dark place to preserve colors and flavors. If no such space is available, store them in dark-colored sealable jars.

**6.** To store large pieces of herbs for use in herbal baths and wreaths, place thoroughly dried branches in large plastic bags and seal with a rubber band. Store in a dark place or in a cardboard box. You can also store large pieces in plastic buckets or fiberboard barrels with tight-fitting lids.

Last but not least, label each container with its contents and date of harvest, especially if you freeze your herbs. Once frozen, herbs are hard to differentiate.

## Freezing Herbs

Another good way to preserve many culinary herbs is to freeze them. This method is quick and easy, and a frozen herb's flavor is usually closer to fresh than a dried herb's flavor.

### How to Freeze Herbs

**Method 1:** Separate herbs into small shoots or leaves; chop with a knife or scissors. Pack herbs in screw-top jars or sealable plastic bags. Squeeze out as much air as possible and freeze immediately.

**Method 2:** Place herb pieces in a blender or food processor with an equal amount of water and process. Pour into ice cube trays, and freeze. You can also freeze whole leaves or flowers in the cube. When solid, transfer cubes to a sealable plastic bag and return to the freezer.

### Herbs to Freeze

| | | |
|---|---|---|
| Basil | Fennel | Peppermint |
| Borage | Geranium, Scented | Rosemary |
| Cayenne Pepper | Lemon Balm | Sage |
| Chervil | Lovage | Savory, Summer |
| Chives | Marjoram | Sorrel, French |
| Coriander | Nasturtium | Spearmint |
| Costmary | Oregano | Tarragon |
| Dill | Parsley | Thyme |

You may freeze leaves whole or processed. Freeze mint or scented geranium leaves whole; float the frozen herbs in punches and other cold drinks. Pestos of basil and other herbs freeze well in ice cube trays. Later, when you want to use the pesto, simply pop out the cube and thaw. You can also freeze herbal butters easily with this technique.

## Candying Herbs

Another method of preserving herbs is to candy them. Try this simple recipe. Air-dry stems, leaves, flowers, or roots you wish to candy. In a saucepan, add 1 cup sugar to ½ cup water. Cook on low heat, stirring constantly until clear. Partly cool and stir in 4 teaspoonsful of gum arabic. Chill. Dip each plant part into the chilled mix, using your finger to spread it over the entire surface. Place pieces on a cake rack to dry, turning them once after 12 hours. When dry, store candied herbs in tightly covered containers.

## Salting Herbs

This seemingly unusual method harkens to the days of our pioneer

ancestors and provides a unique method of preserving herbs. In a stoneware crock, alternate ½ inch of fresh, chopped herbs and ½ inch of noniodized salt. Pound herbs with a wood mallet or jar to eliminate air spaces. You can use both the herbs and the salt for seasoning after a month.

| Herbs for Oils | | |
|---|---|---|
| Arnica* | Fennel | Rosemary |
| Basil | Garlic | St. John's Wort* |
| Cayenne Pepper | Garlic Chives | Savory |
| Comfrey* | Ginger | Tarragon |
| Coriander | Marjoram | Thyme |
| Dill | Mint | Turmeric |

*Do not consume

| Herbs for Vinegars | | |
|---|---|---|
| Basil | Fennel | Raspberry |
| Burnet | Garlic | Rosemary |
| Cayenne Pepper | Horseradish | Savory |
| Chives | Marjoram | Tarragon |
| Dill | | Thyme |

## Preserving Herbs in Oil, Butter, Vinegar, and Liquor

Some herbs lose their flavor after they're exposed to air, but they will retain it if stored in oil, vinegar, or liquor. Horseradish and

ginger are good examples. To preserve horseradish, grate the root to a fine paste and loosely pack it in small jars. Mix with 1 teaspoon of salt dissolved in 1 cup of white vinegar. Stir well to eliminate air pockets and seal in jars with tight lids. Prepare fresh ginger root in the same manner, but cover it with whiskey.

To preserve an herb's flavor in oil, gently heat olive, peanut, or other vegetable oil until warm and fragrant. Pour into a glass jar to which you have added fresh herb sprigs or leaves. Allow the oil to cool, then cover and store in a cool, dark place for about six months. See chapter 3 for herbal oil recipes for medicinal and culinary use.

Like flavored oils, herb butters are easy to make. Combine about 1 tablespoon of minced fresh herbs with ½ cup of softened butter. Wrap the mixture in plastic and store it in the refrigerator for up to one month or in the freezer for up to three months.

Herbal-flavored vinegars add magic to salads and vegetables. Use any vinegar—white, white wine, red wine, apple cider, or rice. Pour the vinegar into a clean glass jar to which you've added chopped fresh herbs. Cover and let it sit two to four weeks. Chapter 3 describes herbal vinegars with culinary and medicinal uses.

An herb's flavor may also be preserved in brandy, vodka, or wine. Add 3 to 12 2-inch sprigs to a pint of spirits and store for several weeks until the herb's flavors have permeated the liquor.

## Preserving Herbs with Glycerine and Desiccants

If you wish to use herbs for crafts, try preserving them with glycerine or desiccants. Desiccants are moisture-absorbing substances such as sand, borax, and silica gel. (You can purchase borax at a grocery store and silica gel at a craft store.)

To preserve with glycerine, mix 1 part glycerine (available at most drugstores) and 2 parts hot water in a jar and stir well. Cut fresh herb stems at an angle with a sharp knife or scissors, and arrange the plants in the jar in 3 or more inches of liquid. Leave the herbs in this solution, refilling the mixture as the plants absorb it. You'll notice a color change as the glycerine slowly rises into the leaves. After two weeks to a month, remove the herbs from the solution. Store herbs in a dry place so the glycerine does not attract water. Herbs preserved this way remain pliable for several years.

Sand has been used for centuries to preserve plants. The finest grade of sand, available from many craft stores, is an excellent nontoxic desiccant. Silica or borax may be toxic to eat, so keep these out of reach of children and pets.

For drying flowers with a desiccant, choose a wide, shallow container. Fill the container with about 1 inch of desiccant and add the flowers. Cover the flowers and leaves; use a spoon for intricately textured petals. After five to ten days, your flowers and leaves should be dried.

## Pressing Herbs

Another way to preserve herbs is to press them. The best time to pick flowers and leaves for pressing is midday, after the dew has evaporated. Avoid harvesting herbs on humid or rainy days. If you must harvest in damp weather, pick whole stems and stand them in water until the flower heads are dry. Pick flowers, buds, and leaves in good condition. Look for varying sizes, colors, and textures and unusual shapes. Slice any large pieces with a razor blade so they are no thicker than ⅛ inch.

You can press herbs a number of ways. The simplest method is to place flowers and leaves between the pages of an old phone book, leaving at least 15 pages between each page of plant material to absorb moisture. If you need extra pressure, place several heavy books on the phone book. After about six to eight weeks, your plants should be thoroughly dried. You can also use a plant press; instructions for making your own appear below.

### How to Make a Plant Press

Cut two pieces of plywood ⅜ inch thick and 10¾ inch square. Drill ³⁄₁₆-inch holes in each corner about ¾ inch from the sides. Sand the boards and apply two coats of matte. Place one board atop the other and insert a ¼×8-inch fully threaded bolt in the corner holes; leave about a 6-inch gap between the boards. Affix washers and wing nuts loosely.

You can use newspaper or blotting paper to absorb the moisture from the plant material. You need 12 sheets of newspaper or 4 sheets of blotting paper for each layer. Cut the paper into rectangles 9×10 inches. Also cut thin, corrugated cardboard into rectangles 9×10 inches. To create the layers, lay down a piece of cardboard, then either two sheets of blotting paper or six sheets of newspaper. Place flowers and leaves on the paper. Place two more sheets of blotting paper or six more sheets of newspaper over the plants, then cover with another piece of cardboard. Continue building the layers. When the press is filled, screw the bolts down to apply pressure.

# Chapter Three

# Herbal Preparations

Y ou've grown your herbs, gathered them, and dried them. The next step is to prepare them. As a budding herbalist, you may start to perspire at the thought of brewing up a batch of herbs. Maybe you're conjuring visions of Macbeth's witches, burbling and cackling as they stir an odorous cauldron in a Scottish glen. Or perhaps you're telling yourself you just don't have the time to spend preparing herbal potions. Well, don't sweat it. Preparing herbs is simple and easy—not to mention economical.

Herbalists use herbs to spur our bodies to heal naturally. The goal of the herbalist is to release the volatile oils, antibiotics, aromatics, and other healing chemicals an herb contains. You can use dried, powdered herbs to make pills, capsules, and lozenges or add herbs to water to brew infusions, or teas. You can soak herbs in alcohol, vinegar, or glycerine to produce long-lasting tinctures. You can combine herbs with sugar or other sweeteners to transform bitter herbs into delectable syrups, jellies, and conserves. You can mash herbs for poultices and plasters. Or you can harness the healing powers of herbs by heating them in oil to make salves, balms, liniments, and creams.

## Making Your Own Medicines

Lay out all the cooking, storage, and labeling materials you'll need to prepare your herbal home remedies. Advance planning prevents last-minute disasters. You don't want to be in the middle of an herbal recipe only to realize that you forgot to buy glycerine to preserve your syrup, for example.

First, decide which type of preparation you intend to make. Second, gather only the amount of herbs you need to complete the recipe. In most cases, you'll require no more than an ounce of a single herb. Salves and other preparations made with oil tend to keep better in small batches. If you intend to save these medicines for longer than a few months, keep them refrigerated.

## Teas

One of the easiest and most popular ways of preparing an herbal medicine is to brew a tea. There are two types of teas: infusions and decoctions. If you have ever poured hot water over a tea bag, you have made an infusion; an infusion is simply the result of steeping herbs in hot water. A decoction is the result of boiling herbs gently in water. When you simmer cinnamon sticks and cloves in apple cider, you're making a decoction.

In general, delicate leaves and flowers are best infused; boiling may cause them to lose the volatile essential oils. To prepare an

*Gather all the materials you'll need to make your herbal preparations before you begin.*

### Herbs for Teas

**Flowers:** Chamomile, elder flower, hops (strobiles), lavender, red clover, yarrow

**Leaves:** Basil, bilberry, blackberry, borage, butcher's broom, catnip, costmary, gentian, geraniums, ginkgo, gotu kola, horehound, horsetail, hyssop, lemon balm, meadowsweet, motherwort, mullein, nettle, parsley, passion flower, peppermint, plantain, raspberry, rosemary, sage, shepherd's purse, skullcap, spearmint, thyme, vervain, willow

**Berries:** Elderberry, hawthorn, juniper, rose hips

**Seeds:** Anise, caraway, coriander, dill, fennel, milk thistle

**Bark:** Cherry, cinnamon, cramp bark, slippery elm

**Root/Rhizome:** Astragalus, black cohosh, blue cohosh, burdock, comfrey, dandelion, echinacea, elecampane, ginger, ginseng, goldenseal, hydrangea, licorice, marshmallow, Oregon grape, valerian, yellow dock

**Stems:** Ephedra, horsetail, oat straw

**Rind:** Lemons, limes, oranges, or other citrus fruits

infusion, use 1 teaspoon of dried herbs per 1 cup of hot water. (If you use fresh herbs, use 1 to 2 teaspoons or more.) Pour the hot water over the herbs in a pan or teapot, cover with a lid, and allow to steep for about ten minutes. Strain and drink. Finely cut herbs in tea bags steep much faster—in about five minutes. You can make your own herbal tea bags, too. Tie up a teaspoon of herbs in a small muslin bag (sold in most natural food stores) or piece of cheesecloth, and drop it in a cup of hot water. Let the tea steep for 15 minutes. To make larger quantities of hot infusions, use 5 tablespoons of herbs per gallon of water.

Extremely volatile herbs such as peppermint and lemon balm lose a lot of essential oils with high heat. These herbs can be infused with cold water. It is easy to recognize volatile herbs because they are highly fragrant. Allow a cold tea to infuse overnight. These herbs are suitable for making the popular "sun" tea. Using 1 teaspoon of herbs per cup of water, put herbs and water in a jar, and place in the sun for a couple of hours. Strain and serve.

Roots, barks, and seeds, on the other hand, are best made into decoctions because these hard, woody materials need a bit of boiling to get the constituents out of the fiber. Fresh roots should be sliced thin. To prepare a medicinal decoction, use 1 teaspoon of herbs per cup of water, cover, and gently simmer for 15 to 30 minutes. Strain the decoction. Use glass, ceramic, or earthenware

*To decoct an herb root such as this fresh ginger root, slice it thin, then boil it gently to extract its constituents.*

pots to make your decoction: Aluminum may taint herbal teas. A tea will remain fresh for several days in the refrigerator.

To preserve teas, make a concentrated brew, three times as strong as an ordinary remedy. Then add one part of drinking alcohol (not rubbing alcohol) or glycerine to 3 parts of the infusion. Store in covered container. When ready to use, dilute with 3 parts water.

How much of an infusion or decoction should you take at one time? In general, drink 1 cup three times a day. A rule of thumb is, if you notice no benefits in three days, change the treatment or see your doctor or herbalist. Rely on professional care immediately in the case of potentially life-threatening conditions, such as difficulty breathing, irregular heartbeat, allergic reactions, or severe injuries.

## Lemon Mint Blend

This remedy is excellent for colds.

*¼ cup dried peppermint leaves*
*¼ cup dried lemon balm leaves*
*3 Tbsp dried organic lemon rind, grated*

Combine ingredients. Bring 1 cup of water to a boil. Remove from heat, and steep 1 to 2 Tbsp of the herb mixture in the water for 15 minutes; strain and drink. This tea is delicious either hot or iced.

## Stomach Remedy

Here's a remedy that can quiet stomach discomfort, from indigestion to a spastic colon.

*1 Tbsp dried chamomile flowers*
*1 tsp fennel seeds*
*2 Tbsp dried mint leaves*

Combine ingredients. Steep 1 tsp of the mixture in 1 cup of hot water for 15 minutes; strain and drink.

*Relax with a cup of herbal tea made from herbs you've grown yourself. Adding mint to teas made with less palatable herbs improves their flavor.*

## Coffee Substitute Decoction

This hot beverage is the perfect substitute for coffee if you're trying to kick the caffeine habit. If you take your coffee with cream, you can even add milk or a milk substitute, such as soy or rice milk, to this brew.

*3 oz dandelion root*
*1 oz roasted chicory root*
*1 oz cinnamon bark*
*1 oz licorice root, shredded (optional)\**
*2 oz organic orange peel*
*½ oz carob powder*
*1 heaping tsp nutmeg*

Combine the herbs. Gently simmer 1 tsp of the herb mixture in 1 cup water for 15 minutes. Remove from heat and steep 15 minutes longer. Strain and drink.

\*Licorice is not recommended for individuals with high blood pressure.

## Tinctures

Another popular way of making herbal medicines is to produce a tincture, an herb extracted in alcohol, glycerine, or vinegar. These solvents are strong enough to release the herbs' chemical constituents without heat. (A combination of alcohol and water is sometimes used because some herbs' constituents are more easily extracted in water, others in alcohol.) Tinctures can be added to hot or cold water to make an instant tea or mixed with water for external use in compresses and foot baths. The advantage of tinctures is that they have a long shelf life and they're available for use in a pinch to make teas or to add to oils or salves to create instant healing ointments. You can even apply an alcohol or vinegar tincture to the skin as a compress to treat bruises, sprains, and skin conditions. Dilute with an equal amount of cool water. Soak a cloth in the solution and bathe the skin. Use a hot or cold compress as the situation dictates.

## Making Tinctures

Commercial tinctures are made by carefully weighing the ingredients and adjusting them according to the individual herb. However, with common kitchen utensils and very little effort, you can

*Use your favorite herbs, dried or fresh, to make tinctures. Tinctures require very little effort to make, and they last a long time.*

*To make your own herbal teas, tinctures, vinegars, and oils, start with a mortar and pestle, clean containers, and dried herbs.*

easily prepare suitable tinctures for your own use. First, clean and pick over dried or fresh herbs, removing any insects or damaged plant material. Remove leaves and flowers from stems. Cut or chop the plant parts you want to process into small pieces, or chop them in a blender or food processor. Cover with just enough drinking alcohol to completely submerge the herbs. The spirit most commonly used is 80 to 100 proof vodka. Some herbs, such as ginger and cayenne, require the higher alcohol content to fully extract their constituents.

Puree the plant material and transfer it to a glass jar. After the plant material settles, make certain the alcohol covers the plants, and add more alcohol if it does not. This is especially important if you use fresh herbs. Plant materials exposed to air can mold or rot. Store the jar at room temperature out of sunlight, and shake the jar every day. After two weeks, strain the liquid with a kitchen strainer, cheesecloth, thin piece of muslin, or paper coffee filter. If particles eventually settle after the tincture has been stored, shake the mixture to redistribute them. Tinctures will keep for many years without refrigeration.

## Dandelion Root Tincture

Place dried, chopped dandelion roots in a food processor with enough 80 to 100 proof vodka to process. Once blended, store in a glass jar, shake daily, and strain in two weeks. Take ½ to 1 tsp three times a day before meals for chronic constipation, poor digestion, or urinary tract problems, or as a spring tonic.

Because the usual dose of a tincture is 30 drops, you receive enough herb to benefit from its medicinal properties with very little alcohol. If you're allergic to alcohol—or simply don't wish to use it—try making vinegar- or glycerine-based tinctures. Vinegar and glycerine dissolve plant constituents almost as effectively as spirits. Glycerine is available at most pharmacies.

## Vinegar Tinctures

Vinegar, which contains the solvent acetic acid, is an alternative to alcohol tinctures. You can use herbal vinegars medicinally or dilute them with more vinegar to make great-tasting salad dressings and

*Whether you use them medicinally or to dress up a salad, herbal vinegars are easy to make. These eye-catching samples make great gifts, too.*

marinades. Use any vinegar, such as apple cider, rice vinegar, red wine vinegar, or balsamic vinegar.

Vinegar is also a potent antifungal agent and makes a good athlete's foot soak when combined with antimicrobial herbs.

## Athlete's Foot Vinegar

*2 garlic bulbs*
*¹/₂ cup fresh or dried calendula petals*
*¹/₄ cup fresh comfrey root*
*Hulls of 3 fresh black walnuts, chopped, or ¹/₂ oz black walnut tincture*
*Vinegar, about 2 cups*
*2 tsp tea tree oil*

Place garlic in a blender along with the calendula petals, comfrey root, and black walnut hulls or tincture. Pour enough vinegar over the herbs to blend. Pour the mixture into a jar, and add tea tree oil. Keep in a dark place for two weeks. Strain. Shake well before using.

To treat athlete's foot, dab solution on affected area several times a day. You may wish to wear dark socks when undergoing this treatment as the black walnut can stain white socks.

## Kitchen Vinegar

This preparation tastes great on salads, stir-fries, and marinades, and it contains antibacterial properties as well. Gather fresh leaves, such as oregano and basil, and place in a blender. Pour vinegar over the herbs and blend. Bottle and allow to sit for two weeks. Strain out the herbs or leave them in the preparation. For a nice presentation, you may add a whole sprig of the herb, a cayenne pepper, or several lemon or orange rinds. This vinegar keeps well for at least a year unrefrigerated.

## Vinegar of the Four Thieves

Here's a recipe handed down from the Middle Ages. Herbal lore has it that four men caught ransacking empty homes infested with bubonic plague were tried before a court in Marseilles. Asked by the judge how the men had avoided contracting the plague, the accused men said they had washed themselves with a special herbal vinegar. The thieves were granted freedom in return for the recipe.

You can add this vinegar to a bath, or take 1 teaspoon internally—no more than 1 tablespoon an hour—to protect yourself during flu season.

*2 quarts apple cider vinegar*
*2 Tbsp lavender*
*2 Tbsp rosemary*
*2 Tbsp sage*
*2 Tbsp wormwood*
*2 Tbsp rue*
*2 Tbsp mint*
*2 Tbsp garlic buds, unpeeled*

Cover the herbs with vinegar. Keep at room temperature for two weeks. Strain and bottle. You can also make a vinegar syrup by adding 4 ounces of glycerine. Sweeten to taste.

## Glycerine Tinctures

The advantage of using a glycerine-based tincture is that it does not contain alcohol. The disadvantage is that glycerine doesn't dissolve a herb's constituents as well as alcohol does.

To make a glycerine tincture, mix 4 ounces water and 6 ounces glycerine. Pour the mixture over 1 ounce of dried or fresh chopped herbs in a clean jar. As with alcohol tinctures, make sure the herbs are submerged under the glycerine and water mixture. Shake daily. Let stand at room temperature for two weeks, then strain and bottle.

## Pills and Capsules

We have come to rely on pharmaceutical pills to cure many of our ailments. There is nothing inherently wrong with taking pills. But if you're uncomfortable with the notion of ingesting synthetic chemicals, you can turn to herbal capsules, tablets, or lozenges. Capsules and tablets provide a convenient method of ingesting herbs that have strong, harsh flavors. They're also an alternative for people who do not enjoy drinking herbal teas or using alcohol-based tinctures. You can buy capsules and tablets at a natural food store or make your own.

## Capsules

You can find empty gelatin capsules at health food stores, mail-order herbal houses, and some pharmacies. Fill the capsules with powdered herbs. Remember, it's best to store your herbs whole, then powder them immediately before encapsulating them. You can powder them with a mortar and pestle or in a coffee grinder or food processor. If the method you use does not produce a fine powder, strain the herbs through a sieve or strainer first.

Fill half the capsule with the powdered herb and pack tightly. A chopstick is a good tool for packing the powder into the capsule. Close with the other capsule half. Many natural food stores also sell capsule makers that speed up the process.

*Decorative as well as useful, mortars and pestles come in a variety of shapes and sizes.*

## Pills

To make herb pills, simply blend powdered herbs with a bit of honey to bind the mixture. Then just pinch off bits of the resulting sticky substance and roll into balls. (If the balls seem too moist, roll them in a mixture of slippery elm and licorice powder to soak up excess moisture.) Dry the herbal pills in a dehydrator, an oven set to preheat, or outdoors on a warm day covered with a cloth. Store the dried pills in an airtight container.

*A sampling of herbal remedies: capsules, powders, and tinctures.*

## Relaxation Pills

These pills contain herbs commonly recommended to reduce tension and calm anxiety. The pills may also help relieve tension headaches.

| | |
|---|---|
| *Skullcap* | *Chamomile* |
| *Valerian* | *Peppermint* |
| *Rosemary* | *Honey* |

Combine equal parts of powdered skullcap, valerian, rosemary, chamomile, and peppermint. Blend with enough honey to bind. Roll off pill-sized pieces, dry, and store in a tightly sealed container.

# Lozenges

To make herbal lozenges, combine powdered herbs with sugar and a mucilaginous binding agent such as marshmallow root, licorice root, or slippery elm bark.

### Throat Lozenges

*3 Tbsp licorice powder*
*3 Tbsp slippery elm powder*
*1 Tbsp myrrh powder*
*1 tsp cayenne powder*
*Honey as needed*
*20 drops orange essential oil*
*2 drops thyme essential oil*
*Sugar*
*Cornstarch*

Mix herbal powders. Stir in honey until a gooey mass forms. Add essential oils. Mix very well. Spread the paste on a marble slab or other nonstick surface coated with sugar or cornstarch. With a rolling pin, roll the mixture flat to about the thickness of a pan-

cake. Sprinkle with sugar and cornstarch. With a knife, cut into small, separate squares. Or pinch off pieces and roll into ¼-inch balls. Flatten the balls into round lozenges. Allow lozenges to air-dry in a well-ventilated area for 12 hours. Suck on lozenges to help soothe sore throats or calm coughs.

# Syrups

In syrup form, even the most bitter herbs taste good. Syrups are ideal for soothing sore throats and respiratory ailments. You can make herbal syrups by combining sugar, honey, or glycerine with infusions, decoctions, tinctures, herbal juices, or medicinal liquors. (Refined sugar makes a clearer syrup with a better flavor.) Preserve syrups by refrigerating or adding glycerine.

Make syrups in small quantities. To make a simple syrup, dissolve the sweetener of your choice in a hot herb infusion. You can add herbal tinctures to increase the syrup's medicinal value. Add 1 to 2 ounces of tincture to the following formula if you wish.

### Herbal Syrup

*¼ cup sugar or honey*
*1½ cups strong herb infusion*
*½ cup glycerine*

Combine sweetener and infusion in a pan and bring mixture to a boil. Add glycerine. Pour mixture into clean bottles and let cool. Keep refrigerated. Makes about 2 cups of syrup.

# Topical Preparations

It is fairly simple to create your own herbal skin preparations. Commercial oils, salves, creams, and lotions often contain byproducts and chemicals you may not wish to use. When you make your

*One way to make herbal syrup is to combine an herbal infusion, tincture, or juice with honey.*

own topical preparations, you can tailor the recipes to suit your particular needs. Use your favorite kind of oil or your favorite scent. See chapter 7 for additional recipes for herbal skin preparations.

## Herbal Oils

Oils provide a versatile medium for extracting herbal constituents. Olive, almond, canola, and sesame oils are good choices, but any vegetable oil will do. Select an oil with a light fragrance that won't overpower the herbs. Avoid mineral oil. You can consume herbal oils in recipes or salads, or massage sore body parts with medicinal oils. Add herbs to the oil of your choice, allow to sit for a week, strain, and bottle. Refrigerate oils you plan to use in cooking.

*Make an herbal oil with a single herb or a combination of herbs. This basil oil will also contain garlic and cayenne pepper.*

## Massage Oil for Sore Muscles

*5 or 6 cayenne peppers*
*1 cup vegetable oil*
*¼ tsp clove essential oil*
*¼ tsp eucalyptus essential oil*
*¼ tsp mint essential oil*

Chop cayenne peppers and place in a jar. Cover with vegetable oil. Make sure the peppers are completely covered. Store oil in a warm, dark place. Strain after one week. Add the essential oils.

Massage on sore muscles. Be careful not to get this oil in your eyes or open wounds—it will sting like the dickens. Wash your hands after using this oil.

## Salves

Salves, also called ointments, are fat-based preparations used to soothe abrasions, heal wounds and lacerations, protect babies' skin from diaper rash, and soften dry, rough skin and chapped lips.

### Herbs to Soften and Heal Skin

| | | |
|---|---|---|
| Aloe vera | Comfrey | Marshmallow |
| Calendula | | Slippery elm |

### Herbs for Sore Muscles

| | | |
|---|---|---|
| Arnica | Eucalyptus | Rosemary |
| Calendula | Ginger | St. John's wort |
| Chamomile | Juniper berries | Wintergreen |
| | Lavender | |

Salves are made by heating an herb with fat or vegetable oil until the fat absorbs the plant's healing properties. Beeswax is then added to the strained mixture to give it a thicker consistency.

Kept in a cool place, salves last at least a year. You can preserve a salve even longer by adding a few drops of tincture of benzoin, poplar bud tincture, or glycerine. (Benzoin and glycerine are available in pharmacies; poplar bud tincture is available in some health food stores.) Make salves in small batches to keep them fresh. Store in tightly lidded jars.

The key ingredient of salves is herbal oil. Make your oil out of the herb of your choice, as described on page 30. Calendula oil makes a wonderful all-purpose healing salve. St. John's wort can be used to treat swelling and bruising in traumatic injuries. Garlic oil can be used to prepare a salve to treat infectious conditions. To turn the oil into a salve, melt ¾ ounce beeswax in 1 cup herbal oil.

You can purchase beeswax from health food stores, beekeeping supply stores, and mail-order companies. Grated beeswax melts faster; use a grater or food processor to grate it. Refrigerate the wax before grating to make the job easier. (Wash utensils with very hot water to remove all the beeswax.)

*To make a salve, first make an herbal oil. Allow it to sit for at least a week, then strain and add beeswax or other hardener.*

Warm the herbal oil, then add the beeswax. When the beeswax melts, pour the salve into containers before the blend starts to harden. If you wish, add 500 IU of vitamin E per ounce to increase the salve's healing properties and help preserve the salve, or add a teaspoon of benzoin or poplar tincture for every cup of herbal oil to help preserve it. Other possible additives are 1 to 2 tablespoons of cocoa butter

## Herbal Salves

### Herbs for Salves

| | | |
|---|---|---|
| Arnica | Goldenseal | Plantain |
| Comfrey | Marshmallow | Slippery elm |
| Elder flower | | Yarrow |

### Salve Ingredients

**Oil bases:** Lard, vegetable or nut oils such as almond, coconut, peanut, and olive oil

**Additives:** Cocoa butter, lanolin

**Hardeners:** Beeswax

**Natural preservatives:** Benzoin, poplar bud, glycerine, vitamin E

to make the consistency more creamy or ½ to 1 teaspoon hydrous lanolin per cup of herbal oil to give the salve more tack. Lanolin is especially good in a salve for diaper rash.

**Note:** Problems with your salve? Simply reheat it. If your salve is too runny, add a bit more beeswax. If the salve is too hard, use more oil. To test your salve before pouring it into individual containers, pour about a tablespoon of salve in a container and put it in the freezer. This "tester" will be ready in a few minutes.

## All-Purpose Healing Salve

*½ cup comfrey root oil*
*½ cup calendula oil*
*¾ oz beeswax*
*1 Tbsp vitamin E oil*
*20 drops vitamin A emulsion*

Combine the oils and gently warm them. Melt the beeswax into the oils. Add vitamins E and A. Pour into salve containers and let stand about 20 minutes to harden.

# Antifungal Salve

*½ cup garlic oil*
*½ cup calendula oil*
*¾ oz beeswax*
*20 drops tea tree essential oil*
*1 tsp black walnut tincture*

Combine the garlic and calendula oils and gently warm them. Melt the beeswax into the oils. Add the essential oil and tincture. Stir well. Pour into salve containers while still warm.

# Juniper Berry Ointment

This ointment is good for wounds, itching, and scratches.

*1 cup juniper berries*
*2 cups oil (olive, peanut, wheat germ, or lanolin)*
*2-3 Tbsp beeswax*

Simmer berries in oil. Melt beeswax into the oil and berry mixture. Strain and pour into jars.

## Liniments

A liniment is a topical preparation that contains alcohol or oil and stimulating, warming herbs such as cayenne. Since liniment is for external use only, sometimes isopropyl, or rubbing, alcohol is used instead of grain alcohol. Do not take products made with rubbing alcohol internally.

### Herbs for Liniments

| | | |
|---|---|---|
| Cayenne | Ginger | Peppermint |
| Clove | Marjoram | Rosemary |
| Eucalyptus | | Wintergreen |

Liniments warm the skin and turn it red temporarily. It is best to test your tolerance to liniments by rubbing a small amount on your wrist to make sure it does not burn. To enhance the heat, cover the area with a cloth after application.

# Liniment for Arthritis, Lung Congestion, and Sore Muscles

*½ oz cayenne pods, chopped*
*½ oz cloves, powdered*
*1 oz eucalyptus leaves, chopped*
*1 cup isopropyl alcohol*
*60 drops wintergreen essential oil*
*20 drops peppermint essential oil*
*20 drops clove essential oil*

Soak first three ingredients in alcohol for two weeks, then strain. Add essential oils. Stir well. Massage liniment into area affected by arthritis, onto back and chest for congestion, or on sore muscles.

## Lotions

A lotion contains oil and another liquid. Add essential oils for therapeutic purposes or to give the lotion your favorite scent.

# Healing Lotion

*½ oz calendula tincture*
*1 oz comfrey tincture*
*1 oz wheat germ oil*
*3 oz aloe vera gel or fresh pulp*
*¼ tsp vitamin C crystals*
*½ tsp essential oil, if desired*

Combine ingredients in a bottle and shake vigorously. Refrigerate if made with fresh aloe pulp.

# Creams

Creams contain water or other water-soluble liquids. They are less greasy than salves and liniments. Making a cream is similar to making mayonnaise or gravy: Slowly add liquid to the wax and oil solution until the ingredients combine smoothly.

To help preserve creams, add a few drops of benzoin tincture or vitamin E, or store in the refrigerator.

## Calendula-Lavender Cream

*2 oz comfrey oil*
*2 oz calendula oil*
*½ tsp hydrous lanolin\**
*½ oz beeswax*
*2 oz distilled water or rose water*
*¹⁄₁₆ oz borax powder*
*¼ tsp lavender oil*

Combine and heat comfrey and calendula oils. Melt lanolin and beeswax in oil mixture. In another pot, gently warm water and dissolve borax in it. Remove both mixtures from heat. Place oil-wax mixture in blender or food processor. Add the borax and water mixture very slowly, constantly blending, until all the water has been added. Constantly push hardened top edge of mixture back into blender or processor. Add lavender oil; blend until thickened. Pour into jars. Store any extra cream in the refrigerator.

You can replace the water in this recipe with fresh plant juices, technically called succus, if they are available. Succus is usually preserved with 20 percent alcohol. But be aware that cream made from fresh plant juices tends to last only 6 to 12 months.

\*Hydrous lanolin is available in pharmacies.

# Compresses and Poultices

You can use compresses to treat headaches, rashes, itching, and swollen glands, among other conditions. To make a compress, soak a cloth in a strong herbal tea, wring it out, and place it on the skin. Soak a cloth with strong peppermint tea to treat rashes that itch and burn. Soak a cloth with arnica or St. John's wort tincture and hold against a sprained ankle. A lavender compress relieves the itchy eyes caused by allergies.

To make a poultice or plaster, mash herbs with enough water to form a paste. Place the herb mash directly on the affected body part and cover with a clean white cloth or gauze.

## Mustard Poultice

A mustard poultice is a time-honored therapy: Your great-grandmother may have used mustard poultices and plasters to treat congestion, coughs, bronchitis, or pneumonia. A mustard poultice, or plaster, immediately improves discomfort in the chest and actually helps to treat infectious conditions—a much-needed therapy in the days before antibiotics. It works mainly by increasing circulation, perspiration, and heat in the affected area.

The person receiving the treatment should sit or lie comfortably. To prepare a mustard poultice, mix ½ cup mustard powder with

## Compresses and Poultices

### Herbs for Compresses

| Arnica | Lavender | Sage |
|---|---|---|
| Garlic | Marjoram | St. John's wort |
| Ginger | Peppermint | Witch hazel |

### Herbs for Poultices

| Comfrey | Mustard | Plantain |
|---|---|---|
| Marshmallow | Oatmeal | Slippery elm bark |

1 cup flour. Stir hot water into the mustard and flour mixture until it forms a paste. Spread the mixture on a piece of cotton that you have soaked in hot water. Cover with a second piece of dry cotton material. Lay the moist side across the person's chest or back. Leave the moist side on for 15 to 30 minutes; promptly remove if the person experiences any discomfort. The procedure is likely to promote perspiration and reddening of the chest.

## Comfrey Poultice

Use a poultice made of fresh comfrey root or leaves to help heal cuts, abrasions, and other injuries to the skin. Place several chunks of comfrey in a blender with enough distilled water to process. Blend into a wet mass. Place the mashed comfrey directly against the skin. Leave on about a half hour. Use the comfrey poultice several times a day for an initial injury. Poultices last several days in the refrigerator. Although comfrey helps knit many minor wounds, serious injuries should be examined by a physician.

## Herbal Baths for Feet and Hands

The skin absorbs the healing properties of many herbs, so you can treat many conditions by soaking in a herbal bath. Add a pint of herbal infusion or decoction to water in a basin, and soak your hands or feet. See chapter 7 for recipes for soothing herbal baths.

## A Word About Buying Herbal Preparations

Making herbal remedies yourself is very satisfying, but if you need an herbal remedy in a pinch, purchase your herbal preparations. Before you buy, you should know a few basics about commercial herbal remedies.

When buying herbs in capsule or tablet form, it's often impossible to assess the quality of the herbs. A naturopathic physician, an herbalist, and individuals who have used the product are good sources of information. It's always wise to take the time to learn about the herbs you are considering. Make sure they are indicated for the condition you wish to treat or prevent, and make sure you understand the appropriate therapeutic dosage.

Increasingly, herb suppliers are "standardizing" the products they sell to consumers. This means these herbal preparations have been tested to determine the type and amount of at least one chemical constituent contained in the plant. Standardization sounds like a good idea. But the practice has its pros and cons.

The good news is that standardization ensures the potency of an herbal product. Many of the healing properties of *Ginkgo biloba*, for example, are thought to reside in chemicals called heterosides. Thus, if you buy a standardized ginkgo preparation, you can be fairly certain you're getting a sufficient amount of heterosides. The problem is, ginkgo also contains other compounds. Should we standardize for all chemicals? If we discover more active constituents in the next decade, will they all need to be standardized? If so, we can expect to pay plenty for the herbs we buy.

Another problem with standardization is that as we study the medicinal effects of herbs, we're learning that healing may result not from a single element contained in a plant, but from a complex combination of constituents. Standardization implies that an herb is good only for the standardized constituent. But herbs contain many nourishing substances; unlike drugs, herbs are not administered to produce a single chemical effect. If we begin to value plants for their standardized chemicals only, it won't be long before pharmaceutical companies are isolating extracts and packaging them as drugs. And that's not what herbal medicine is about.

If you want to avoid pharmaceutical side effects and live in harmony with the world around you, the best way to treat minor ailments is to grow your own herbs and make your own medicines. That way you can be absolutely certain you're taking safe, organic remedies. Of course, you should never attempt to diagnose a serious illness and treat it yourself. In such cases, seek advice from a physician. But for headaches, colds, or minor cuts and scrapes, pay a visit to nature's pharmacy.

# Chapter Four

# Know Your Herbs

In a smoky hut at the edge of a clearing, an old woman mumbles an incantation as she wraps a boy's broken leg in a poultice of comfrey leaves. When she is done, she mumbles thanks to the spirits who have guided her, and smiles to reassure the boy's anxious parents. By spring, the boy will be running and jumping with the other children in the village.

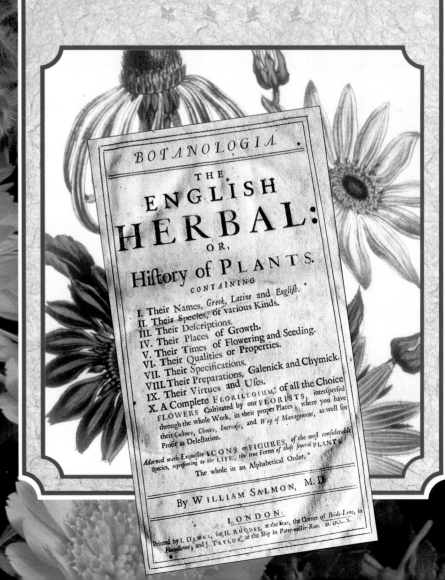

From earliest times, human beings have been captivated by the mystical, seemingly magical ability of herbs to heal and nurture us. The Bible is rife with references to herbal healing: "Go up into Gilead and take Balm...." Jeremiah 46:11; "And Isaiah said, 'Take a lump of figs.' And they took it and laid it on the boil, and he recovered...." 2 Kings 20:7.

Those who had knowledge of herbal healing were revered by their neighbors. In an age before science, these simple healers meant the difference between life and death. After the Industrial Revolution, as the population became urbanized and science evolved, interest in herbs waned.

But in the last 30 years, as those of us who live in industrialized nations have grown more health-conscious and less willing to turn to synthetic drugs, herbal medicine has enjoyed a resurgence in popularity. Pharmaceuticals, though lifesavers in countless cases, are not without side effects. As more people strive to lead more natural lives, they are looking in increasing numbers to herbs as natural remedies. In doing so, they are participating in an ancient healing tradition.

*An aloe plant from* **Herbarium Blackwellianum,** *1750.*

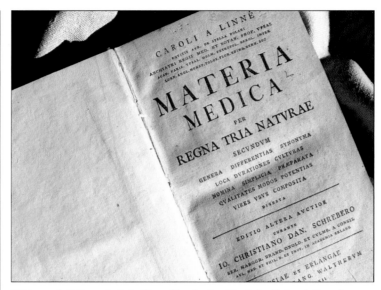

*This early* **Materia Medica** *(Latin for* **On Medicine***) listed medicinal plants.*

## Western Herbalism

The pagan tribes of Europe were quick to recognize the healing value of herbs. According to the Doctrine of Signatures, one of the earliest of herbal medical theories, attributes of plants mirror certain physiologic conditions in man. Oil turns blood-red when infused with the flowers of St. John's wort. Thus, Europeans reasoned, the herb must be good for treating wounds. As Western medicine evolved, this principle developed further, and herbs were used to treat symptoms associated with diseases.

## Homeopathic Herbalism

Homeopathy, which developed in Europe 200 years ago, is based on a belief that "like treats like." Thus, a homeopathic physician prescribes extremely minute doses of herbs or other agents that cause the symptoms of a particular disease. The homeopath, then, uses herbs to encourage the body to fight off illness and heal itself.

## Eastern Herbalism

For more than 5,000 years, Chinese physicians have used herbs not to suppress disease symptoms, as we do currently in the West, but to encourage the body to correct imbalances that may be causing the illness. Healers in China and other Asian countries use herbs to boost qi (sometimes written as chi and pronounced chee), the life force they believe animates all living things. If you visit a

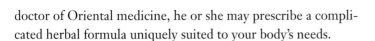
doctor of Oriental medicine, he or she may prescribe a complicated herbal formula uniquely suited to your body's needs.

## Ayurvedic Herbalism

Equally ancient is the practice of Ayurveda, which developed in India millennia ago and also uses herbs to balance the body's systems. Ayurveda is derived from two Sanskrit root words. Ayur comes from ayus, meaning totality of life; veda means knowledge. The goal of Ayurvedic medicine is to heal body, mind, and spirit. An Ayurvedic physician prescribes herbs to tone and nurture your particular body type and constitution.

## Using Medicinal Herbs Safely

Today, it seems, more people than ever are turning to herbs for sustenance and healing. Most herbs are safe to use in moderate amounts. But unless your ailment is minor—a common headache, for example—never attempt to diagnose yourself. If you do use herbs medicinally, be sure you know what you're taking and the effect it is intended to have on you. And don't take herbs—or any medicine—without making sure the herb is appropriate for your condition. In other words, do your homework. This is especially important if you're pregnant or nursing because anything you ingest affects your child.

*Pills and tinctures prepared for use as homeopathic remedies.*

If you use prescription medications regularly, you should seek advice from a naturopathic physician or herbalist before using herbs medicinally. Blood thinning medications, in particular, may interact with herbs, other drugs, and even some foods and are the drug class most often responsible for hospitalization due to adverse side effects. Also note that children and the elderly sometimes require lower doses of herbs.

## Herb Profiles

This section describes some of the most common and popular herbs in use today. Each profile includes an illustration and a description of the plant's growth habits; site preferences; propagation methods; and appropriate harvest, preservation, and storage techniques. You will also find notes on each herb's culinary, cosmetic, decorative, and medicinal uses. Height and spread indicate size normally reached by a mature plant. Keep in mind that figures are approximate; ultimate size depends on climate, soil, and light conditions. Varietal differences also may account for variance.

---

### Herbs to Use with Caution or to Avoid

These herbs should be used with caution when taken internally:

| | | |
|---|---|---|
| Angelica | Blue Cohosh | Licorice |
| Black Cohosh | Ephedra | Rue |
| | Juniper | |

These herbs should not be taken internally:

| | | |
|---|---|---|
| Arnica | Comfrey | Wormwood |
| | Tansy | |

See herb profiles for specific precautions regarding these and other herbs.

---

The common name of each herb appears first, followed by its scientific name—the plant's genus (the first, capitalized name) and species (the second, lowercase name). It's important to identify plants by their scientific names because many plants share a common name—the angelicas, for example—but their uses may differ significantly. Or one herb may have many different names: Bilberry is sometimes called huckleberry or whortleberry. Using the botanical names is the only way to specifically identify an herb. The herbs appear in alphabetical order by their common name.

*The frontispiece from a 1732 pharmacopeia,* Corpus Pharmaceutico Chymico Medicum.

*An antique pharmacy seed cabinet.*

Botanists have recently revised some of the family names of herbs. Because much of the information you'll find on herbs will continue to use the older, common family name, we've included it in parentheses after the new, revised name.

Use this section to learn more about the herbs that interest you. Use the at-a-glance format to find the information you need to make a garden plan. You won't find some of the most talked-about Chinese herbs such as astragalus at your local nursery, but these popular plants are available through a few mail-order sources.

The herbs profiled on pages 140–143 are not usually found in gardens but are, nonetheless, botanicals prized for their medicinal or culinary attributes. Although your area may not provide the proper conditions under which to grow them, you can purchase many of the herbs listed here in bulk or commercial preparations at health food stores and some pharmacies.

# Glossary

**Acid soil:** A pH content of less than 6.5

**Alkaline soil:** A pH content of more than 7.3 (Most herbs thrive in an alkaline soil.)

**Alterative:** Gradually and favorably alters a medical condition

**Analgesic:** Relieves pain

**Annual:** Grows and dies in one season

**Antacid:** Neutralizes excess stomach acids

**Antibiotic:** Destroys or inhibits growth of microorganisms such as those that cause infectious diseases

**Antipyretic:** Reduces fever

**Antiseptic:** Prevents growth of bacteria

**Antispasmodic:** Prevents or relaxes muscle spasms

**Astringent:** Dries, constricts, and binds inflamed or draining tissues

**Biennial:** Completes its life cycle in two growing seasons

**Bitter:** Plant with a sharp, sometimes unpalatable taste that stimulates appetite and enhances digestion

**Carminative:** Relieves gas and pain in the bowels

**Compress:** Cloth soaked in an herbal tea and applied externally

**Cultivar:** Cultured variety of plant

**Cutting:** Leaf, bud, or portion of stem or root removed from a plant and used to form a new plant

**Deciduous:** Plant or tree that sheds its leaves at the end of the growing season

**Decoction:** Tea made by boiling the tough, woody parts of a plant

**Demulcent:** Protects damaged or inflamed tissues

**Diaphoretic:** Induces sweating

**Diuretic:** Increases urine flow

**Evergreen:** Bears foliage throughout the year

**Expectorant:** Assists in expelling mucus from lungs and throat

**Genus:** Botanical name for a group of closely related plants

**Herbaceous:** Perennials with nonwoody stems, which die down at the end of the growing season

**Infusion:** Tea made by steeping an herb's leaves or flowers in hot water

**Laxative:** Promotes bowel movements

**Mucilage:** Gelatinous substance found in some herbs

**Mulch:** Covering, often of wood chips, laid down to warm or protect the soil around a plant

**Nervine:** Calms tension and nourishes the nervous system

**Perennial:** Lives from year to year

**pH scale:** System for measuring the acidity or alkalinity of soil

**Pinnate:** Leaf that resembles a feather

**Poultice:** Plant matter applied to injured or inflamed skin

**Propagate:** To cause plants to reproduce

**Rhizome:** Underground stem that creeps horizontally

**Rootstock:** Crown and root system of herbaceous perennials

**Runner:** Stem that spreads along the soil surface

**Salve:** Healing ointment

**Sedative:** Quiets the nervous system and promotes sleep

**Shrub:** Perennial with branched, woody stems

**Species:** Classification applied to a plant within a genus

**Stimulant:** Increases circulation

**Sucker:** Shoot that grows up from below ground level

**Tincture:** Herbal extraction of a plant, usually with alcohol

**Tonic:** Improves overall function of a particular organ or tissue

**Tuber:** Root or underground stem

**Umbel:** Flat-topped mass of small flowers on stalks

**Variety:** Natural or cultivated variation of a species

# Aloe

**Perennial**

**Botanical Name:** *Aloe vera* or *A. barbadensis*

**Family:** Liliaceae

**Height:** 1–5 ft. with flowering stalk

**Spread:** 1–3 ft.

**Description:** *Aloe vera* is the most common of the more than 300 species of aloe. Resistant to salt and drought, this very hardy herb can be found on rocky shorelines or dunes or intermingled with other vegetation just about anywhere. A common houseplant, aloe is characterized by pointed, fleshy leaves that exude a mucilaginous (gelatin-like) sap when broken. Aloe produces yellow to orange-red tubular flowers that grow to 1 inch. The herb is native to East Africa and widely cultivated in Egypt, the Near East, Bermuda, Spain, the Bahamas, the Caribbean, South America, southern Florida, and Texas.

**Ease of Care:** Easy

**Cultivation:** Aloe needs neutral, average, well-drained soil with filtered sun to shade. In good soil and a warm climate, an aloe plant will thrive for years. It is not frost-hardy; it survives to zone 3. The plant's fleshy, spiky leaves make aloe a good ornamental garden plant.

**Propagation:** Aloe's tiny black seeds can germinate in about four weeks but often take many months. The best way to obtain new plants is to remove suckers or offshoots from the mother plant when they have grown 1 to 2 inches for an indoor plant and 6 to 8 inches for an outdoor plant. The herb takes two to three years to flower. Aloe is sold in nurseries throughout the country.

**Uses:** This common plant has many uncommon virtues. Cleopatra is said to have massaged fresh aloe gel into her skin every day to preserve her beauty. And, indeed, modern clinical studies show that aloe is one of the best herbs for soothing skin and healing burns, rashes, frostbite, and severe wounds. It is also used to treat eczema, dandruff,

acne, ringworm, gum disease, and poison oak and ivy. Aloe is found commercially in a number of creams and lotions for softening and moisturizing skin. It works by inhibiting formation of tissue-injuring compounds that gather at the site of a skin injury. The plant contains chrysophanic acid, which is highly effective in healing abrasions. Some compounds from aloe show promise in the laboratory as potential cancer fighters.

**Part Used:** Sap from fleshy leaves. Cut the outermost (oldest) leaves first. Aloe produces new leaves from its center.

**Preservation:** Use fresh leaves. To preserve, add vitamin C powder or liquid.

**Precautions:** Aloin, the yellow portion of aloe just under the leaf's peel, is a strong laxative that may cause severe cramping and diarrhea, so use aloe cautiously internally and always with a carminative such as ginger, fennel, or coriander. Commercial aloe juice has this property removed, so it is safe to drink as recommended on

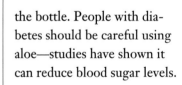

the bottle. People with diabetes should be careful using aloe—studies have shown it can reduce blood sugar levels.

**Medicinal Use:** Break off a leaf, slice it down the middle, and rub the gel on the skin. To make a poultice of aloe, place the cut leaf on the burned or affected area, and wrap it with gauze. You can also apply store-bought gel or juice. Remove the yellow section if you juice your own aloe for internal use. Take up to ¼ cup a day of pure aloe sweetened with fruit juice, or follow the directions for aloe juice.

# Angelica

**Biennial**

**Botanical Name:**
*Angelica archangelica*

**Family:** Apiaceae (Umbelliferae)

**Height:** 5–6 ft., in flower

**Spread:** 3 ft.

**Description:** This large, boldly attractive plant produces lush growth, making it a striking focal point for your garden. Angelica looks much like a very large celery or parsnip plant. This herb produces large white umbel flower heads and decorative yellow-green seedpods. Often you'll find angelica growing near seas, streams, and mountain brooks and in marshes, swamps, and moist meadows. It is native to Syria and possibly Europe but now cultivated elsewhere, including the United States.

**Ease of Care:** Moderate

**Cultivation:** Angelica likes a cool, moist location and average to well-drained soil. It will grow in sun but prefers partial shade.

**Propagation:** Seeds must be no more than 6 months old to germinate. Sow them in late fall. Scatter seeds on top of soil and lightly cover with additional soil. Plant seeds directly in the garden, or transplant seedlings. Mature angelica plants do not like to be moved.

**Uses:** For centuries, peasants gathered angelica because it was purported to ward off evil spirits. Early physicians prescribed angelica for a number of illnesses. Angelica syrup was taken as a digestive aid, and American Indians used angelica to treat lung congestion and tuberculosis. Today angelica is used primarily to treat digestive and bronchial conditions and as an expectorant and cough suppressant. It has antibacterial, antifungal, and diaphoretic (induces sweating) properties. It also increases

menstrual flow. Japanese studies have shown that a related species of angelica has anti-inflammatory properties that may be useful in an arthritis treatment. In China, the Asian species is prescribed to improve liver function in people with cirrhosis and chronic hepatitis, to regulate menstruation, and to relieve menopausal symptoms. Studies have shown that compounds from Chinese angelica may also have cancer-fighting properties.

Commercially, angelica roots and seeds are used to flavor Benedictine and Chartreuse liqueurs, gin, vermouth, and some brands of tobacco. The herb's distinctive flavor is also found in fresh or dried leaves and stems. Add very small amounts of fresh leaves to salads, fruits, soups, stews, desserts, and pastries.

Add the flowers to fresh floral arrangements. The herb dyes wool a dark green.

**Part Used:** Leaves, seeds, stems, root

**Preservation:** Harvest roots during the plant's first fall or second spring, leaves throughout summer, stems anytime, and seeds when ripe. Stems may be candied or frozen. Hang-dry or freeze leaves.

**Precautions:** Don't attempt to gather wild species of angelica; they look a lot like water hemlock, which is extremely toxic. Angelica increases menstrual flow, so avoid it if you're pregnant. It contains chemicals called psoralens, which can cause some sensitive people to develop a rash when exposed to sunlight; some people get dermatitis when handling the leaves. Use small amounts of the herb since it can act strongly on the nervous system. If angelica causes you any problems, discontinue use.

**Medicinal Use:** Use angelica root in tea, tincture, or pill form. Take ¼ to ½ teaspoon (1 to 2 droppers full) of tincture and up to 1 cup of tea daily.

# Anise

**Annual**

**Botanical Name:**
*Pimpinella anisum*

**Family:** Apiaceae
(Umbelliferae)

**Height:** 1½–2 ft.

**Spread:** 8 in.

**Description:** Anise produces feathery leaves and a lacy flower umbel on slender, weak stems. The plant strongly resembles dill. It is native to Egypt and the Mediterranean region and widely cultivated in Europe, India, Mexico, Russia, and the United States.

**Ease of Care:** Moderate

**Cultivation:** Anise prefers full sun and average, light, dry soil. Sow seed in the garden, or transplant seedlings when small. Like dill, anise grows best in rows or clumps so its weak multiple stems can support one another. It takes at least four months of warm, frost-free weather to grow seeds to maturity. In northern areas, the growing season is usually not long enough for anise to produce seeds.

**Propagation:** Sow seed in early spring. Because the plant produces a long taproot, it is difficult to transplant.

**Uses:** Anise has been considered a valuable herb since at least the 6th century B.C. The Romans cultivated the plant for its distinctive fragrance and flavor, which is similar to licorice. They also used anise extensively as a medicine. For centuries, anise was used to induce a mother's milk to flow, to ease childbirth, and as an aphrodisiac. Today herbalists recommend anise to aid digestion and prevent gas. Because it loosens bronchial secretions and reduces coughing, anise is often found in cough syrups and lozenges. And the herb has some antimicrobial properties.

Anise is a prime ingredient in many ethnic cuisines, including Scandinavian, Greek, East Indian, Arabic, and Hispanic foods. The herb intensifies the flavor of pastries, cakes, and cookies, and it complements eggs, stewed fruit, cheese, spinach, and carrots. Use leaves whole in salads or as a garnish. Anise cookies are a traditional Christmas treat in Europe. Dried leaves make a pleasant-tasting tea, and the herb has been used to flavor liqueurs, including the well-known Greek ouzo. With its licorice-like taste, it is used to flavor most of the "licorice" candy in the United States and other candies as well.

Anise seed is a wonderful addition to sachets, and, commercially, the essential oil adds scent to perfumes and soaps and flavors toothpastes and mouthwashes. Dogs love the smell of anise—in greyhound racing, the artificial hare is scented with anise.

**Part Used:** Seeds, leaves

**Preservation:** Harvest during late summer when seeds ripen. To collect seeds, hang-dry seed heads in paper bags in a warm, dry place. Store in tightly sealed containers.

**Precautions:** Although anise has been recommended to treat morning sickness, the herb has an estrogenlike property. Pregnant women should avoid any herbs or drugs that might have an estrogenic effect. The essential oil can be narcotic and toxic, so use it carefully.

**Medicinal Use:** Anise is rarely used alone but makes a great flavoring in teas and tinctures, and it is a popular addition to cough syrups.

# Arnica

**Perennial**

**Botanical Name:**

*Arnica montana*

**Family:** Asteraceae (Compositae)

**Height:** 1–2 ft.

**Spread:** 10 in.

**Description:** Arnica, also called leopardsbane, mountain tobacco, and wolfsbane, is found in mountainous regions. The herb is indigenous to Europe and Siberia, but it has been naturalized in southwestern Canada and the western United States. Other species of arnica can be found from Alaska to New Mexico. The plant grows from a horizontal, dark brown root and produces round and hairy stems. These send up as many as three flower stalks with blossoms that resemble daisies and appear from June to August. Lance-shaped, bright green, and toothed, arnica's leaves appear somewhat hairy on their upper surfaces. The oval lower leaves grow to 5 inches long.

**Ease of Care:** Moderate

**Cultivation:** Arnica requires sandy, dry soil with humus and full sun. It prefers acidic soil but will grow in most beds as long as they are well drained. Some species of arnica tolerate light shade, including *A. cordifolia* and *A. latifolia.*

**Propagation:** New arnica plants may be produced by means of division, cuttings, or seeds.

**Uses:** The next time your calves ache after a strenuous morning run, try massaging them with an arnica liniment. European herbalists and American Indians have long recognized arnica's abilities to soothe and relax sore, stiff muscles. More than 100 commercial drug preparations in Germany contain arnica. The herb is also used to make homeopathic remedies. The flower is the most potent part of the plant, but sometimes the leaves are also used.

Arnica's healing powers have been attributed to two chemicals, helenalin and arnicin, which have anti-inflammatory, antiseptic, and pain-relieving properties. Arnica also increases blood circulation.

**Part Used:** Flowers, leaves

**Preservation:** The plant is best used fresh. Gather flowers in midsummer, just as they reach their blooming peak. Preserve them in alcohol to make a liniment.

**Precautions:** The helenalin in arnica causes dermatitis in a few people after repeated applications. Discontinue use if you develop any skin problems. Otherwise, arnica is safe for topical use. But do

not ingest arnica. Taken internally, the herb can irritate the kidneys and the digestive tract, cause dizziness, and elevate blood pressure.

**Medicinal Use:** Arnica is available in tinctures, salves, and ointments to treat minor wounds, sprains, and bruises. You can lay a compress made with arnica tea or the diluted tincture on such injuries, or place a compress on the stomach to relieve abdominal pain. To make an arnica oil, heat 1 ounce of flowers in 10 ounces of any vegetable oil for several hours on low heat. Strain and let the oil cool before applying it to bruises or sore muscles.

# Astragalus

**Perennial**

**Botanical Name:**
*Astragalus membranaceus*

**Family:** Fabaceae
(Leguminosae)

**Height:** 4 ft.

**Spread:** 1½ ft.

**Description:** Known as milk-vetch root in the West and huang qi in the East, this plant produces symmetrical oblong, pointed leaves. Astragalus is a member of the legume family, which includes lentils, beans, clover, and licorice. Its Latin name, *membranaceus,* refers to the root, which is full of membranes that pull apart easily and shred into pieces.

**Ease of Care:** Moderate

**Cultivation:** Astragalus is not yet found in most herb gardens, but it is gaining popularity as its use in North America increases. In Asia, it is cultivated commercially or gathered in the wild. Plants can be purchased through mail order from a few nursery sources.

**Propagation:** Astragalus roots may be divided or grown from seed.

**Uses:** Here in the West we're just beginning to appreciate the healing properties of astragalus, an herb that has been revered in Asia for more than 2,000 years. Compiled by Chinese physicians in the first century A.D., *The Divine Husbandman's Classic of the Materia Medica* lists astragalus as its number-one health-giving plant. Chinese physicians believe that astragalus is a tonic for the lung and spleen. Because of its immune-system–enhancing properties, astragalus is often prescribed for people with "wasting" diseases such as fatigue or loss of appetite due to chronic illness, or for people who need to strengthen their body's systems. It is also used to treat chronic diarrhea. It is not uncommon in China to use astragalus extracts to fight several kinds of cancer. It is used in Chinese hospitals to lessen the side effects of chemotherapy and radiation; studies have also found it improves survival rates of cancer patients.

Astragalus is an excellent diuretic. It lowers fevers and has a beneficial effect on the digestive system. Other illnesses for which herbalists use astragalus include arthritis; diabetes; inflammation in the urinary tract; prolapsed uterus, stomach, or anus; uterine bleeding and weakness; water retention; and skin wounds that refuse to heal.

Astragalus' ability to lower blood pressure is probably due to the gamma-aminobutyric acid it contains, which dilates blood vessels. Other chemicals in the root have been found to strengthen the lungs.

**Part Used:** Root

**Preservation:** The root is harvested in the fall and dried.

**Precautions:** None

**Medicinal Use:** Drink up to 2 cups, four times a day, to strengthen the immune system and improve general health. If using astragalus tincture, take up to ½ teaspoon (2 droppers full), four times a day.

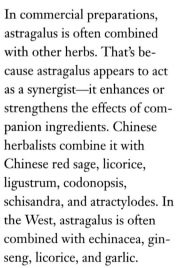

In commercial preparations, astragalus is often combined with other herbs. That's because astragalus appears to act as a synergist—it enhances or strengthens the effects of companion ingredients. Chinese herbalists combine it with Chinese red sage, licorice, ligustrum, codonopsis, schisandra, and atractylodes. In the West, astragalus is often combined with echinacea, ginseng, licorice, and garlic.

# Basil

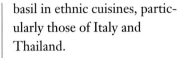

**Annual**

**Botanical Name:**
*Ocimum basilicum*

**Family:** Lamiaceae (Labiatae)

**Height:** 1½ ft.

**Spread:** 10 in.

**Description:** Basil produces a neat, dense growth, with bright-green, triangular leaves. You can even clip basil into a neat hedge. A compact dwarf variety, Spicy Globe, makes an outstanding edging or an attractive container plant. Purple Ruffles and Dark Opal are dramatic purple-leaved varieties. Green Ruffles has a great lime-green color. And lemon basil adds lemon flavor to foods. Basil is native to India, Africa, and Asia and cultivated in France, Egypt, Hungary, Indonesia, Morocco, Greece, Bulgaria, the former Yugoslavian nations, and Italy. In the United States, it is widely grown in California and in kitchen gardens all over the country.

**Ease of Care:** Easy

**Cultivation:** Basil prefers full sun and semi-rich, moist soil. It will grow in partial shade but gets "leggy" (it grows sparsely and doesn't fill out).

**Propagation:** Sow seeds when soil is warm, or get a head start by planting seeds indoors and transplanting seedlings after the danger of frost is past.

**Uses:** A member of the mint family, basil is recommended to aid digestion and expel gas. It's also good for treating stomach cramps, vomiting, and constipation. It has been found to be more effective than drugs to relieve nausea from chemotherapy and radiation. In India, *O. sanctum* is used to prevent stomach ulcers, colitis, asthma, and high blood pressure. Basil has a slight sedative action and sometimes is recommended for nervous headaches and anxiety. Studies show that extracts of basil seeds have antibacterial properties. Basil contains vitamins A and C as well as antioxidants, which prevent cell damage. One study found that basil increases production of disease-fighting antibodies up to 20 percent. It also combats the herpesvirus.

In Malaysia, basil is used to expel intestinal worms. Clinical studies show that basil essential oil is, indeed, effective in killing parasites.

In the kitchen, basil's rich, spicy flavor—something like pepper with a hint of mint and cloves—works wonders in pesto, tomato sauce, salads, cheese dishes, eggs, stews, vinegars, and all sorts of vegetables. Often you'll find basil in ethnic cuisines, particularly those of Italy and Thailand.

Strongly fragrant, basil is used in sachets and potpourri. A basil infusion used as a hair rinse adds luster to the hair and helps treat acne and itching skin. Basil essential oil is found in perfumes and toilet waters, lotions, shampoos, and soaps. Added to the bath, it produces an invigorating soak.

**Part Used:** Leaves

**Preservation:** Take prunings and use fresh leaves any time. Harvest basil when buds are about to blossom—when the plant is at its flavor peak—and hang-dry. Basil retains its flavor best when frozen or stored in oil or vinegar.

**Precautions:** Used in moderation, basil is quite safe.

**Medicinal Use:** Basil is rarely used to make tea, except for lemon basil, which has a delightful taste. Basil tinctures are not readily available, but you can make your own, or simply add basil to foods.

# Bilberry

**Perennial**

**Botanical Name:**

*Vaccinium myrtillus*

**Family:** Ericaceae

**Height:** 1–2 ft.

**Spread:** 3–4 ft.

**Description:** Bilberry is a deciduous shrub with thin, creeping stems. Leaves are bright green, alternate, and oval. Flowers are pale green to pink and appear from late spring to late summer, followed by purple fruit. Native to Europe, northern Asia, and North America, the herb is found in woodlands, forests, and moorlands. One of more than 100 members of the genus *Vaccinium*, bilberry is related to blueberries and huckleberries.

**Ease of Care:** Moderate

**Cultivation:** A wild herb, bilberry requires acidic, peaty soil and sun or filtered shade.

**Propagation:** New plants may be grown from rooted cuttings in spring or fall.

**Uses:**
Bilberry contains vitamins A and C and was a folk remedy in Scandinavia to prevent scurvy and treat nausea and indigestion. The berries were once steeped in gin and taken as a digestive tonic. They are a popular Russian remedy for colitis and stomach ulcers because they decrease inflammation in the intestines and protect the lining of the digestive tract. The herb has astringent, antiseptic, and tonic properties, making it useful as a treatment for diarrhea.

Berries contain flavonoid anthocyanidins, which have a potent antioxidant action and protect body tissues, particularly blood vessels. Several studies have shown that bilberry extracts stimulate blood vessels to release a substance that helps dilate (open) veins and arteries. Bilberries may keep platelets from clumping, thus preventing clotting and improving circulation. The berry may help prevent many diabetes-related conditions caused by poor circulation.

Because they contain a substance that slightly lowers blood sugar, the leaves are a folk remedy to manage diabetes. However, you should not use the leaves to self-treat diabetes. German researchers are investigating the leaves as a treatment for gout and rheumatism.

Bilberry preparations may be particularly useful for treating eye conditions and have been prescribed for diabetic retinopathy, cataracts, night blindness, and macular degeneration. In England, World War II pilots were given bilberry jam to improve their eyesight. Modern European prescription medications that contain bilberry are used to improve eyesight and circulation.

Bilberry has also been used to flavor liqueurs. The berries yield a blue dye.

**Part Used:** Fruit, leaves

**Preservation:** Gather fruit when ripe and use fresh, or freeze.

**Precautions:** None with the fruit. The leaves contain chemicals that irritate the liver.

**Medicinal Use:** Eat the herb's nutrient-rich, tart fruit raw, or make it into jam, jelly, or syrup (the most common way to buy bilberry). You can also use bilberry capsules, tea, or tincture. Take 2 to 6 capsules a day. Take ½ to 1 teaspoon tincture (2 to 4 droppers full) up to three times a day. Take 1 to 2 teaspoons of the syrup a day, or follow label directions.

# Black Cohosh

**Perennial**

**Botanical Name:**
*Cimicifuga racemosa*

**Family:** Ranunculaceae

**Height:** 3–6 ft. (flower stalk)

**Spread:** 2 ft.

**Description:** Related to buttercup, larkspur, and peony, black cohosh is a leafy herb with knotty black roots and a smooth stem. Also known as snakeroot, the plant produces small, multiple white flowers in midsummer on tall stalks. Black cohosh grows in the eastern United States and Canada.

**Ease of Care:** Moderate

**Cultivation:** Black cohosh is a wild plant that prefers rich soil and forest conditions. Seeds take two to four weeks to germinate and are best stratified.

**Propagation:** Sow seed in spring; divide roots in spring or fall.

**Uses:** North American Indians used black cohosh to treat fatigue, sore throat, arthritis, and rattlesnake bite, but the herb's primary use historically was as a medicine to ease childbirth. Nine-teenth-century American

herbalists also recommended black cohosh for fever and menstrual cramps. Black cohosh is a diuretic, expectorant, astringent, and sedative, but today it is most often recommended for treating symptoms of menopause. The herb seems to have an estrogenic effect by binding to estrogen receptors in the body. Black cohosh contains the anti-inflammatory salicylic acid (the main ingredient of aspirin) and has been used for a variety of muscular, pelvic, and rheumatic pains, especially those caused by nervous tension. Herbalists in China use a related species, *C. foetida*, to treat headache, measles, and gynecologic problems.

**Part Used:** Root

**Preservation:** Harvest the roots in the fall; cut them lengthwise and dry.

**Precautions:** An overdose of black cohosh may cause dizziness, diarrhea, abdominal pain, vomiting, visual dimness, headache, tremors, and a depressed heart rate. Don't use it if you have a heart condition. Because the herb seems to affect hormones, don't use it if you're pregnant.

**Medicinal Use:** Black cohosh has a bitter taste, so mix it with other, more palatable herbs if you drink it as a tea. Black cohosh tinctures contain more active ingredients than teas. Take up to 1 teaspoon (4 droppers full) of tincture or 2 cups of tea a day.

# Blue Cohosh

**Perennial**

**Botanical Name:**
*Caulophyllum thalictroides*

**Family:** Berberidaceae

**Height:** 1–3 ft.

**Spread:** 1½ ft.

**Description:** Blue cohosh is a bluish-green, deciduous plant that flowers in June to August, producing yellow-green clusters of blooms on tall stalks. Blue cohosh is native to North America and grows from New Brunswick to Manitoba and south to Alabama. You may encounter blue cohosh in woods and along stream banks.

**Ease of Care:** Moderate

**Cultivation:** The herb likes rich, moist, humusy soil and shade.

**Propagation:** Sow seeds in spring; if you plant them in fall, they may germinate the following spring. Divide rhizomes in spring or fall. Seeds and rhizomes are available through mail order from wild flower and herb sources.

**Uses:** American Indians considered blue cohosh a panacea for women's ailments. Over the centuries and up to the present time, the herb has been used to treat uterine abnormalities and relieve menstrual cramps. Before the introduction of forceps, American obstetricians used blue cohosh to help induce labor.

In the past, herbalists also used blue cohosh to treat bronchitis, rheumatism, and irregular menstruation. They also combined it with other herbs, including motherwort and partridge berry, for women in the last few weeks of pregnancy to promote smooth labor. It was listed as an "official" medicine in the *U.S. Pharmacopoeia* until 1936.

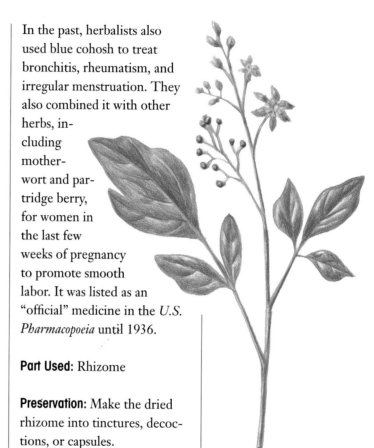

**Part Used:** Rhizome

**Preservation:** Make the dried rhizome into tinctures, decoctions, or capsules.

**Precautions:** Blue cohosh contains several strong compounds. It can constrict coronary blood vessels, so do not use it if you have a history of stroke or have high blood pressure, heart disease, or diabetes. The powdered rhizome irritates mucous membranes, so handle it with care; don't inhale it or get it in your eyes. And don't take blue cohosh during labor unless you are working with an herbalist or midwife knowledgeable about herbs. Above all, do not eat the berries: They are poisonous!

**Medicinal Use:** Use blue cohosh in tincture, tea, or pill form. Take ⅛ to ¼ teaspoon (½ to 1 dropper full) of tincture or drink ½ cup of tea, one to four times a day.

# Borage

**Annual** (with **Biennial** characteristics)

**Botanical Name:**
*Borago officinalis*

**Family:** Boraginaceae

**Height:** 2–2½ ft.

**Spread:** 1½ ft.

**Description:** The herb's basal rosette of long, spear-shaped leaves produces tall stems covered with attractive, bright-blue, star-shaped flowers that hang downward. All parts of the plant are covered with bristly "hairs." Borage is a nice addition to any flower garden. Although usually grown as an annual, the plant will often overwinter in mild climates for a second growing season. Borage is native to Europe, Asia Minor, northern Europe, and Africa. It has become naturalized in Great Britain and is found widely in North America, often in waste places and along roads.

**Ease of Care:** Easy

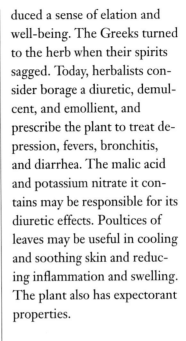

**Cultivation:** Borage prefers a dry, sunny location in poor to ordinary, well-drained soil. It is difficult to transplant; if you must do so, move the plant when it is young.

**Propagation:** Sow seed in early spring or late fall.

**Uses:** Celtic warriors drank borage wine because they believed it gave them courage. Romans thought borage produced a sense of elation and well-being. The Greeks turned to the herb when their spirits sagged. Today, herbalists consider borage a diuretic, demulcent, and emollient, and prescribe the plant to treat depression, fevers, bronchitis, and diarrhea. The malic acid and potassium nitrate it contains may be responsible for its diuretic effects. Poultices of leaves may be useful in cooling and soothing skin and reducing inflammation and swelling. The plant also has expectorant properties.

The crisp flavor of borage flowers complements cheese, fish, poultry, most vegetables, salads, iced beverages, pickles, and salad dressings. You can eat small amounts of young leaves: Steam well or sauté as you would spinach so the leaves are no longer prickly. You can also candy the flowers.

**Part Used:** Flowers, leaves

**Preservation:** Pick blossoms as they open and use them fresh or candied. Young leaves are good for fresh use. Because borage flowers lose much of their flavor when dried, preserve them in vinegar to use later.

**Precautions:** Borage is safe to use in moderation. Claims that it may harm the liver have not been substantiated, but you may want to limit how much you use; the herb contains the same type of alkaloids as comfrey. Some researchers strongly suggest not eating the leaves, which contain higher amounts of pyrrolizidine alkaloids than the flowers do.

**Medicinal Use:** Use the flowers in foods and the leaves in poultices.

# Burdock

**Biennial** (may be grown as an **Annual**)

**Botanical Name:** *Arcium lappa, A. minus*

**Family:** Asteraceae (Compositae)

**Height:** To 6 ft.

**Spread:** 3 ft.

**Description:** This stout, coarse herb has many branches, each topped by numerous flowers, which appear in summer. The seed burrs cling to anything that rubs against them. The large leaves grow to 20 inches. Native to Eurasia, burdock has become naturalized throughout North America. You're likely to find burdock in fields and vacant lots, especially in damp areas.

**Ease of Care:** Easy

**Cultivation:** A wild plant, burdock prefers average, moist, deep, loose, and well-drained soil and full sun, but it will grow in filtered sun.

**Propagation:** Burdock is grown easily from seed sown in the spring. Seedlings transplant well, but older plants are more difficult to relocate because they produce long taproots.

**Uses:** If you've ever returned from an outdoor romp with your pet and discovered burrs clinging tenaciously to the cuffs of your trousers and your pet's fur, you've encountered burdock, an herb whose primary use is as a blood purifier. The root is also considered a diuretic, diaphoretic, and laxative. It has also been used to treat psoriasis, acne, and other skin conditions. Research has found that several compounds in burdock root inhibit growth of bacteria and fungi. A poultice of leaves is effective in healing bruises, burns, and swellings. The Chinese also use burdock root to treat colds, flu, measles, and constipation and burdock seeds to treat skin problems. Herbalists use burdock to treat liver disorders.

Burdock also contains a substance called inulin, a starch that is easily digested. Burdock root tastes like a marriage of potato and celery; eat it fresh, steamed, or sautéd, treating it much like a carrot. Eat young stalks raw or steam them as you would asparagus. Burdock root is a staple of Japanese cuisine and sold in Japanese grocery stores, often under the name gobo root.

**Part Used:** Root, leaves, seeds

**Preservation:** Dig roots in the plant's first fall or second spring; use them fresh or dry. Gather leaves before flowers bloom. Gather seeds after they ripen.

**Precautions:** Only one case of a problem with burdock has been reported; however, it is believed the tea used was probably contaminated with the toxic belladonna.

**Medicinal Use:** Burdock may be consumed as a vegetable, dried for tea, or tinctured. Drink up to 2 cups of tea a day. Take ½ to 1 teaspoon tincture up to three times a day.

# Burnet

**Perennial**

**Botanical Name:**
*Poterium sanguisorba*

**Family:** Rosaceae

**Height:** 1½ ft., in flower

**Spread:** 1 ft.

**Description:** A ground-hugging rosette of dark green leaves forms the plant, from which thin, 1- to 1½-foot stems arise to produce handsome purple flower heads. Burnet makes a good edging plant. Also called salad burnet, the plant is native to western Asia and Europe and has become naturalized in North America.

**Ease of Care:** Easy

**Cultivation:** Burnet prefers full sun in average soil, although rich soil improves its flavor, making it less bitter. Burnet prefers an alkaline soil; if your soil is very acidic, add lime.

**Propagation:** Sow seed. Burnet self-sows easily after its first planting.

**Uses:** Herbalists have used burnet for at least 2,000 years. Useful to control bleeding, burnet's name, in fact, means "to drink up blood." Nineteenth-century Shakers used burnet for healing wounds. And the herb is considered helpful in treating vaginal discharges and diarrhea. Burnet leaves contain vitamin C and tannins; the latter gives it astringent properties. It relieves indigestion and diarrhea. Practitioners of traditional Chinese medicine use the root topically on wounds and burns to reduce inflammation and the risk of infection. It is also used to treat gum disease. While burnet is rarely used medicinally in North America, Europeans and Russians still use it in their folk medicine. It is used to heal ulcerative colitis as a folk remedy in Northern Europe and Russia. Apparently, its medicinal properties are due to more than simply the astringent tannins it contains. Russian research shows that the leaves improve circulation to the uterus, especially in pregnant women. The leaves also have immune-enhancing properties that may help correct some abnormalities during pregnancy.

In the kitchen, use tender, young, well-chopped leaves in salads, vinegars, butters, and iced beverages. Add leaves to vinegars, marinades, and cheese spreads. And flowers make attractive garnishes.

**Part Used:** Leaves, flowers

**Preservation:** Burnet does not dry well. Harvest leaves in early autumn and preserve them in vinegar.

**Precautions:** Although Russian studies show its value during pregnancy, use only small amounts unless a health practitioner recommends it.

**Medicinal Use:** Apply in compresses to heal wounds and stop bleeding. Add the leaves to foods.

# Butcher's Broom

**Perennial**

**Botanical Name:**
*Ruscus aculeatus*

**Family:** Liliaceae

**Height:** 4 ft.

**Spread:** To 3 ft.

**Description:** For 300 years—from the 16th to 19th centuries—butcher's broom was associated with the meat industry. Butchers used the leaves to repel vermin and animals. Later, they made "brooms" from the plant to scrub chopping blocks. With its waxy green leaves and scarlet berries, butcher's broom has been used to decorate meats at Christmas; indeed, another name for the herb is box holly. Found naturally from the Azores to Iran, butcher's broom is an erect evergreen, with prickly leaves and whitish or pinkish flowers that appear from mid-autumn to late spring. Its round berries are scarlet or yellow. Butcher's broom is found in woodland thickets on poor, dry, rocky soil.

**Ease of Care:** Easy

**Cultivation:** Cultivate butcher's broom in regular garden soil. An attractive plant, it is available at many nurseries, sold as an ornamental.

**Propagation:** Seeds, cuttings

**Uses:** Butcher's broom enjoys a venerable history as a medicinal herb. The ancient Greeks recommended butcher's broom for treating kidney stones, gout, and jaundice.

Today, butcher's broom is experiencing a comeback. There is scientific evidence it may have value in treating circulatory problems, such as varicose veins and hemorrhoids. In German studies, it decreased the inflammation of varicose veins, helped to tighten them, and encouraged the blood to flow up the legs. In addition to strengthening blood vessels, the plant reduces fever and increases urine flow.

**Part Used:** Leaves

**Preservation:**
Harvest leaves when the plant goes into flower. Dry or use fresh.

**Precautions:** Butcher's broom may elevate blood pressure; do not use if you have high blood pressure.

**Medicinal Use:** Drink 2 to 3 cups of tea a day to treat circulation problems or take ½ teaspoon tincture (2 droppers full) a day. Butcher's broom is often combined with other herbs that are good for circulation, such as gingko and hawthorn.

# Calendula

**Annual**

**Botanical Name:** *Calendula officinalis*

**Family:** Asteraceae (Compositae)

**Height:** 1–2 ft.

**Spread:** 1 ft.

**Description:** Calendula produces coarse, bright green leaves attached to brittle stems. The plant grows rapidly and blooms abundantly throughout summer, until the first frost. Also called pot marigold, the herb's flower colors range from bright yellow to vivid orange. (It is not a true marigold.) Calendula is a cheerful addition to any garden and makes an attractive potted plant. Calendula is found naturally from the Canary Islands through southern and central Europe. It is cultivated widely around the world.

**Ease of Care:** Easy

**Cultivation:** Calendula enjoys full sun and average, well-drained soil. Be on the lookout for insects, which adore calendula.

**Propagation:** Sow seed outdoors in early spring or indoors about seven weeks before the last frost.

**Uses:** The Romans grew these plants to treat scorpion bites. In accordance with the Doctrine of Signatures, calendula's yellow flowers were believed to be an effective treatment for jaundice. The herb is used today to treat wounds, skin conditions, and peptic and duodenal ulcers. Calendula's primary use is to heal the skin and reduce swelling. Apply calendula to sores, cuts, bruises, burns, and rashes. It even soothes the discomfort of measles and chicken pox—simply make a double strength tea and wash over the skin eruptions. It also helps prevent and relieve diaper rash. Calendula induces sweating, increases urination, and aids digestion. Researchers have found that compounds in calendula may be useful in treating cancer. It has traditionally been used to treat tonsillitis and any condition related to swollen lymph glands, including breast cancer. It is also an excellent treatment for infection due to *Candida albicans.* Calendula tincture is used topically on varicose veins, bruises, and sprains.

In the kitchen, add a few calendula flowers to salads and sandwiches. Powdered yellow flowers may substitute for saffron's color (they once were used to color butter, custards, and liqueurs), although go easy—they have a bitter taste. The flowers produce a bright yellow dye and are commercially grown. Dry flowers for potpourri. A calendula rinse brings out highlights in hair. It is a popular ingredient in skin cream and lotions, baby oils, and salves.

**Part Used:** Flowers

**Preservation:** Dry whole flowers or remove petals from their green backs and spread them thinly on screens to dry. Stir while drying to prevent petals from molding.

**Precautions:** None

**Medicinal Use:** To treat thrush, an infection with the *Candida* organism that appears in the mouth, swab the area with a tincture diluted in an equal amount of distilled water. Calendula is rarely drunk as a tea. A strong infusion, however, makes a good compress. For a poultice, mash fresh flowers and apply to the skin. To make calendula oil, crush dried or wilted flowers, then heat in olive oil for a few hours on low heat. Strain.

# Caraway

**Biennial**

**Botanical Name:** *Carum carvi*

**Family:** Apiaceae (Umbelliferae)

**Height:** 2 ft.

**Spread:** 8 in.

**Description:** Although caraway is a biennial, some varieties behave as annuals, going to seed in their first year. Caraway is characterized by fine-cut leaves that resemble the foliage of carrots. White umbels develop in the plant's second year to produce distinctively flavored seeds. Native to the Middle East, Asia, and central Europe, caraway has become naturalized in North America.

**Ease of Care:** Moderate

**Cultivation:** Caraway grows best in a light, average, well-drained soil in full sun, although it tolerates partial shade. Plant in place; caraway produces a long taproot and does not transplant easily.

**Propagation:** Sow seeds outdoors in early spring or late summer.

**Uses:** Caraway seeds were found in ancient tombs, indicating the plant was used at least 5,000 years ago. As a medicine, caraway is used—most often as a cordial—to relieve an upset stomach and dispel gas. Caraway water has long been given to babies with colic. A compress soaked in a strong infusion or the powdered and moistened seed relieves swelling and bruising. But you may be most familiar with caraway from eating sauerkraut, rye crackers, and rye bread—foods that rely heavily on its strong aroma and taste. Add caraway seeds to beef dishes, stews, and breads. Add leaves to salads and soups. The herb complements eggs, cheese, sauces, barley, oats, pork, and fish, as well as cabbage, beets, spinach, potatoes, peas, cauliflower, turnips, and zucchini. Cooking it a long time can make it bitter, so add caraway no more than 30 minutes before a dish is done. It also makes children's medicines more tasty. The essential oil is added to soaps, cosmetics, perfumes, and mouthwashes and used to flavor liqueurs in Germany, Scandinavia, and Russia.

**Part Used:** Leaves, seeds, root

**Preservation:** Cut plants at ground level when seeds ripen. Hang-dry seed heads in paper bags in a cool, dry place. Store seeds in tightly sealed containers. In its first fall or spring, dig up roots, clean, and store in a cool, dark area.

**Precautions:** None

**Medicinal Use:** The most popular way to use caraway medicinally is in food. It is rare to find anyone using it by itself as a tincture or tea, but sometimes it flavors tinctures or syrups.

# Catnip

**Perennial**

**Botanical Name:** *Nepeta cataria*

**Family:** Lamiaceae (Labiatae)

**Height:** 3–4 ft.

**Spread:** 2 ft.

**Description:** Also called cat-mint, this herb produces fuzzy, gray-green, triangular leaves in pairs along abundant branches. The leaves give off a pungent scent when crushed. From July through September, catnip produces white flowers with purple or pink spots. The herb is native to the Eurasian region and naturalized throughout North America and elsewhere.

**Ease of Care:** Easy

**Cultivation:** Catnip grows well in full sun to partial shade, in average to sandy, well-drained soil.

**Propagation:** Sow seed in spring or fall; take cuttings in early summer.

**Uses:** Your cat may go crazy over catnip, but the herb has actually been used as a mild sedative for about 2,000 years. The Romans harvested catnip, and colonists carried the herb

to America, where it quickly became naturalized. Catnip tea aids digestion, promotes sleep, and treats colds, nervousness, and headaches. Its most important use is as a sedative that is safe enough even for children and the elderly. Catnip contains sedative constituents similar to valerian, another popular herbal relaxant. One of catnip's most famous uses is to treat colic in babies—a condition for which it has been used for hundreds of years. It also makes a good tea for treating indigestion associated with anxiety or nervousness. The tea treats measles and chicken pox when used both internally

and topically. An infusion applied to the skin relieves hives and other rashes. The herb increases perspiration, reduces fevers, and increases menstrual flow. But catnip finds its greatest commercial value in the pet industry, as filling for cat toys. Cats react differently than humans do to the herb; they find it very stimulating, not sedating at all. The herb's fragrance also repels many insects.

**Part Used:** Leaves

**Preservation:** Gather leaves in late summer just before the plant blooms. Hang-dry plants, remove leaves from stems, and store in airtight containers.

**Precautions:** None

**Medicinal Use:** Catnip is usually combined with other herbs in a tea or tincture. For indigestion or for use as a gentle sedative, mix it with chamomile and lemon balm. For a stronger muscle and nerve relaxant, mix it with valerian or skullcap. Take up to 4 cups of tea or 1 teaspoon (4 droppers full) of tincture a day.

# Cayenne Pepper

**Perennial**

**Botanical Name:**

*Capsicum annuum*

**Family:** Solanaceae

**Height:** 1–3 ft.

**Spread:** 1 ft.

**Description:** Cayenne's angular branches and stems may look purplish. Its red pod-like fruits are extremely hot. Flowers, which appear in drooping clusters on long stems, are star-shaped and yellowish-white. Leaves are long and elliptical. Cayenne grows naturally in the tropics, but gardeners in most parts of the United States can grow it with success.

**Ease of Care:** Easy

**Cultivation:** Unless you live in an area that rarely experiences freezing temperatures, it's best to plant cayenne in containers you can bring inside when temperatures drop, or grow it as an annual. The plant grows best in rich soil. If your soil is average, fertilize it with compost, rock phosphate, or wood ashes. Cayenne likes full sun.

Give your plants lots of water during early stages of growth. Mulching protects them from drought.

**Propagation:** Because cayenne has a long growing season (up to 18 weeks), start plants indoors if propagating from seed. Transplant seedlings 12 to 18 inches apart, and allow 3 feet between rows.

**Uses:** Cayenne has many medicinal uses. The main ingredient in cayenne is capsaicin, a powerful stimulant responsible for the pepper's heat. Although it can set your mouth on fire, cayenne, ironically, is good for your digestive system and is now known to help heal ulcers! It reduces substance P, a chemical that carries pain messages from the skin's nerve endings, so it reduces pain when applied topically. A cayenne cream is now in use to treat psoriasis, postsurgical pain, shingles, and nerve damage from diabetes. It may even help you burn off extra pounds. Researchers in England have found that about ¼ ounce of cayenne burns from 45 to 76 calories by increasing metabolism.

Taking cayenne internally stabilizes blood pressure. You can apply powdered, dry cayenne as a poultice over wounds to stop bleeding. And in the kitchen, cayenne spices up any food it touches. A new use for cayenne is as a "pepper spray," used by both the public and many police forces.

**Part Used:** Fruit

**Preservation:** Pick cayenne peppers after the fruits have turned red. Dry immediately and store in a cool, dry place. You can also freeze cayenne peppers or preserve them in oil or vinegar.

**Precautions:** Overexposure to the skin can produce pain, dizziness, and a rapid pulse. Alcohol or fat, such as whole milk, neutralizes the reaction. If you touch a pepper and then rub your eyes or nose, you could inflame those sensitive tissues.

**Medicinal Use:** Add a pinch of cayenne powder to other herbal infusions to treat colds and influenza. Simmer 3 table-

spoons cayenne in 1 cup of cider vinegar. Do not strain. Shake before using. Take 1 teaspoon (4 droppers full) straight or add it to ½ cup warm water or tea for colds, flu, or sore throat. You can also combine cayenne with other heating herbs such as peppermint, eucalyptus, cinnamon, rosemary, and thyme in liniments for sore muscles or lung congestion.

# Chamomile, German

**Annual**

**Botanical Name:**
*Matricaria recutita*

**Family:** Asteraceae
(Compositae)

**Height:** 2 ft.

**Spread:** 4–6 in.

**Description:** These small, fine-leaved plants look almost like ferns, but the herb's abundant, small, daisy-type flowers have an apple scent. German chamomile looks much like its cousin, Roman chamomile *(Chamaemelum nobile)*, but German chamomile is an annual and must be grown from seed each spring. Roman chamomile may spread to form a lush mat, which can be mowed regularly. Both chamomile species are native to Europe, Africa, and Asia and have become naturalized in North America. Chamomile is widely cultivated. There are other species of chamomile, including several that are indigenous to North America.

**Ease of Care:** Moderate

**Cultivation:** Chamomile grows in full sun, in average to poor, light, dry soil. Plant several chamomiles; single plants are too small to have any impact in a garden.

**Propagation:** Sow seed in early spring; divide in the spring or fall.

**Uses:** Chamomile is one of the world's best-loved herbs. The herb produces a pleasant-tasting tea, which has a strong aroma of apples. The early Egyptians valued chamomile and used it to cure malaria and bring down fevers. The ancient Greeks called on chamomile to relieve headaches and treat illnesses of the kidney, liver, and bladder. Today herbalists prescribe the herb to calm nerves and settle upset stomachs, among its other uses.

Chamomile's medicinal properties derive from its essential oils. The herb has three primary medicinal uses: an anti-inflammatory to reduce swelling and infection; an anti-spasmodic to relieve digestive upsets, headaches, and menstrual cramps; and an anti-infective for cleansing wounds. Chamomile is often found in creams and lotions to soothe sensitive or irritated skin and treat rashes and skin allergies. Cosmetics employ it to reduce puffiness, especially around the eyes. It reduces the swelling that results from allergies or colds. It is used on bruises, sprains, and varicose veins and almost any time the skin becomes inflamed. Chamomile infusions make excellent skin cleansers. Use chamomile both internally and topically to relieve muscle pain. Its calming action not only relieves pain but also induces sleep and relieves nervous indigestion—

it has been used to calm children and babies for hundreds of years. Chamomile reduces gastric acid, which helps prevent or speed healing of ulcers. It even shows immune-system activity. Chamomile's fragrant aroma makes it a good addition to potpourri and flower arrangements.

**Part Used:** Flowers

**Preservation:** Harvest flowers when fully open. Hang-dry plants; screen-dry flowers.

**Precautions:** Chamomile flowers may cause symptoms of allergies in some people allergic to ragweed and related plants, although the risk of this is quite low.

**Medicinal Use:** Drink as much chamomile tea as you wish. Use up to 1½ teaspoons (6 droppers full) of tincture a day. You can also take chamomile as pills, or use it in a vinegar or skin cream. Use a chamomile compress, poultice, or tincture on bruises and inflammation. Add a few drops of essential oil to creams, lotions, or a bath.

# Chaste Tree

**Perennial**

**Botanical Name:**
*Vitex agnus castus*

**Family:** Verbenaceae

**Height:** To 20 ft.

**Spread:** 6 ft.

**Description:**
Chaste tree is a small tree, with opposite leaves divided into lanceolate leaflets. Its small flowers are lavender or lilac. Native to southern Europe, the herb has been naturalized in warm regions.

**Ease of Care:** Easy

**Cultivation:** Chaste tree likes sandy or loamy, well-drained soil and full sun.

**Propagation:** Sow seed in spring; layer or take young woody cuttings in spring.

**Uses:** During the Middle Ages, monks used chaste tree to diminish their sexual drive, hence the herb's common name, monk's pepper. Today chaste tree, which is often referred to as Vitex, is used primarily to treat women's discomforts. The flavonoids in chaste tree produce a progesterone-like effect. The herb may raise progesterone levels by acting on the brain. Chaste tree helps to normalize and regulate menstrual cycles, reduce premenstrual fluid retention, reduce some cases of acne that may flare up during PMS or menstruation, reduce hot flashes, and treat menopausal bleeding irregularities and other menopausal symptoms. It is also useful in helping dissolve fibroids and cysts in the reproductive system and may be used for treating some types of infertility.

Chaste tree may be used after childbirth to promote milk production. It is a slow-acting herb and may take months to take effect.

**Part Used:** Berries

**Preservation:** Gather berries after they ripen; dry or tincture.

**Precautions:** Because of its complex hormonal actions, be cautious using chaste tree during pregnancy. It may also interfere with hormonal drugs. Little information is available about the physiologic activity of chaste tree in men.

**Medicinal Use:** Drink 3 to 4 cups of tea a day. Take ½ to 1 teaspoon (2 to 4 droppers full) tincture up to two times a day.

# Chives

**Perennial**

**Botanical Name:**
*Allium schoenoprasum*

**Family:** Liliaceae

**Height:** 8–12 in.

**Spread:** 8 in.

**Description:** Chives produces tight clumps of long, thin, grasslike leaves that resemble those of onion in appearance and taste. The herb produces abundant, small, rose-purple, globe-shaped flower heads in early summer. Chives may be planted as edging, grown alone, or grown with other plants in containers. The herb is native to Greece, Sweden, the Alps, and parts of northern Great Britain. It is widely cultivated elsewhere.

**Ease of Care:** Easy; it is drought-tolerant, and most insects ignore it.

**Cultivation:** Chives prefers an average to rich soil but manages in almost any soil. The herb grows best in full sun to partial shade. Chives makes a good ornamental plant in the garden. Chives may also be grown as a potted plant indoors at any time of the year. Several new varieties have been developed to produce thicker bunches and longer-lasting flowers. Chives is said to complement growth of carrots, grapes, roses, and tomatoes. The herb deters Japanese beetles and may prevent companion plants from developing black spot, scab, and mildew.

**Propagation:** Sow seed or divide at any time during the growing season.

**Uses:** Archaeologists tell us that chives has been in use for at least 5,000 years. By the 16th century, it was a popular European garden herb. Chives' few medicinal properties derive from the sulfur-rich oil found in all members of the onion family. The oil is antiseptic and may help lower blood pressure, but it must be consumed in fairly large quantities. Chives' pleasant taste—like that of mild, sweet onions—complements the flavor of most foods. Use fresh minced leaves in dishes containing potatoes, artichokes, asparagus, cauliflower, corn, tomatoes, peas, carrots, spinach, poultry, fish, veal, cheese, eggs, and, of course, in cream cheese atop your bagel or in sour cream on a baked potato. Add chives at the last minute for best flavor. Flowers are good additions to salads and may be preserved in vinegars.

**Part Used:**
Leaves, flowers

**Preservation:**
Harvest leaves any time by trimming off the top one third. Mince leaves and freeze them to obtain full flavor since they do not dry well. Or dry them in the refrigerator to help preserve their color and taste. (Commercial chives are freeze-dried.) Pick flowers before seeds appear and preserve in vinegar.

**Precautions:** None

**Medicinal Use:** The best way to derive chives' benefits is to add minced leaves liberally to cooked dishes or use a chive vinegar.

# Comfrey

**Perennial**

**Botanical Name:**
*Symphytum officinale*

**Family:** Boraginaceae

**Height:** 3 ft.

**Spread:** 1 ft.

**Description:** Comfrey is a hardy, leafy plant that dies down in winter and comes back strong in spring. The herb produces roots that are black outside and white inside and exude a mucilaginous substance when crushed. Various species of comfrey have purple-pink flowers and appear from May through the first frost. The herb is native to Europe and Asia and has become naturalized on every continent. Comfrey is found along stream banks and in moist meadows.

**Ease of Care:** Easy

**Cultivation:** Comfrey prefers rich to average soil and full sun or partial shade but will grow almost anywhere. The herb is easy to grow, but it is very invasive and difficult to eradicate, so plant it where you can contain it. Once established, comfrey requires little maintenance, but you will have it there forever!

**Propagation:** Sow seed in spring, divide in fall, take cuttings any time. Set plants 3 feet apart.

**Uses:** Comfrey has been regarded as a great healer since at least around 400 B.C., when the Greeks used it topically to stop bleeding, heal wounds, and mend broken bones. The Romans made comfrey poultices and teas to treat bruises, stomach disorders, and diarrhea. Today herbalists continue to prescribe comfrey for bruises, wounds, and sores. Allantoin, a compound found in comfrey, causes cells to divide and grow, spurring wounds to heal faster. It also inhibits inflammation of the stomach's lining. Comfrey has been recommended for treating bronchitis, asthma, respiratory irritation, peptic ulcers, and stomach and intestinal inflammation. Studies show it inhibits prostaglandins, substances that cause inflammation. It was once promoted as a salad green and potherb; however, internal use of comfrey has become a much-debated topic.

In cosmetic use, comfrey soothes and softens skin and promotes growth of new cells. Comfrey is found in creams, lotions, and bath preparations. It dyes wool brown.

**Part Used:** Root, leaves

**Preservation:** Dig comfrey roots in late summer or fall.

**Precautions:** There is some evidence that excessive consumption of comfrey root, especially *Symphytum uplandicum*, contributes to liver damage, though this has not been confirmed. Several people who consumed comfrey have experienced liver damage. It has been suggested that other substances they took simultaneously may have interacted adversely with the comfrey. Use comfrey root topically only until it receives a clear bill of health. Comfrey contains pyrrolizidine alkaloids, which are responsible for its harmful effects. The dried leaf contains no pyrrolizidine alkaloids; it is considered relatively safe to use as tea and does contain some of the healing allantoin. The fresh leaves contain very little pyrrolizidine, especially the large, mature leaves.

**Medicinal Use:** If using dried root, chop or grind it and dissolve it in hot water to release mucilage for external use. Don't boil comfrey or you'll break down the healing allantoin. You'll notice that most skin salves contain comfrey, so add comfrey root or leaves to oils, salves, and lotions. You can apply a poultice of grated comfrey root or a compress cloth soaked in comfrey tea to sunburns and other skin irritations.

# Coriander

**Annual**

**Botanical Name:** *Coriandrum sativum*

**Family:** Apiaceae (Umbelliferae)

**Height:** 2–3 ft.

**Spread:** 6 in.

**Description:** Coriander's bright green, lacy leaves resemble those of flat-leaved Italian parsley when they first spring up from seed, but they become more fern-like as the plant matures. Coriander, also called cilantro and Chinese parsley, flowers from middle to late summer. The herb is native to the eastern Mediterranean region and southern Europe. It is widely cultivated in Morocco, Mexico, Argentina, Canada, India, and the United States, especially in South Carolina.

**Ease of Care:** Easy

**Cultivation:** Coriander prefers average, well-drained soil in full sun. Protect fragile stalks from wind. Coriander may enhance growth of anise.

**Propagation:** Sow seed in spring after soil is warm.

**Uses:** Coriander has been cultivated for 3,000 years. The Hebrews, who used coriander seed as one of their Passover herbs, probably learned about it from the ancient Egyptians, who revered the plant. The Romans and Greeks used coriander for medicinal purposes and as a spice and preservative. The Chinese believed coriander could make a human immortal. Throughout northern Europe, people would suck on candy-coated coriander seeds when they had indigestion; chewing the seeds soothes an upset stomach, relieves flatulence, aids digestion, and improves appetite. Poultices of coriander seeds have been used to relieve the pain of rheumatism. The Chinese prescribe the tea to treat dysentery and measles. Coriander relieves inflammation and headaches. But its most popular medicinal use has been to flavor strong-tasting medicines and to prevent intestinal gripping common with some laxative formulas.

Coriander's leaf flavor is a cross between sage and citrus. The herb's bold flavor is common to several ethnic cuisines, notably those of China, southeast Asia, Mexico, East India, Spain, Central Africa, and Central and South America. Add young leaves to beets, onions, salads, sausage, clams, oysters, and potatoes. Add seeds to marinades, salad dressings, cheese, eggs, and pickling brines. Coriander seed is used commercially to flavor sugared confections, liqueurs such as Benedictine and Chartreuse, and gin. Its essential oil is found in perfumes, aftershaves, and cosmetics because of its delightfully spicy scent. It is no longer as popular a cosmetic as it was from the 14th to 17th centuries, but coriander "refines" the complexion and was in the famous *Eau de Carnes* and Carmelite water. It is still used in soaps and deodorants.

**Part Used:** Young leaves, seeds

**Preservation:** Harvest only fresh, young leaves, and freeze them promptly or preserve them in vinegar. Harvest seeds when they start to turn brown. Cut a whole plant and hang-dry upside down inside paper bags to catch seeds.

**Precautions:** Very large doses are narcotic, but it is unlikely you could eat the quantity needed to produce this effect.

**Medicinal Use:** Coriander leaves and seeds are almost exclusively eaten, although occasionally the seed is used to flavor medicine.

# Costmary

**Perennial**

**Botanical Name:**
*Chrysanthemum balsamita*

**Family:** Asteraceae
(Compositae)

**Height:** 2½–3 ft.

**Spread:** 2 ft.

**Description:** Costmary produces basal clusters of elongated oval leaves. The herb sends up tall flower stems that produce clusters of unremarkable blooms. When leaves are young and fresh, they smell spicy; the scent changes to balsam when the leaves are dried. The herb is native to western Asia. Although it's rarely found growing in the wild, it is cultivated throughout Europe and North America.

**Ease of Care:**
Easy

**Cultivation:** Costmary prefers fertile, well-drained soil in full sun to partial shade.

**Propagation:** Divide as needed and every few years as clumps become large.

**Uses:** Costmary flourished in English gardens and was used to spice ale. The herb is antiseptic and slightly astringent and has been used in salves to heal dry, itchy skin. It promotes urine flow and

brings down fevers. Although rarely used for this purpose today, its principle medicinal use was as a digestive aid and to treat dysentery, for which it was included in the *British Pharmacopoeia*. The cosmetic water was commonly used to improve the complexion and as a hair rinse. Costmary is good for acne and oily skin and hair.

Costmary's flavor complements beverages, chilled soups, and fruit salads. You can add dried leaves to potpourri, sachets, and baths, or slip them in books to deter bugs that eat paper—this was once a common practice. Dried branches have been used to make herbal baskets.

**Part Used:** Leaves

**Preservation:** Pick leaves any time. Hang-dry to preserve. Dried costmary retains its scent for a long time.

**Precautions:** None

**Medicinal Use:** Costmary is rarely used medicinally, but you could make a tea of the leaves. However, the tea tastes bitter, so add sweeter herbs such as lemon balm and mint.

# Cramp Bark

**Perennial**

**Botanical Name:**
*Viburnum opulus*

**Family:** Caprifoliaceae

**Height:** To 13 ft.

**Spread:** 6 ft.

**Description:** A relative of black haw and sloe, cramp bark was introduced to England in the 16th century from Holland, where it is known as guelder rose. Also called highbush cranberry or snowball tree, cramp bark has multiple branches that produce three to five lobed, shiny leaves. White flowers appear from early to middle summer, followed by scarlet berries that eventually turn purple. The tree is native to Europe, North Africa, and northern Asia and has become naturalized elsewhere, particularly in Canada and the northern United States. Cramp bark may be found in woodland clearings in wet, loamy soil.

**Ease of Care:** Easy, once established

**Cultivation:** Cramp bark likes moist, average to rich soil and full sun.

**Propagation:** Cramp bark grows from seed, although seeds need stratification and may take months to germinate. New shrubs also grow from hardwood cuttings. The easiest way to obtain the herb is to buy a plant from the nursery—it is a popular landscape plant.

**Uses:**
Cramp bark's name tells you how the tree is used. American Indian women relied extensively on cramp bark to ease the pain of menstrual cramps and childbirth. An early American formula known as Mother's Cordial was given to women in childbirth. Cramp bark is used to halt contractions during premature labor and prevent miscarriage. It has also been used to prevent uterine hemorrhaging.

An antispasmodic, cramp bark may reduce leg cramps, muscle spasms, and pain from a stiff neck. Nineteenth-century herbalists often prescribed cramp bark as a sedative and muscle relaxant. The herb's medicinal actions may be attributed in part to a bitter called viburnin, as well as valerianic acid (also found in valerian), salicosides (also found in willow bark), and an antispasmodic constituent. Clinical studies indicate cramp bark may be useful in treating cardiovascular problems, reducing blood pressure and heart palpitations, and fighting influenza viruses. Cramp bark is considered an astringent as well.

The tree's cooked berries taste somewhat like cranberries, which is why it is often called cranberry tree or bush. In Scandinavia, liquor is distilled from the fruit. A Russian brandy, *nastoika*, made with the berries is used as a stomach ulcer remedy. From a species that grows in Japan, the Japanese make a vinegar to treat cirrhosis of the liver.

**Part Used:** Root, bark

**Preservation:** Dig roots in summer or fall. Peel bark from the root and dry or tincture. Gather trunk bark in April or May, and tincture or dry.

**Precautions:** Do not eat fresh berries, which contain viburnin and may cause indigestion. The toxicity dissipates when berries are cooked.

**Medicinal Use:** Use under the care of a physician or herbalist during pregnancy. Use cramp bark with herbs such as wild yam and other uterine relaxants in tea, pills, or tinctures. As a general antispasmodic, blend in with sedative herbs such as valerian. Take up to 1½ teaspoons (about 6 droppers full) of tincture or 6 cups of tea a day to relieve muscle spasms.

# Dandelion

**Perennial**

**Botanical Name:**
*Taraxacum officinale*

**Family:** Asteraceae
(Compositae)

**Height:** 6–12 in.

**Spread:** 1 ft.; may become
invasive

**Description:** Long considered a lawn pest, dandelion produces a taproot that is white on the inside and dark brown on the outside. You're probably familiar with the bright yellow flowers that top dandelion's hollow stems. Flowers appear in late spring and close at night. Dark green leaves are jagged and grow close to the ground in a rosette. Native to Europe and Asia, dandelion has become naturalized throughout temperate regions.

**Ease of Care:** Easy

**Cultivation:** Dandelion is a wild plant that likes nitrogen-rich soil but will grow just about anywhere. The herb prefers full sun to partial shade.

Dandelion is said to enhance growth of fruit trees.

**Propagation:** Collect seeds from the wild and sow in spring.

**Uses:** The Arabs were the first to introduce dandelion's healing and nutritive abilities to the Europeans through their writing. By the 16th century, dandelion was considered an important culinary and blood-purifying herb in Europe. The root is used to treat liver diseases, such as jaundice and cirrhosis. It also is considered beneficial for building up blood and curing anemia.

Dandelion root's diuretic properties may help lower blood pressure and relieve premenstrual fluid retention. Unlike most diuretics, it retains potassium rather than flushing it from the body. Clinical studies have favorably compared dandelion's actions with the frequently prescribed diuretic drug Furosemide. Dandelion roots contain inulin and levulin, starchlike substances that are easy to digest, as well as a bitter substance (taraxacin) that stimulates digestion. Dandelion roots, stems, and leaves exude a white sticky resin that dissolves warts, if applied repeatedly.

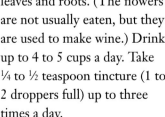

Wine made from dandelion flowers tastes like sherry. An Arabian dish, yublo, contains the flower buds and oil, flour, honey, and roses. The roasted ground root makes a good coffee substitute. Dandelion leaves are rich in minerals and vitamins, particularly vitamins A, B₂, C, and K and calcium. Add young leaves to salads, or sauté them as you would spinach. The English sometimes put the flowers in sandwiches. Dandelion makes a tonic bath and facial steam. Its flowers produce a yellow dye.

**Part Used:** Root, leaves, flowers

**Preservation:** Gather leaves in the spring, flowers in the summer, and roots in the fall.

**Precautions:** The white latex in fresh dandelion is caustic and may cause skin irritation and digestive disturbances, so dry the root before using.

**Medicinal Use:** Supplement your diet with fresh dandelion leaves and roots. (The flowers are not usually eaten, but they are used to make wine.) Drink up to 4 to 5 cups a day. Take ¼ to ½ teaspoon tincture (1 to 2 droppers full) up to three times a day.

# Dill

**Annual**

**Botanical Name:**
*Anethum graveolens*

**Family:** Apiaceae
(Umbelliferae)

**Height:** 2–3 ft.

**Spread:** 6–12 in.

**Description:** Dill produces
fine-cut, fernlike leaves on
tall, fragile stems. It is a
blue-green annual with attractive yellow flower umbels and yellow-green seed
heads. The herb blooms
from July through
September. Native to the
Mediterranean region and
southwest Asia, it has become naturalized through-
out North America.

**Ease of Care:**
Easy

**Cultivation:** Dill likes light,
moist, sandy soil in full sun.
Because it does not transplant
well, sow in place and thin as
needed. Grow dill in clumps or
rows, so fragile stems can support each other. Some gardeners believe dill enhances the
growth of cabbage, onions, and
lettuce.

**Propagation:** Sow seed in late
fall or early spring. Plant at
three-week intervals during
spring and early summer for a
fresh supply all season.

**Uses:** Dill derives from an old
Norse word meaning "to lull,"
and, indeed, the herb once was
used to induce sleep in babies
with colic. Herbalists also use
dill to relieve gas and to stimulate flow of mother's milk. Dill
stimulates the appetite and settles the stomach, but the seeds
have also been chewed to
lessen the appetite and stop the
stomach from rumbling—
something that parishioners
found useful during all-day
church services. In India, it is
used to treat ulcers, fevers,
uterine pain, and problems
with the eyes and kidneys, usually in a formula with other
herbs. In Ethiopia, the seeds
are chewed to relieve a
headache.

Add minced dill leaves to salads and use as a garnish. Seeds
go well with fish, lamb, pork,
poultry, cheese, cream, eggs,
and an array of vegetables,
including cabbage, onions,
cauliflower, squash, spinach,
potatoes, and broccoli. Of
course, dill pickles would not
be the same without dill seed
and weed. The herb is particularly popular in Russia and
Scandinavia. Its taste somewhat resembles caraway, which
shares a similar chemistry.

**Part Used:** Leaves, seeds

**Preservation:** Clip fresh leaves
as needed. Flavor is best re-
tained for later use if frozen;
pick leaves just as flowers
begin to open. For seeds, harvest entire plants when seed
heads begin to turn brown.
Hang-dry upside down in
paper bags to catch seeds.

**Precautions:** None

**Medicinal Use:** By far, the most
popular way to use dill is to in-
corporate it into your food to
aid digestion. Although you
could use it in an herb tea,
sweeter digestive herbs such as
anise are preferred. An essential oil is available; however, it
is used mostly by the food industry.

# Echinacea

**Perennial**

**Botanical Name:**
*Echinacea purpurea*

**Family:** Asteraceae (Compositae)

**Height:** To 4 ft.

**Spread:** 2 ft.

**Description:** Also known as purple coneflower, echinacea resembles the black-eyed Susan. The herb produces long black roots and stout, sturdy stems covered with bristly hairs. Cone-shaped flower heads, which appear from middle to late summer, are composed of numerous tiny purple florets surrounded by deep pink petals. Leaves are pale green to dark green. Echinacea is native to prairies from southern Canada to Texas.

**Ease of Care:** Easy

**Cultivation:** Echinacea prefers average, well-drained soil and full sun to light shade. The herb may fall prey to leaf spot or Japanese beetles.

**Propagation:** Sow seed in spring. Mulch in winter. Dig up the plant about every four years, divide, and replant in fertilized soil.

**Uses:** American Indians used echinacea extensively to treat the bites of snakes and poisonous insects, burns, and wounds; the root facilitates wound healing. (Sometimes the seeds are combined with the roots for medicinal use.) Echinacea is prescribed to treat various infections, mumps, measles, and eczema. A compound in echinacea prevents damage to collagen in the skin and connective tissues when taken internally. Recent studies suggest that, applied topically, echinacea may treat sunburn.

Today, echinacea root is used primarily to boost the immune system and help the body fight disease. Besides bolstering several chemical substances that direct immune response, echinacea increases the number and activity of white blood cells (the body's disease-fighting agents), raises the level of interferon (a substance that enhances immune function), increases production of substances the body produces to fight cancers, and helps remove pollutants from the lungs. Many studies support echinacea's ability to fend off disease.

Another species, *E. angustifolia*, is used interchangeably with *E. purpurea* although the chemistry of the two species is slightly different.

**Part Used:** Root, seeds, leaves; flowers and seed heads for crafts

**Preservation:** Harvest roots after the plant begins to die back in the fall. Replant the crown after you have taken the root. Dry or tincture.

**Precautions:** Echinacea has been shown to be very non-toxic and safe even for children. Some herbalists believe echinacea should not be used by people with auto-immune disorders such as lupus or rheumatoid arthritis because their immune systems are already overstimulated.

**Medicinal Use:** Take capsules, tea, or tinctures. Most herbalists recommend large, frequent doses at the onset of a cold, flu, sinus infection, or other illness. For acute infection, take ¼ teaspoon (1 dropper full) of tincture every 1 to 3 hours for a day or two, then reduce the dosage. Take echinacea three times a day for several weeks; then abstain for several weeks before using again. Echinacea is often used alone but may be combined with other anti-infection and immune-stimulating herbs.

# Elderberry

**Perennial**

**Botanical Name:**
*Sambucus nigra*

**Family:** Caprifoliaceae

**Height:** 12–50 ft.

**Spread:** To 20 ft.; may become invasive

**Description:** Elderberry comprises about 13 species of deciduous shrubs native to North America and Europe. European settlers brought elderberry plants with them to the American colonies. Its flowers are white and plate-shaped, the leaves are pinnate (resembling a feather) and may be toothed, and its fruit appears in purple-blue clusters.

**Ease of Care:** Easy to grow; may require maintenance since it likes to sprawl

**Cultivation:** Elderberry prefers fertile, moist soil and full sun to partial shade. Propagate the suckers or grow plants from seeds or cuttings.

**Uses:** Elderberry has probably been used medicinally and nutritively for as long as human beings have gathered plants.

Evidence of elderberry plants has been uncovered in Stone Age sites. Ancient people used elderberries to dye their hair black. The wood of old stems is still used to make musical instruments by Native Americans and Europeans.

In the kitchen, the berries are used to make jams, jellies, chutneys, preserves, wines, and teas. For decades, elder flower water was on the dressing tables of proper young ladies who used it to treat sunburn and eradicate freckles. It is still sometimes used in Europe for these purposes. Yellow and violet dyes are made from the leaves and berries, respectively.

Medicinally, elderberry has been used as a mild digestive stimulant and diaphoretic. Elder flowers decrease inflammation so are often included in preparations to treat burns and swellings and in cosmetics that reduce puffiness. The berries have been used traditionally in Europe to treat flu, gout, and rheumatism as well as to improve general health. Several tales attribute longevity to the elderberry.

Recent studies in Israel found the berry is a potent antiviral that fights influenza virus B, the cause of one of the common forms of flu. Recognizing that it has long been used as a flu remedy, researchers at the Hebrew University Hadasah Medical Centre in Jerusalem conducted clinical studies and found the berry reduced fever, coughs, and muscle pain within 24 hours. After taking an elderberry syrup only two days, almost two-thirds of those with influenza reported complete recovery. The Centre also found that elderberry stimulates the immune system. The berries are currently under investigation for their ability to inhibit the herpes and Epstein-Barr viruses as well as HIV, the virus that causes AIDS. The berries are also rich in compounds that improve heart and circulatory health.

**Part Used:** Berries, flowers

**Preservation:** Pick flowers in full bloom. Use them fresh or dried. Harvest berries when juicy and ripe.

**Precautions:** The elderberry that bears blue fruit is perfectly safe to eat, although large quantities of the raw berries can cause some indigestion and act as a laxative. Cooking the berries before eating them cancels this action. The leaves, bark, and root, on the other hand, are slightly toxic and should not be used internally. Don't use the elder plant that bears red berries: This plant is a different species (*Sambucus pubens*).

**Medicinal Use:** Drink the flower tea freely. Take up to 3 cups of tea or 1 teaspoon (4 droppers full) of tincture made from the berry. Elderberry is also available in juices.

# Elecampane

**Perennial**

**Botanical Name:**
*Inula helenium*

**Family:** Asteraceae
(Compositae)

**Height:** 4–6 ft.

**Spread:** 2 ft.

**Description:** Also known as wild sunflower, velvet dock, scabwort, and horseheal, elecampane is a tall, attractive plant. Sturdy, with a round, coarse, woolly stem, elecampane produces blooms that resemble sunflowers. Elecampane's leaves are toothed and bristly on the upper surface, velvety on the underside. Elecampane ranges from central and southern Europe to northwest Asia. It has been naturalized in many parts of North America—from Nova Scotia to North Carolina and west to Missouri. Often, it's found in damp soil, near ruins, and along roadsides or woodland edges.

**Ease of Care:** Easy

**Cultivation:** Elecampane likes moist, moderately fertile soil or a well-drained clay loam in full sun to partial shade.

**Propagation:** Elecampane may be started from seeds sown indoors in late winter and transplanted later. You can also obtain new plants from offshoots or 2-inch root cuttings taken from a mature plant in autumn. Use moist, sandy soil to cover the cuttings, and keep them in a cool room. By early spring, the roots should develop into plants.

**Uses:** Elecampane's Latin name, *helenium*, refers to the legend that Helen of Troy carried a handful of elecampane on the day Paris abducted her, sparking the Trojan War. Perhaps she carried it because she had worms: Elecampane has been used for centuries to expel parasites in the digestive system, and today we know it contains a compound that expels intestinal worms.

But elecampane has been used most often for treating respiratory diseases. It is especially good for shortness of breath and bronchial problems. Early American colonists grew it for use as an expectorant; in Europe, people with asthma chewed on the root. Indian Ayurvedic physicians prescribe elecampane for chest conditions. In China, the plant is known as hsuan-fu-hua and is used to make syrup, lozenges, and candy to treat bronchitis and asthma.

European studies show that elecampane promotes menstruation and may be useful in reducing blood pressure. The herb also has been shown to have some sedative effect. The root is added to many medicines and used as a flavoring for sweets. Cordials and sugar cakes are still made from it in parts of Europe. You'll find the flower heads in dried craft arrangements.

**Part Used:** Root

**Preservation:** Harvest plant roots in the fall of the plant's second year, after it has gone through two hard frosts. Harvest seed heads for crafts.

**Precautions:** Avoid elecampane if you're pregnant, as the herb has been used traditionally to promote menstruation. Studies have shown that a small dose of elecampane lowers blood sugar levels in animals, but higher doses raise them. Thus, people with diabetes should be careful when using the herb. People occasionally develop a rash from skin contact with the herb.

**Medicinal Use:** Take as tea, tincture, or pills. Make into syrup or lozenges for coughs. Elecampane is often mixed with other herbs that are good for the lungs, such as mullein, licorice, and plantain.

# Evening Primrose

**Biennial**

**Botanical Name:**
*Oenothera biennis*

**Family:** Onagraceae

**Height:** 3–6 ft

**Spread:** 1½ ft.

**Description:** Some people are so busy during the day they don't have time to enjoy their herb gardens until after the moon rises. If you're one of those folks, evening primrose is the perfect herb for your garden. Its clear yellow flowers unclasp and blossom in the evening. Later in the growing season, evening primrose flowers may remain open during the day. Evening primrose flowers from early summer to mid-autumn. The stem is sturdy, rough, hairy, and reddish; its seeds round, beige, and oily. The plant's leaf is long, oval, pointed, and a mid-green color.

**Ease of Care:** Easy

**Cultivation:** Don't try to grow evening primrose indoors. The plant needs a sunny, open site, with well-drained soil.

**Propagation:** Sow seeds in spring to early summer; thin to 12 inches by autumn.

**Uses:** The boiled root of evening primrose, which tastes something like a sweet parsnip, may be pickled or tossed raw in salads. The plant once was grown in monasteries; more recently scientists have found that the seeds contain

a rare substance called gamma-linoleic acid (better known as GLA), which may have value in treating multiple sclerosis, thrombosis, premenstrual symptoms, menopausal discomfort, alcohol withdrawal, hyperactivity, and psoriasis. In one study, more than half the study participants found that their PMS symptoms completely disappeared when they used evening primrose. In another study, more than half the arthritis patients who took evening primrose oil also found relief. The oil, when combined with zinc supplements, improves dry eyes and brittle nails, although it often takes two to three months to notice improvement in these conditions. Leaves and bark have been used to ease cough spasms.

The Highland Psychiatric Research Group in Scotland discovered evening primrose helps regenerate damaged liver cells. It is also thought to prevent liver damage, stop alcohol from impairing brain cells, and lessen the symptoms of a hangover. Research is underway to determine if it can protect cells

against HIV, the virus that causes AIDS.

**Part Used:** Seed, leaves, stems

**Preservation:** Wait two years to dig up the roots.

**Precautions:** None

**Medicinal Use:** Purchase oil of evening primrose in capsules and follow package directions. The capsules are expensive, but many people find they can reduce the recommended dose after a period of use. Unfortunately, the oil cannot be obtained from the seeds at home—a special process is required to extract it.

# Fennel

**Perennial**

**Botanical Name:**
*Foeniculum vulgare*

**Family:** Apiaceae
(Umbelliferae)

**Height:** 4–7 ft.

**Spread:** 3 ft.

**Description:** With its feathery leaves, fennel looks much like a large version of its relative, dill. This fairly hardy perennial flowers from June through October. Sweet fennel (*F. vulgare dulce*), the variety sold in grocery stores, produces celerylike stalks known as finochhio. Both varieties taste similar to anise or licorice. Fennel is native to the Mediterranean region and widely naturalized elsewhere. It loves to grow by the ocean and near streams.

**Ease of Care:** Easy

**Cultivation:** Fennel likes alkaline soil; you can add lime if soil is very acidic, although the herb is not fussy. Grow in full sun to partial shade in well-drained, average soil. Shelter fennel from heavy winds because the plant's fragile stems blow over easily.

**Propagation:** Sow seeds in late fall or early spring.

**Uses:** The Greeks gave fennel to nursing mothers to increase milk flow. Early physicians also considered fennel a remedy for poor eyesight, weight loss, hiccups, nausea, gout, and many other illnesses. Fennel is a carminative (relieves gas and pain in the bowels), weak diuretic, and mild digestive stimulant. Herbalists often recommend fennel tea to soothe an upset stomach and dispel gas. It aids digestion, especially of fat. In Europe, a popular children's carminative is still made with fennel, chamomile, caraway, coriander, and bitter orange peel. Fennel is also a urinary tract tonic that lessens inflammation and helps eliminate kidney stones.

Fennel tastes like a more bitter version of anise. Use leaves in salads and as garnishes. You can eat tender stems as you would celery, and add seeds to desserts, breads, cakes, cookies, and beverages. Mince bulbs of sweet fennel and eat raw or braise. Fennel complements fish, sausage, duck, barley, rice, cabbage, beets, pickles, potatoes, lentils, breads, and eggs. Add it to butters, cheese spreads, and salad dressings. Fennel essential oil is found commercially in condiments, liqueurs, and aromatherapy cosmetics such as creams, perfumes, and soaps. It has a reputation for improving the complexion and decreasing wrinkles. A fennel infusion acts as a skin cleanser and antiseptic. It reduces bruising when applied topically. The herb dyes wool shades of yellow and brown.

**Part Used:** Leaves, seeds

**Preservation:** Snip leaves any time to use fresh, or freeze. Harvest whole plants just before they bloom, and hang to dry. To harvest seeds, cut down plants when seeds turn brown. Hang-dry in paper bags to catch seeds.

**Precautions:** Fennel has mild estrogenic properties, so avoid it if you're pregnant. Very large amounts can overstimulate the nervous system. Be especially careful using the essential oil.

**Medicinal Use:** Use fennel in food and herb teas. It is sometimes used in formulas to treat digestion or urinary tract problems. Laxative formulas may use fennel to ease the activity of the intestines and reduce gas and bloating. Make a facial cream with fennel seeds, lavender, and rosemary.

# Feverfew

**Perennial or Biennial**

**Botanical Name:**
*Tanacetum parthenium*
(formerly *Chrysanthemum parthenium*)

**Family:** Asteraceae (Compositae)

**Height:** To 2 ft.

**Spread:** 1–2 ft., spreading

**Description:** Feverfew is an erect herb that produces a branched root and many stems. Its multiple flowers are small and white, with yellow centers, like its cousin, the daisy, and it looks somewhat like chamomile. Flowers appear from midsummer through fall. Feverfew's leaves are yellowish green with a bitter scent. The herb is native to central and southern Europe and has become naturalized throughout temperate regions, including North and South America. Feverfew reportedly grew abundantly around the Parthenon in Athens; hence its botanical name *parthenium*.

**Ease of Care:** Easy

**Cultivation:** Feverfew prefers average, well-drained soil and full sun to partial shade.

**Propagation:** Sow seeds or divide roots in spring. Take cuttings in fall or spring.

**Uses:** Feverfew's common name derives from the Latin *febrifugia*, which means "driver out of fevers." The Romans used the herb extensively for this purpose, and the Greeks employed it to normalize irregular contractions in childbirth. Today feverfew leaves are best known for their ability to fight headaches, particularly migraines. The herb's constituents relax blood vessels in the brain and inhibit secretion of substances that cause pain. Feverfew is most effective when used long-term to prevent chronic migraines, but some people find it helpful when taken at the onset of a headache. When patients at the Department of Medicine and Haemotology in Nottingham, England, ate fresh feverfew leaves for three months, they had fewer migraines and less nausea when they did experience one. Their

blood pressure was reduced, and they reported feelings of well-being. Feverfew also is reported to reduce inflammation in joints and tissues. It has been prescribed for treating menstrual cramps.

Pyrethrin, an active ingredient, is a potent insect repellent. Feverfew's leaves and stems produce a dye that is greenish-yellow.

**Part Used:** Leaves, flowers

**Preservation:** The best time to gather leaves is just before flowering, but you can harvest them throughout the summer. Tincture to retain the maximum amount of medicine.

**Precautions:**
Feverfew may cause stomach upset. Chewing raw leaves regularly may irritate the mouth. Tinctures and capsules do not

cause such irritation. Because feverfew relaxes blood vessels, it may increase blood flow during menstruation. Some people develop allergic reactions after prolonged exposure to it.

**Medicinal Use:** The best way to take feverfew for migraines is to eat three or four leaves a day. Be forewarned that the leaves are bitter. If raw leaves irritate your mouth, are too bitter, or are unavailable, take 1 to 3 capsules (preferably with freeze-dried feverfew) or ½ to 1 teaspoon (2 to 4 droppers full) of tincture daily. Commercial preparations are usually made from leaves but may also contain flowers. Drink up to 3 cups of tea a day. Combine with other, more palatable, herbs, such as mint, to improve the taste. Recent studies show that the flowers are also effective medicinally.

# Garlic

**Perennial or Biennial**

**Botanical Name:**
*Allium sativum*

**Family:** Liliacea

**Height:** To 2 ft.

**Spread:** 6 in.

**Description:** Like its cousin the onion, garlic produces a compound bulb composed of numerous cloves encased in a papery sheath. Flowers are small and white to pinkish. Long, slender green leaves arise from the bulb. The herb may have originated in southern Siberia; it is cultivated extensively around the world.

**Ease of Care:** Easy

**Cultivation:** Garlic likes rich, deep, well-drained soil and full sun. Garlic contains fungicides and is thought to repel pests from companion plants.

**Propagation:** Sow seeds in the fall or plant cloves in early spring for a midsummer harvest. Plant cloves with the pointed side up.

**Uses:** Garlic has been prized for millennia, used by the Egyptians, Hebrews, Romans, Greeks, and Chinese. Garlic is one of the most extensively researched and widely used of plants. Its actions are diverse and affect nearly every body system. The herb boasts antibiotic, antifungal, and antiviral properties and is reported to be effective against many influenza strains, as well as herpes simplex type I. During World War I, field physicians applied garlic juice to infected wounds. Allicin, which gives garlic its distinctive odor, is as effective as a 1 percent penicillin solution in destroying bacteria, fungi, and yeast.

Garlic has been used to treat streptococcal infections, dysentery, whooping cough, and even tuberculosis. Several of garlic's sulfur compounds are noxious to parasites. Garlic inhibits blood clotting and keeps platelets from clumping, which improves blood flow and reduces the risk of stroke. It reduces cholesterol levels, making it a preventive for heart diseases. One study found that people who regularly ate garlic had almost half as many heart attacks. Garlic lowers blood pressure by relaxing vein and artery walls, keeping them open to improve blood flow. Constituents in garlic appear to increase insulin levels and lower high blood sugar levels.

Chinese scientists are investigating garlic's potential as a preventive treatment for stomach cancer. And a recent University of Minnesota study suggests that women who eat garlic may lower their risk of colon cancer.

Garlic's strong oniony taste has endeared it to cooks all over the world. You may add garlic to butters, cheese spreads, breads, all sorts of vegetables, stuffings, sauces, marinades, salad dressings, stews, soups, and meat dishes. Dried flower heads make an interesting addition to floral arrangements.

**Part Used:** Cloves

**Preservation:** Harvest garlic when tops turn brown in midsummer; dry in a cool, dark spot.

**Precautions:** Some people who consume large amounts of garlic feel nauseous or hot or have gas and bloating. Garlic juice may irritate the skin or mucous membranes of sensitive people.

**Medicinal Use:** One of the best ways to consume garlic is to eat it raw. When cooked, the stronger the flavor is, the more medicinal value it has. You can also take 1 to 2 capsules of garlic two to three times a day. Take ¼ teaspoon (1 dropper full) of garlic tincture in a glass of water, two to four times a day. A good antifungal treatment is to use garlic vinegar (garlic tincture made with vinegar).

# Gentian

**Perennial**

**Botanical Name:** *Gentiana lutea*

**Family:** Gentianaceae

**Height:** To 3 ft.; occasionally taller

**Spread:** 1 ft.

**Description:** Also called bitter root, gentian produces an interesting-looking root that may grow 1 to 2 feet long and 1 to 2 inches thick. Fresh roots are pale yellow; roots have a strong, perhaps disagreeable odor and are extremely bitter. Gentian's leaves, found at each stem joint, are smooth, waxy, and oval and light to medium green. The herb produces abundant, oblong fruit capsules.

**Ease of Care:** Moderate

**Cultivation:** Gentian likes neutral to acid soil that is moist and well drained. The plant requires partial shade. Once satisfactorily transplanted, the plants require little attention. But they need abundant moisture and shelter from cold, dry winds and direct sunshine.

Once a year, refresh the bed with acid soil or peat moss. If the temperature in your area dips well below freezing, mulch gentian with hay or evergreen boughs to protect it.

**Propagation:** It's possible, though difficult, to grow gentian from seeds, which require frost or stratification to germinate. Even then, they may take up to a year to produce seedlings. For most gardeners, the best bet is to start gentian plants from crown divisions or transplanted roots.

**Uses:** Gentian root has been prized as a digestive bitter for more than 3,000 years—the Egyptians, Arabs, Greeks, and Romans used it. In India, Ayurvedic doctors used gentian to treat fevers, venereal disease, jaundice, and other illnesses of the liver. Colonists in Virginia and the Carolinas discovered Indians using a gentian decoction to treat back pain. Chinese physicians use it to treat digestive disorders, sore throat, headache, and arthritis. Gentian, moreover, has been used to increase menstruation, thus easing painful periods.

Today, gentian is used commercially to make liqueurs, vermouth, digestive bitters, and aperitifs. Gentian is also a primary ingredient of Moxie, a patent medicine popular in the late 19th century that is still sold in New England as a soft drink. The herb's bitterness increases gastric secretions and helps a sluggish appetite or poor digestion. It is especially useful for problems digesting fat or protein. Researchers in Germany found that it cures heartburn, intestinal inflammation, and general indigestion. It also destroys several types of intestinal worms.

**Part Used:** Root; flowers in dried arrangements

**Preservation:** Dig up gentian roots in late summer or autumn, then dry them slowly to cure them. Harvest flowers as soon as they bloom, and dry them for use in decorations.

**Precautions:** Don't take gentian if you are pregnant. Although no studies have shown it is dangerous, gentian has been used to promote menstruation. Gentian also contains constituents that may elevate blood pressure. Although the Food and Drug Administration has approved gentian for use in foods and alcoholic beverages, large doses may cause nausea and vomiting. The gentian violet sold in pharmacies is *not* made from gentian: It is a very potent chemical used to treat skin infection.

**Medicinal Use:** Gentian is rarely made into tea because it is so bitter. If you use gentian tincture, take ¼ to 1 teaspoon (1 to 4 droppers full) diluted in a small amount of water, 30 minutes before meals. To make gentian bitters, infuse 3 ounces of chopped gentian root in 1 pint of brandy and strain after two weeks. Dilute with water before taking. Take ¼ to 1 teaspoon at a time.

# Geranium, Scented

**Perennial**

**Botanical Name:**

*Pelargonium graveolens*

**Family:** Geraniaceae

**Height:** 2 ft.

**Spread:** 1 ft.

**Description:** Botanically, these fragrant plants are not really geraniums, but pelargoniums. The leaves are frilly, soft, and well-veined; if you rub against them they emit a distinctive fragrance. The flowers are pink and unscented. The leaves of the different species come in a variety of shapes and sizes. Native to South Africa, the scented geranium has become naturalized in the eastern Mediterranean region, India, Australia, and New Zealand. The plant is widely cultivated.

**Ease of Care:** Moderate

**Cultivation:** A tender plant, the scented geranium will not tolerate freezing temperatures. It needs rich, dry, loamy, well-drained soil and light shade.

**Propagation:** The plants are best started from cuttings in spring or summer and transplanted after two to three weeks.

**Uses:** You could call the scented geranium the potpourri plant. The herb comes in a wide variety of fragrances, including rose, apple, lemon, lime, apricot, strawberry, coconut, and peppermint, making it an ideal addition to potpourri and sachets. The plant was considered fashionable in Colonial and Victorian times.

Herbalists sometimes recommend the astringent herb for treating diarrhea and ulcers and to stop bleeding. The essential oil is used to treat ringworm, lice, shingles, and herpes. The pharmaceutical industry uses one of the antiseptic compounds in geranium called geraniol. The leaves of some varieties, including rose, may be used to flavor cookies and jelly. Add other leaves, such as peppermint, to herbal teas. Added to facial steams and baths, they are cleansing and healing to the skin. The scent is popular in men's products—it blends well with woodsy and citrus fragrances. Rose geranium is used in many aromatherapy products for its relaxing and emotional balancing properties. This species is also added to cosmetics to improve the complexion.

The fresh leaves of scented geranium can be added to jellies and fruit dishes or placed on desserts. For a unique herbal treat, place the leaves in the bottom of a buttered cake pan before pouring in the batter. When you turn the finished cake over, it will be decorated with the herb leaves.

**Part Used:** Leaves

**Preservation:** Gather leaves at any time and use fresh or dry. Gather flowers as soon as they bloom.

**Precautions:** None

**Medicinal Use:** Scented geranium is used most often as an essential oil—usually rose geranium is the only one sold as "geranium." Dilute the essential oil in vegetable oil, lotion, or cream for skin care, as a topical medicine, or as a cosmetic. Use the leaves in cooking or to make flavored herb tea.

# Ginger

**Perennial**

**Botanical Name:**
*Zingiber officinale*

**Family:** Zingiberaceae

**Height:** 1–4 ft.

**Spread:** 1½ ft.

**Description:** This tropical, aromatic herb produces a knotty, buff-colored tuberous rhizome. Leaves are grasslike, and flowers are dense, conelike, greenish-purple spikes with edging. Native to southeast Asia, ginger is cultivated elsewhere, including south Florida.

**Ease of Care:** Easy

**Cultivation:** Ginger requires fertile, moist, well-drained soil and full sun to partial shade. The plant thrives in hot, humid climates, making it suitable for gardens in parts of the American South. Elsewhere, grow ginger in a greenhouse or indoors in a container.

**Propagation:** Purchase green roots from a nursery or Oriental grocery store and plant the "eyes" in loam, sand, peat moss, and compost.

**Uses:** Most every child knows the taste of ginger. It's the prime ingredient in ginger ale, gingerbread, and gingersnaps. But the popular kitchen spice enjoys a rich history as a medicinal herb as well. Ginger is a potent antinausea medication, useful for treating morning sickness, motion sickness, and nausea accompanying gastroenteritis (stomach "flu"). As a stomach calming aid, ginger reduces gas, bloating, and indigestion and aids in the body's absorption of nutrients and other herbs. Ginger is also a valuable deterrent to several types of intestinal worms. And the herb may work as a therapy and preventive treatment for some migraine headaches and rheumatoid arthritis.

Ginger promotes perspiration if ingested in large amounts. Use internally or topically. The herb stimulates circulation, so if you are cold, you can use warm ginger tea to help raise your body heat. Ginger may occasionally promote menstrual flow. It also prevents platelets from clumping and thins the blood, which reduces the risk of atherosclerosis and blood clots. Grated ginger poultices or compresses ease lung congestion when placed on the chest and alleviate gas, nausea, and menstrual cramps when laid on the abdomen.

Ginger is a staple of many cuisines, including those of southeast Asia, India, Japan, the Caribbean, and North Africa. Add the spicy chopped root to beverages, fruits, meats, fish, preserves, pickles, and a variety of vegetables. Use ground ginger in breads, cookies, and other deserts.

**Part Used:** Root (rhizome)

**Preservation:** Pull up ginger 8 to 12 months after you plant it, and remove leafstalks and fibers from the root. Use fresh, or tincture or dry.

**Precautions:** Although ginger is prescribed for nausea, some people develop this symptom after ingesting very large amounts.

**Medicinal Use:** Take up to 6 cups of tea or 1½ teaspoons tincture (6 droppers full) a day. For nausea, take 1 to 2 ginger capsules every 2 to 6 hours. Grate ginger root for a poultice. Ginger is often added to other herb formulas both for its taste and versatile medicinal uses. Ginger is also medicinal when added to foods.

# Ginkgo

**Perennial**

**Botanical Name:**
*Ginkgo biloba*

**Family:** Ginkgoaceae

**Height:** To 100 ft.

**Spread:** 20 ft.

**Description:** This stately deciduous tree produces male and female flowers on separate plants. Female plants produce orange-yellow fruits the size of large olives. In the fall its leaves turn gold. Found throughout the temperate world, ginkgo may be grown in many parts of the United States. It is cultivated extensively.

**Ease of Care:** Easy

**Cultivation:** Ginkgo requires well-drained soil. The trees are largely resistant to insects, drought, and diseases

**Propagation:** Plant saplings in spring.

**Uses:** Ginkgo is one of the oldest species of tree on earth. It is used to treat conditions associated with aging, including stroke, heart disease, impotence, deafness, ringing in the ears, blindness, and memory loss. In many studies, it helped people improve their concentration and memory. Ginkgo promotes the action of certain neurotransmitters, chemical compounds responsible for relaying nerve impulses in the brain. It is even undergoing investigation as a treatment for some mental disorders.

Ginkgo increases circulation, including blood flow to the brain, which may help improve memory. Several studies show it reduces the risk of heart attack and improves pain from blood clots (phlebitis) in the legs. Additional studies show that, in a large percentage of people, ginkgo helps impotence caused by narrowing of arteries that supply blood to the penis; macular degeneration of the eyes, a deterioration in vision that may be caused by narrowing of the blood vessels to the eye; and cochlear deafness, which is caused by decreased blood flow to the nerves involved in hearing.

Constituents in ginkgo are potent antioxidants with anti-inflammatory effects. A current scientific theory attributes many of the signs of aging and chronic disease to oxidation of cell membranes by substances called free radicals, which may arise from pollutants or from normal internal production of metabolic substances. Ginkgo counters destruction of cells due to oxidation. Scientists are also investigating ginkgo as a medicine that one day may help the body accept transplanted organs. Researchers also found it can help children with asthma.

The herb produces chemicals that interfere with a substance called platelet activation factor, PAF, which is involved in organ graft rejection, asthma attacks, and blood clots that lead to heart attacks and some strokes.

**Part Used:** Leaves

**Preservation:** Gather leaves in summer; dry or tincture.

**Precautions:** Ginkgo may cause problems for people with clotting disorders or those who take blood-thinning medications. Extremely large quantities of ginkgo sometimes cause irritability, restlessness, diarrhea, nausea, and vomiting.

**Medicinal Use:** Take 2 to 6 capsules a day (follow package directions) or up to 1 teaspoon (4 droppers full) of tincture a day. The most active ingredients are found in the leaves after they have turned color in the fall.

# Ginseng, American

**Perennial**

**Botanical Name:**
*Panax quinquefolius*

**Family:** Araliaceae

**Height:** 1½ ft.

**Spread:** To 1 ft.

**Description:** American ginseng produces a single stem, a whorl of leaves, and several green-white flowers from June through August. Leaves are toothed; the berries, bright red. American ginseng is indigenous to Manitoba and Quebec and ranges south to Georgia and west through Alabama to Oklahoma. It may be found in hardwood forests on north or northwestern slopes, although years of high demand have made it scarce in the wild.

**Ease of Care:** Difficult

**Cultivation:** Ginseng needs to be pampered but can be grown in home gardens. The herb demands shade and humusy, rich, well-drained loam. Commercially, ginseng is grown in shelters that mimic forests. The plant must be mulched in winter and takes from five to seven years to produce usable roots, which often fall prey to rotting diseases or gophers.

**Propagation:** Ginseng seeds require a cold period of at least four months to germinate. The most common way to grow it is to buy seedlings two to three years old.

**Uses:** The Chinese have used a close relative of American ginseng since prehistoric times. In the United States, colonists grew rich collecting American ginseng and exporting it to China, where the herb enjoys a strong reputation as an aphrodisiac and prolonger of life. Ginseng is an adaptogen, capable of protecting the body from physical and mental stress and helping bodily functions return to normal.

Clinical studies indicate that ginseng may slow the effects of aging, protect cells from free radical damage, prevent heart disease, and help treat anemia, atherosclerosis, depression, diabetes, edema (excess fluid buildup), ulcers, and hypertension. Its complex saponins, ginsenosides, are responsible for most of its actions. They stimulate bone marrow production and immune-system functions, inhibit tumor growth, and detoxify the liver.

Ginseng has many dual roles, for example, raising or lowering blood pressure or blood sugar, according to the body's needs.

Ginseng gently stimulates and strengthens the central nervous system, making it useful for treating fatigue and weakness caused by disease and injury. It reduces mental confusion and headaches.

**Part Used:** Root

**Preservation:** Do not uproot this endangered plant if you're lucky enough to find it growing wild. Purchase products made from cultivated ginseng, or grow your ginseng. Dry the roots or preserve them in alcohol or honey.

**Precautions:** Ginseng is generally considered safe. Side effects of taking quantities of ginseng or mixing it with large amounts of caffeine may include some of the symptoms for which it is prescribed, including insomnia, nervousness, and irritability. Consult a physician or qualified herbalist before using ginseng if you have high blood pressure or are pregnant. Use of ginseng aggravates some cases of hypertension and improves other cases.

**Medicinal Use:** Take about 1 gram of dried root per day. This amount is equivalent to about 4 capsules or 1 to 2 teaspoons tincture (4 to 8 droppers full). Or chew on the whole root. It is also available in a thick concentrated extract to make instant tea and as a sweetened liquid extract. Some herbalists recommend that you take ginseng for several weeks, then stop using it for a week or two for optimum effects.

# Goldenseal

**Perennial**

**Botanical Name:**
*Hydrastis canadensis*

**Family:** Ranunculaceae

**Height:** 1 ft.

**Spread:** 1 ft.

**Description:** Goldenseal is small and erect, with hairy stems growing from a twisted, knotted rhizome that is brown on the outside and bright yellow on the inside. The herb's solitary flowers are white and appear usually in May or June. One or two maple-leaf–shaped leaves appear at the base of the plant. Berries are orange-red and contain two shiny black seeds. Native to North America, the herb is sometimes found in moist, rich woodlands, damp meadows, and forest highlands. Goldenseal is farmed in woodland settings.

**Ease of Care:** Difficult

**Cultivation:** It takes about five years for the root to get large enough to harvest. Overharvesting of wild plants has put goldenseal on the endangered list. (You can use Oregon grape root as an alternative to goldenseal. It also contains goldenseal's active ingredient, berberine, and is much less expensive).

**Propagation:** Sow seeds in fall or stratify them. New plants also grow from root division. You can also purchase roots from mail-order nurseries.

**Uses:** The Cherokee Indians mixed powdered goldenseal root with bear grease and slathered their bodies to protect themselves from mosquitoes and other insects. Pioneers adopted the herb and used it to treat wounds, rashes, mouth sores, morning sickness, liver and stomach complaints, internal hemorrhaging, depressed appetite, constipation, and urinary and uterine problems.

One of goldenseal's active ingredients is hydrastine, which affects circulation, muscle tone, and uterine contractions. The herb is also an antiseptic, astringent, and antibiotic, making it effective for treating eye and other types of infections. Berberine and related alkaloids have been credited with goldenseal's antimicrobial effects. Goldenseal makes a good antiseptic skin wash for wounds and for internal skin surfaces, such as in the vagina and ear; it also treats canker sores and infected gums. The herb has been found to fight a number of disease-causing microbes, including *Staphylococcus* and *Streptococcus* organisms.

Berberine may be responsible for increasing white blood cell activity and promoting blood flow in the liver and spleen. Berberine has been used in China to combat the reduction of white blood cells that commonly follows chemotherapy and radiation treatment for cancer. Studies suggest it may have potential in the treatment of brain and skin cancers.

**Part Used:** Root

**Preservation:** Harvest roots in late fall and dry slowly.

**Precautions:** Hydrastine accumulates in the system and is toxic in large doses. Berberine may lower blood pressure, but hydrastine raises it, so avoid the herb if you have high blood pressure, heart disease, or glaucoma, except under professional guidance.

**Medicinal Use:** You can drink up to 2 cups a day of tea, but the taste is very bitter. Take ½ to 1 teaspoon tincture (2 to 4 droppers full) up to twice a day or dab on minor cuts or sore, inflamed gums.

# Gotu Kola

**Perennial**

**Botanical Name:**
*Centella asiatica*

**Family:** Apiaceae (Umbelliferae)

**Height:** 6 in.

**Spread:** 6 in.; may become invasive

**Description:** Gotu kola is a plant of many names. It produces fan-shaped leaves about the size of an old British penny; hence, its names include Indian pennywort, marsh penny, and water pennywort. Gotu kola is related to carrot, parsley, dill, and fennel but has neither the feathery leaves of its cousins nor the umbrella of tiny flowers they produce.

**Ease of Care:** Moderate

**Cultivation:** Gotu kola grows wild in marshy areas. Although it is a perennial, it grows only as an annual in cool climates. The plant requires moist, rich soil and partial shade. To thrive, gotu kola needs humidity, thus, it's best suited for subtropical climates or a greenhouse.

**Propagation:** Seeds germinate in seven to ten days. The plant may be propagated by means of layering.

**Uses:** Gotu kola is considered a relaxant, nerve tonic, diuretic, anti-inflammatory, and wound healer. The herb has long been regarded as a life extender. Shepherds in Sri Lanka noticed that elephants ate it and lived a long time. Thus, a later proverb reasoned, "Two leaves a day will keep old age away." Indian Ayurvedic physicians have used the plant extensively to treat the problems of aging. There is no evidence to support the theory that gotu kola prolongs life, but some tests have shown that the plant is a sedative and tonic for the nervous system and could help in treating many neurologic and mental disturbances, especially debility stemming from stress. Ayurvedics also use gotu kola to treat asthma, anemia, and other blood disorders.

In India gotu kola has been called brahmi, in honor of the god Brahma. It is reputed to improve memory, and East Indians again note that elephants, which supposedly never forget, consider gotu kola a delicacy.

The plant also has been used internally to treat rheumatism and other inflammatory diseases. In the Orient, physicians employ gotu kola leaves and roots to treat wounds, ulcers, and lesions that don't heal properly, including leprosy lesions. Gotu kola contains a chemical called asiaticoside, which aids in the treatment of leprosy. It also helps prevent scarring, and it has been used successfully in Germany to heal the skin after surgery.

Gotu kola is thought to stimulate the body's immune system. It improves circulation throughout the body—one reason it may improve memory and brain function. It also im-proves varicose veins and other circulation disorders.

**Part Used:** Leaves, stems

**Preservation:** Use fresh leaves anytime. Leaves may also be dried and infused for creams, lotions, and ointments.

**Precautions:** In moderate doses, gotu kola is considered quite safe. Although mice developed tumors after the concentrated chemical asiaticoside was applied to their skin, new evidence demonstrates that a gotu kola tincture inhibits the growth of cancer cells in smaller doses. Don't take gotu kola if you are pregnant or nursing or if you take tranquilizers because gotu kola's sedating properties may interfere with the drug. In extremely large doses, gotu kola is narcotic, producing rashes or dizziness. If you develop these symptoms, stop using the herb.

**Medicinal Use:** Drink at least 2 cups of tea a day. You can also use the tea in a compress for wounds. Take up to ½ teaspoon (2 droppers full) of tincture a day. Eat the leaves fresh.

# Hawthorn

**Perennial**

**Botanical Name:**
*Crataegus laevigata*

**Family:** Rosaceae

**Height:** To 25 ft.

**Spread:** To 10 ft.

**Description:** Like many members of the rose family, hawthorn bears thorns as well as lovely, fragrant flowers and brightly pigmented berries high in vitamin C. As many as 900 species of hawthorn exist in North America, ranging from deciduous trees to thorny-branched shrubs. Hawthorn produces white flower clusters in May. The herb is native to Europe, with closely related species in North Africa and western Asia. It is often found in areas with hedges and deciduous woods.

**Ease of Care:** Easy

**Cultivation:** Hawthorn tolerates a wide variety of soils but prefers ground that is alkaline, rich, loamy, and moist. Hawthorn also likes full sun. The tree sometimes falls prey to aphids and other insects and fungus.

**Propagation:** Sow seed in the spring. Certain varieties of hawthorn must be grafted or budded. Smaller trees transplant better than larger ones. Trees are sold in most nurseries.

**Uses:** Hawthorn has been cherished for centuries. The Druids considered hawthorn a sacred tree. The Pilgrims brought it to America: Mayflower is, in fact, another name for hawthorn.

Hawthorn is an important herb for treating heart conditions. The berries and flowers contain several complex chemical constituents, including flavonoids such as anthocyanidins, which improve the strength of capillaries and reduce damage to blood vessels from oxidizing agents. Hawthorn's ability to dilate blood vessels, enhancing circulation, makes it useful for treating angina, atherosclerosis, high and low blood pressure, and elevated cholesterol levels. Many clinical studies have demonstrated its effectiveness for such conditions—with the use of hawthorn, the heart requires less oxygen when under stress. Heart action is normalized and becomes stronger and more efficient. Hawthorn also helps balance the heart's rhythm and is prescribed for arrhythmias and heart palpitations by European physicians. Although it affects the heart somewhat like the medication digitalis, hawthorn does not have a cumulative effect on the heart.

**Part Used:** Berries, twigs behind the flowers, and flowers

**Preservation:** Gather flowers in spring and tincture. Gather berries in fall and dry or tincture. You can also use berries to make jam or jelly.

**Precautions:** Hawthorn is considered safe and may be used for long periods. Do not self-medicate with hawthorn. Consult a physician or herbalist before taking it, especially if you take prescription heart medication: Hawthorn may intensify the effects of these drugs.

**Medicinal Use:** Take ½ to 1 teaspoon tincture (2 to 4 droppers full) up to five times a day, or drink up to 5 cups of the tea. It is often combined with other heart tonics such as motherwort and garlic.

# Hops

**Perennial**

**Botanical Name:**
*Humulus lupulus*

**Family:** Cannabaceae

**Height:** 20–40 ft.

**Spread:** Spreading vine

**Description:** Like the grape, hops is a quick-growing and quick-spreading vine. Each year a stem grows from the root and begins to twine. After the third year, hops produces a papery, conelike fruit called a strobile. Male and female flowers grow on separate plants and appear from middle to late summer. Hops leaves somewhat resemble grape leaves, hairy and coarse, with serrated edges. A relative of marijuana, hops is native to Europe and can be found in vacant fields and along rivers. The Pilgrims brought hops to Massachusetts, and it quickly spread south to Virginia. Most hops grown in the United States is for the beer industry, which uses hops to flavor its products.

**Ease of Care:** Easy

**Cultivation:** Hops can be grown as a garden plant. Vines also are grown commercially in hopyards on wires strung between poles. Hops requires full sun, deep, humusy, well-drained soil, and good air circulation to prevent mildew from forming.

**Propagation:** Hops may be started from cuttings or suckers taken in early summer from healthy old plants.

**Uses:** If you worked in a hopyard, you might find yourself falling asleep on the job. Hops contains chemicals that depress the central nervous system, making it a useful sedative herb. Abraham Lincoln and England's King George III, notorious insomniacs, reportedly lay their heads on hops-filled pillows to ensure a good night's sleep. Hops' other constituents are antiseptic, antibacterial, and anti-inflammatory, and they slightly increase activity of the female hormone estrogen. Hops has also been used as a pain reliever, fever cure, expectorant, and diuretic. It has been prescribed to treat nervous heart conditions, PMS, menstrual pain, and nervous symptoms of menopause. The Greeks and Romans used hops as a digestive aid. If you have drunk beer, you will be familiar with hops' pleasantly bitter taste. This bitterness makes hops an excellent digestive aid. Since the 9th century A.D., brewers have used hops to flavor and preserve beer. In some Scandinavian countries, weavers make a coarse cloth from hops vine. Dried hops also makes an interesting addition to dried floral arrangements.

**Part Used:** Fruit

**Preservation:** Gather strobiles in summer after they turn an amber color; dry or tincture. Tincturing is the best way to preserve hops. The herb becomes unstable in the presence of light and air and loses some of its flavor and medicinal effectiveness.

**Precautions:** The herb may cause a rash known as hops dermatitis. Avoid hops if you're pregnant because of its hormonal actions.

**Medicinal Use:** Drink hops tea up to three times a day. Take ½ to 1 teaspoon (2 to 4 droppers full) of tincture up to three times a day or take it in pills. Hops is often mixed with other sedative herbs or herbs that help relieve menstrual or menopausal symptoms.

# Horehound

**Cultivation:** Horehound is a hardy plant in zone 4 that prefers deep, well-drained, sandy soil and full sun. It may become invasive.

**Propagation:** Horehound grows easily from seed or division in spring.

**Uses:** When your grandfather had a cold, he may have sucked on a horehound lozenge. The herb has been used for centuries to open clogged nasal passages and alleviate other symptoms associated with the sniffles. One of the Hebrew's ritual bitter herbs, horehound was also prized by the Greeks and Egyptians. Herbalists have employed it to treat hepatitis and jaundice. But horehound's most reliable uses are to soothe sore throats, help the lungs expel mucus, and treat bronchitis. A weak sedative, it also helps normalize an irregular heartbeat. It induces sweating and will lower a fever, especially when infused and drunk as a hot tea.

The herb's primary constituents include an essential oil, tannin, and a bitter chemical called marrubiin. The plant also contains vitamin C, which adds to its ability to fight colds. Horehound has a taste similar to sage and hyssop but more bitter. At one time it was used in England as a bitter to flavor ale. Today some people use the leaves to make an old-fashioned candy called horehound drops.

**Part Used:** Leaves

**Preservation:** Gather leaves before the herb blooms in summer; dry or tincture.

**Precautions:** In very large doses, horehound may cause cardiac arrhythmias.

**Medicinal Use:** If you can handle the bitter taste, drink horehound tea, but more likely you'll use it as a tincture or cough syrup. Take ¼ to ½ teaspoon (1 to 2 droppers full) of tincture up to three times a day. Take the syrup a teaspoon at a time. Horehound preparations typically include other herbs used for lung congestion such as mullein or elecampane. The lozenges often contain anise to improve their taste.

# Horseradish

**Perennial**

**Botanical Name:**
*Armoracia rusticana*

**Family:** Cruciferae

**Height:** 4–5 ft.

**Spread:** 2 ft.

**Description:** Horseradish, a cousin of mustard, produces a long, white tapering root. Its flowers are small and white and appear in mid-summer; its leaves are abundant. Native to southeastern Europe and western Asia, the herb is cultivated widely in North America and naturalized in some areas.

**Ease of Care:** Easy

**Cultivation:** Horseradish prefers average, moist, heavy soil and full sun. Once established, it is difficult to eradicate. Some gardeners believe that planting horseradish near potatoes makes them more disease-resistant.

**Propagation:** Take cuttings 8 to 9 inches long from the root in the spring. Each cutting should have a bud. Place them 12 inches apart in soil that is at least 12 to 15 inches deep.

**Uses:** Have you ever bitten into a roast beef sandwich and thought your nose was on fire? The sandwich probably contained horseradish. Even a tiny taste of this potent condiment seems to go straight to your nose. Whether it's on a roast beef sandwich or in an herbal preparation, horseradish clears sinuses, increases circulation, and promotes expulsion of mucus from upper respiratory passages.

Horseradish has been used as a medicine for centuries. Its chief constituent decomposes upon exposure to air to turn into mustard oil, which gives both horseradish and mustard their heat and flavor. The root contains an antibiotic substance and vitamin C, which are effective in clearing up sinus, bronchial, and urinary infections. Horseradish can make an effective heat-producing poultice that alleviates the pain of arthritis and neuralgia. It also stimulates digestion and has long been eaten with fatty foods to help digest them.

As a condiment, horseradish is widely used. Its sharp mustardy taste enhances mayonnaise, fish, beef, sausage, eggs, potatoes, and beets. Horseradish is used extensively in Eastern European cuisine and is the main ingredient in Dresden sauce. Tender new leaves may be chopped fine and tossed in salads.

**Part Used:**
Root. Fresh root is superior as both medicine and food, but dried horseradish powder will do in a pinch.

**Preservation:** Harvest roots in late fall. Store whole in dry sand in a cool, dark place. Horseradish roots will stay fresh for months. The best way to preserve horseradish is to put it in vinegar or lemon juice right after grating it; the mustard oil produced upon grating is quickly lost otherwise. Use grated horseradish within

three months—it becomes better as it ages. Reconstitute dried horseradish at least 30 minutes before serving.

**Precautions:** Large doses of horseradish may cause an upset stomach, vomiting, or headache. Topical use may cause inflammation. Horseradish's volatile fumes may irritate the lungs if you inhale large quantities on a continuous basis.

**Medicinal Use:** Grate the fresh root in a food processor or blender. Add vinegar and honey or sugar to taste. Spread ¼ teaspoon or less of prepared horseradish on a cracker and eat it. Stir horseradish in a sip of warm water with a little honey and take for hoarseness or head congestion, or take ½ teaspoon tincture (2 droppers full) in warm water. Repeat every hour until the problem clears.

# Horsetail

**Perennial**

**Botanical Name:**
*Equisetum arvense*

**Family:** Equisetaceae

**Height:** 1st stage, 4–8 in.; 2nd stage, to 1½ ft.

**Spread:** 6 in.

**Description:** One of the earth's oldest plant species, horsetail has been around for 200 million years. The herb's name refers to the resemblance of the whorls of its needlelike leaves to a horse's tail. The herb's other common name, scouring rush, derives from the plant's one-time use as a natural scouring pad for pots and pans. Horsetail appears in two stages: In the first, the herb produces a green-yellowish bamboolike stalk; in the second, whorls of threadlike leaves appear around the stalk. Harvest it in this second stage in the spring while it is still young. You're likely to encounter this hardy herb in moist woods, along roads, and in waste places.

**Ease of Care:** Easy

**Cultivation:** Horsetail prefers acidic to neutral, humusy, moist soil and partial shade. You can purchase horsetail at many nurseries. Once it has rooted, it's difficult to eradicate. Try planting the herb in a bucket placed just below the surface of a pond.

**Propagation:** Horsetails are easy to divide. Dig and divide the roots.

**Uses:** Horsetail is high in minerals, particularly silica. The herb contains so much silica, in fact, that you can use it to polish metal. Early Americans used horsetail to scour pots and pans. Horsetail treats water retention, bed-wetting, and other bladder problems, including kidney stones. It is also used to decrease an enlarged prostate. Used externally, it stops bleeding and helps wounds to heal. It was once used to prevent the lungs from scarring in people with tuberculosis.

Because it contains minerals, horsetail strengthens bone, hair, and fingernails. Horsetail infusions—often combined with nettles—are drunk to help broken bones mend. The silica in it encourages the absorption of calcium by the body and helps prevent build-up of fatty deposits in the arteries.

Dried stems are interesting additions to flower arrangements. Horsetail yields a yellowish-green dye.

**Part Used:** Stems, shoots

**Preservation:** Gather very young shoots in spring and cook as you would asparagus. Horsetail branches are also made into infusions and tinctures.

**Precautions:** Make sure your horsetail was not gathered near an industrial site. Horsetail tends to pick up large amounts of nitrates and selenium from the soil. Equisetene, a chemical found in the plant, is a nerve toxin in large doses. It increases in amount as the plant matures, so pick horsetail only in the spring when it is in its second stage. Long-term use of horsetail could result in kidney damage. Do not use horsetail if you have high blood pressure or are pregnant.

**Medicinal Use:** Drink up to 2 cups a day of the tea. Take ½ to 1 teaspoon tincture (2 to 4 droppers full) or 2 capsules up to two times a day. You can buy capsules of horsetail mixed with other herbs and nutrients to strengthen nails and hair. It's best to take horsetail for a week and abstain for two before resuming use. It is usually blended with other herbs such as saw palmetto and nettle root to treat an enlarged prostate.

# Hydrangea

**Perennial**

**Botanical Name:**
*Hydrangea arborescens*

**Family:** Saxifragaceae

**Height:** To 9 ft.

**Spread:** To 6 ft.

**Description:** Native to North America, hydrangea is also known as seven barks because it produces seven separate layers of different-colored bark. In the wild, 23 species are related to this well-known cultivated plant. Many cousins are found in eastern Asia and North, Central, and South America. Hydrangea flowers are pink to deep blue, depending on soil alkalinity levels. The plant flowers from July through September, sometimes later. Leaves are ovate (egg-shaped), toothed, and pointed. In the wild, hydrangea is found in rich woods from New York to Florida and west from Louisiana to Ohio. The plant is highly regarded for its garden beauty.

**Ease of Care:** Easy

**Cultivation:** Hydrangea prefers rich, moist soil and full sun or partial shade.

**Propagation:** Cuttings, layering

**Uses:** Hydrangea root, which contains a number of glycosides, saponins, and resins, is used most often for treating enlarged prostate glands. The herb is employed to treat urinary stones and cystitis, and it can help prevent the recurrence of kidney stones. But you should not self-medicate for urinary or kidney stones, as these conditions require professional medical treatment.

The root is a laxative and diuretic. American Indians used its bark in poultices for treating wounds, burns, sore muscles, sprains, and tumors, and they chewed it for stomach and heart trouble. The leaves also contain some of the medicine but are not as strong as the roots. You can dry the flower heads as well as the individual flowers for use in craft projects. To retain their color, dry them as quickly as possible in a dark place or dry them in silica gel. The flowers are also very attractive when pressed.

**Part Used:** Dried roots and rhizome; flowers for dried flower projects

**Preservation:** Harvest roots in autumn; clean and slice while fresh because the roots become very hard after they dry. Pick the flowers just before they are in full bloom.

**Precautions:** Hydrangea may cause dizziness and indigestion when ingested in large amounts. Lower the dose if this occurs. The wood is reported to cause skin reactions in woodworkers, and the flowers have been known to make children sick when they ate the buds.

**Medicinal Use:** Drink 1 cup of tea, three times a day. If using tincture, take ½ to ¾ teaspoon (2 to 3 droppers full), three times a day. To prevent kidney stones, hydrangea is generally mixed with other herbs such as horsetail, Joe-pye weed, goldenrod, cramp bark, and dandelion. You may also find it combined with saw palmetto, nettle root, horsetail, marshmallow, and other herbs that reduce prostate inflammation.

# Hyssop

**Perennial**

**Botanical Name:**
*Hyssopus officinalis*

**Family:** Lamiaceae (Labiatae)

**Height:** 1½–2 ft.

**Spread:** 1 ft.

**Description:** Hyssop is a compact, aromatic member of the mint family, with many branches and square stems. Its leaves have a minty, somewhat medicinal odor. Blue or violet flowers appear in whorls to form dense spikes at the top of the stem from June through August. Hyssop is native to the Mediterranean and has become naturalized in some areas of North America.

**Ease of Care:** Easy

**Cultivation:** Hyssop prefers light, well-drained soil and full sun. Aside from occasional pruning, the plant requires little care.

**Propagation:** Sow seeds in the spring; take cuttings or divide in the spring or fall.

**Uses:** Hyssop has been a favorite medicinal herb since it was used in ancient Greece. With its strong camphorlike odor, the herb was strewn on floors to freshen homes in the Middle Ages. Hyssop baths were once used in England to treat rheumatism. Hyssop, which has a chemistry similar to horehound, has been used mostly to treat bronchitis, flu, colds, and sore throats. It reduces inflammation, so it makes a good throat gargle. In laboratory tests, it destroys the herpesvirus. A poultice of the fresh leaves promotes healing of wounds. The herb's essential oil is a prime flavoring of liqueurs, including Benedictine and Chartreuse. Add leaves to salads, chicken soup, fruit dishes, lamb, and poultry stuffing. Hyssop essential oil is expensive and found in quality perfumes. Use the herb or essential oil in a cleansing facial steam. Hyssop is said to repel flea beetles and other pests.

**Part Used:** Leaves

**Preservation:** Harvest stems just before flowers open. Hang in a warm, dry place. Harvest flowers as soon as they bloom, and dry or tincture. Harvest only green matter; hyssop's tough woody stems have less oil than the leaves do. Store dried hyssop in tightly covered glass containers or tins.

**Precautions:** Use hyssop in small doses and not at all if you are pregnant or have high blood pressure. It can also induce epileptic seizures. Be especially cautious when using the essential oil, which is more potent than the plant.

**Medicinal Use:** Hyssop is rarely used in tinctures; instead it is added to teas and syrups to treat congestion, colds, and flu. Drink up to 2 cups of tea or take 2 tablespoons of syrup daily.

# Juniper

**Perennial**

**Botanical Name:**

*Juniperus communis*

**Family:** Cupressaceae

**Height:** 2–20 ft.

**Spread:** From 4 ft.

**Description:** Most junipers are low growing, with tangled, spreading branches covered with reddish-brown bark. The many varieties of juniper vary in size, color, and shape. Most cultivated junipers are dwarf varieties. The tree produces male and female flowers on separate plants. Juniper blooms from April through June and produces berries that ripen to a bluish-purple in the tree's second year. The berries are covered with a whitish wax, and its leaves are green, prickly, and needle-shaped. This species is native to Europe and has become naturalized throughout North America.

**Ease of Care:** Easy

**Cultivation:** Hardy trees, Junipers will grow just about anywhere. They prefer full sun and sandy or light, loamy soil. To produce berries, you must grow both male and female plants. Once established, junipers require little care.

**Propagation:** Sow seed in the spring or fall, but germination may take two to three years. In late summer, take cuttings, which root easily if kept moist. Seedlings, available at nurseries, may be transplanted at any time of year, although they do better in early spring or fall.

**Uses:** The berries give gin its distinct flavor. American Indians used the leaves and berries externally to cure infections, relieve arthritis, and treat wounds. Adding a handful of crushed juniper leaves to a warm bath soothes aching muscles. A compress of juniper berries is sometimes recommended for gout, rheumatoid arthritis, and nerve, muscle, joint, and tendon pain. The berries were once chewed by doctors to ward off infection when treating patients. Chewing them also improves bad breath.

Juniper's essential oils relieve coughs and lung congestion. Its tars and resins treat psoriasis and other skin conditions. In both treatments, juniper has a warming, circulation-stimulating action. Juniper also relieves gas in the digestive system, increases stomach acid, and is a diuretic. The essential oil in its berries has antiseptic properties and is sometimes used for chronic urinary tract infections.

In the kitchen, you can use juniper berries to flavor patés and sauerkraut. Crushed berries spice game dishes, stews, sauces, and marinades. Toss juniper branches on the grill to impart a distinctive smoky taste to meats.

**Part Used:** Berries, leaves

**Preservation:** Harvest leaves at any time; wear gloves because leaves are prickly. Harvest only ripe berries. It takes live berries two years to ripen and turn dark blue. Spread berries on a screen and dry until they turn black. Tincture crushed juniper berries or store whole.

**Precautions:** Don't use juniper if you're pregnant or have a kidney infection or chronic kidney problems. Overdose symptoms may include diarrhea, intestinal pain, kidney pain, blood in urine, rapid heartbeat, and elevated blood pressure. Some hay fever sufferers develop allergic reactions to juniper. Don't use juniper if you develop any reactions. Use the essential oil externally only and with caution since it is very potent.

**Medicinal Use:** Drink up to 1 cup of tea a day. Take the tea or tincture for one week, then abstain for one or two. Take 10 to 20 drops of tincture no more than four times a day. To make a massage oil, dilute juniper berry essential oil with vegetable oil. Rub on the skin over the urinary tract or digestive tract.

# Lavender

**Perennial**

**Botanical Name:**
*Lavandula angustifolia*

**Family:** Lamiaceae (Labiatae)

**Height:** 2–4 ft.

**Spread:** 2–3 ft.

**Description:** Lavender is a bushy plant with silver-gray, narrow leaves. It produces abundant 1½- to 2-foot flower stalks topped by fragrant and attractive purple-blue flower clusters. The plant flowers in June and July. An outstanding addition to any garden design, the herb also makes a nice edging or potted plant. There are a number of species and cultivars of lavender. Differences focus primarily on flower color (some have white, others, pink flowers), size, and growth habits. Munstead, a smaller variety of lavender, may be clipped to form a low hedge. Lavender is native to the Mediterranean, but the herb is cultivated around the world.

**Ease of Care:** Easy

**Cultivation:** Lavender prefers full sun in well-drained, sandy to poor, alkaline soil.

**Propagation:** Sow seed in spring; take cuttings or layer before the plant flowers.

**Uses:** Perhaps the smell of lavender reminds you of soap. That's because lavender is a prime ingredient of many soaps. Its name, in fact, derives from the Latin "to wash." The Romans and Greeks used lavender in the bath. Lavender is also found commercially in shaving creams, colognes, and perfumes. It is used in many cosmetics and aromatherapy products because it is so versatile, and its fragrance blends so well with other herbs. Studies show that the scent is very relaxing. Lavender's scent is also a remedy for headache and nervous tension.

Lavender cosmetics are good for all complexion types. It is an excellent skin healer: It promotes the healing of burns, abrasions, infected sores, and other types of inflammations, including varicose veins. It is also a popular hair rinse. The herb is a carminative (relieves gas and bowel pain) and antispasmodic. It is most often used for sore muscles in the form of a massage oil. As recently as World War I, lavender was used in the field as a disinfectant for wounds; herbalists still recommend it for that purpose. Lavender destroys several viruses, including many that cause colds and flu. It also relieves lung and sinus congestion. Lavender flowers may be added to vinegars, jellies, sachets, and potpourri. Place a sprig of lavender in a drawer to freshen linens. And dried flowers make wonderful herbal arrangements, although they are fragile.

**Part Used:** Leaves, flowers, branches

**Preservation:** Harvest flowers when they are in the late bud stage, just before they bloom. Hang to dry.

**Precautions:** None

**Medicinal Use:** It is rare to find lavender included in herbal teas, tinctures, or pills, but the essential oil is one of the most popular for use in skin care preparations. A few drops can be added to creams, salves, lotions, or the bath. Lavender makes an excellent compress for a headache, sore eyes, or a skin injury. For sinus and lung congestion, use a lavender steam. Add a strong lavender infusion or a couple drops of the essential oil to a quart of warm water for a douche to treat vaginal infections with *Candida* fungus.

# Lemon Balm

**Perennial**

**Botanical Name:**
*Melissa officinalis*

**Family:** Lamiaceae (Labiatae)

**Height:** 3 ft.

**Spread:** 1–2 ft.

**Description:** Lemon balm is an attractive plant with shield-shaped leaves that smell strongly of lemon. Like most mints, the herb produces square stems and flowers from July through September. Lemon balm is native to Europe and North Africa but has become naturalized elsewhere, including many parts of the United States. It is cultivated throughout the world.

**Ease of Care:** Easy

**Cultivation:** Lemon balm prospers in full sun but will also do well in partial shade. It likes a well-drained or moist, sandy soil. The plant grows abundantly. It attracts honeybees but repels other insects. Lemon balm is susceptible to developing powdery mildew, so avoid overhead watering if this is a problem. It is susceptible to frost and may need to be mulched during the winter in a cold climate.

**Propagation:** Sow seeds or divide in autumn or early spring; take cuttings in spring and summer. However, lemon balm self-seeds so profusely, you may need only to transplant it once it is established.

**Uses:** This venerable herb has been used for at least 2,000 years. Homer mentions balm in his epic *Odyssey*. And Greek and Roman physicians prescribed it to treat the bites of scorpions and dogs. But lemon balm's real fans were the Arabs, who believed it was good for heart disorders and dispelling melancholy. Colonists brought lemon balm to America. Thomas Jefferson grew it at Monticello, and many Old Williamsburg recipes call for its use. Lemon balm was an important medicine well into the 19th century. The herb acts as a mild tranquilizer and is used to soothe a nervous stomach or minor heart palpitations. Its calming effect combined with its antihistamine action make it an excellent choice for relieving mild headaches; it's especially useful for children.

Researchers have found that a mixture of lemon balm and valerian is as effective as some tranquilizers, without the side effects. The scent alone has long been used to reduce nervous tension. Compounds in it may even prove useful to people with hyperthyroidism, although the herb itself won't replace thyroid medication. And its essential oil reduces risk of infections by inhibiting growth of bacteria and viruses. Recent studies show it is particularly effective against the herpesvirus. It is also effective against flu and colds.

In the kitchen, this herb, with its lemony-mint flavor, complements salads, fruits, marinated vegetables, poultry and stuffing, punch, fish marinades, and an assortment of vegetables, including corn, broccoli, asparagus, and beans. Lemon balm is employed commercially to flavor liqueurs such as Benedictine and Chartreuse. Lemon balm infusions cleanse the skin and help clear up acne. You may add leaves to your bath—or even polish furniture with them.

**Part Used:** Leaves

**Preservation:** Harvest in midsummer and hang branches to dry, or spread leaves on screens.

**Precautions:** None

**Medicinal Use:** You can enjoy lemon balm tea freely. It is delicious hot or iced, by itself or mixed with other herbs. It is often blended with chamomile and mint as a digestive aid, for relaxation, or to give to children as a calmative.

# Licorice

**Perennial**

**Botanical Name:**
*Glycyrrhiza glabra*

**Family:** Fabaceae (Leguminosae)

**Height:** To 3 ft.

**Spread:** 2 ft.

**Description:** Licorice sends out stolons that create a tangled mass of taproots. The herb flowers in mid-summer; in climates with a long growing season, the herb produces a fruit pod clustered in a prickly pod. Licorice is native to the Mediterranean region, northern India, and southwest Asia. It is cultivated in Greece, Iran, Iraq, India, Spain, Syria, and Russia.

**Ease of Care:** Moderate

**Cultivation:** Licorice prefers neutral, well-drained, sandy soil and full sun to partial shade. In cold climates, take the plants inside during the winter. Licorice will handle only a light frost.

**Propagation:** Sow seed in early spring or late fall; take cuttings from suckers.

**Uses:** Licorice has been a popular flavoring for millennia. Archaeologists have determined that the Assyrians and Egyptians used it. Licorice's main constituent, glycyrrhizin, is 50 times sweeter than sugar. Although the herb was once a popular candy flavoring, most of the licorice candy made in the United States is actually flavored with anise. Licorice is used commercially in pastries, ice cream, puddings, soy sauce, soy-based meat substitutes, and tobacco.

As a medicine, licorice was also used by the Greeks and Romans and is still one of the most popular Chinese herbs. In the United States, licorice is in cough syrups and drops. The herb is also used to sweeten mouthwash and toothpaste. A laxative, this soothing herb has also been prescribed for stomach and bowel inflammation and peptic ulcers. Licorice reduces stomach acid and encourages the stomach to protect itself from acid. Carbenoxolene, a compound derived from licorice, was, until recently, the drug of choice to treat ulcers. Another form of licorice, deglycyrrhizinated licorice, shows promise as a future drug. Studies show it can be as effective as Tagemet and Zantac. Licorice has estrogenic effects and is useful for treating menopausal symptoms and normalizing an irregular menstrual cycle. Licorice is also an antiviral and decongestant and is used to treat dermatitis, colds, and infections. It enhances the immune system, and it may have anti-tumor properties. Several clinical studies indicate it may be useful to treat herpes, a viral condition which currently has no cure.

Like the adrenal hormone cortisone, it decreases inflammation, so it is used to reduce the symptoms of rheumatoid arthritis and other inflammatory disorders but without cortisone's side effects. And while cortisone therapy depletes the adrenal glands, licorice encourages them to function better and relieves adrenal exhaustion. Studies show licorice neutralizes liver toxins and increases the liver's ability to store glycogen, which provides muscles with energy.

**Part Used:** Root

**Preservation:** Dig roots in late autumn or early winter. Leave sections of the root in the soil to sprout the next year. Dry licorice in shade.

**Precautions:** Licorice may raise blood pressure in people who have hypertension. It may cause headaches, shortness of breath, bloating, and fluid retention in high doses or with long-term use of low daily doses. Avoid licorice if you're pregnant. Do not use as a daily laxative as it can cause excessive potassium loss.

**Medicinal Use:** Take licorice in the form of syrup, tea, tincture, or pills. Use no more than 1 cup of tea or ⅛ teaspoon (½ dropper full) of tincture a day. You can also chew on the dried roots.

# Lovage

**Perennial**

**Botanical Name:** *Levisticum officinalis*

**Family:** Apiaceae (Umbelliferae)

**Height:** 4–6 ft.

**Spread:** 2 ft., spreads

**Description:** A large plant, lovage produces glossy, dark green leaves that resemble those of celery. The herb flowers in June and July. It is native to southern Europe and has become naturalized throughout North America.

**Ease of Care:** Easy

**Cultivation:** Lovage likes moist, rich, acidic soil. It will grow in full sun or partial shade. Because it dies down in winter, mark its place in the fall to avoid digging the roots and damaging the plant.

**Propagation:** Sow seeds in late summer; divide in autumn or early spring.

**Uses:** Herbalists have recommended lovage to increase urine flow, reduce gas and bowel pain, and treat sore throat, kidney stones, and irregular menstruation. Lovage also is used to treat stomachaches, headaches, obesity, and boils. The hot tea induces sweating.

The taste of lovage's leaves, stems, and seeds resembles that of celery but is much sharper. Use leaves in salads, soups, stews, and sauces. Dried and powdered, they make a tasty addition to herbal salt substitutes. Stems may be cooked, puréed, candied, or eaten raw like celery. Add seeds to pickling brines, cheeses, salad dressings, potatoes, tomatoes, chicken, poultry stuffings, and rice. It also flavors some alcoholic beverages.

**Part Used:** Leaves, stems, seeds

**Preservation:** Harvest fresh leaves as needed. Pick for later use just before the plant begins to bloom. Blanch whole leaves and freeze, or mince and freeze in cubes. Or you can dry lovage by hanging the stems in bundles. Pick seed heads when they turn brown. Hang them upside-down in paper bags to catch seeds.

**Precautions:** Do not use lovage if you are pregnant or have any kidney problems.

**Medicinal Use:** Lovage is sometimes used medicinally, but its most common use is as an addition to foods or condiments. The food industry uses lovage essential oil.

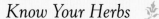

# Marjoram

**Perennial** (often grown as an **Annual**)

**Botanical Name:**
*Origanum majorana* or *Majorana hortensis*

**Family:** Lamiaceae (Labiatae)

**Height:** 1 ft.

**Spread:** 8 in.

**Description:** Marjoram is a bushy, spreading, fairly hardy perennial that is grown as an annual in freezing climates. It produces small, oval, gray-green, velvety leaves and knotlike shapes that blossom into tiny white or pink flowers from August through September. The herb makes an attractive potted plant that may be brought inside when temperatures fall. Native to southwest Asia, marjoram has become naturalized in Mediterranean regions and is cultivated widely in North America.

**Ease of Care:** Easy

**Cultivation:** Like its cousin oregano (*Origanum vulgare*), marjoram likes average to sandy, well-drained alkaline soil and full sun. If your winters are severe, grow marjoram as an annual or in pots that may be brought indoors. If you keep it outdoors, shelter it from the cold.

**Propagation:** Sow seed indoors a few weeks before the last frost and transplant outdoors after the soil has warmed; take cuttings in spring.

**Uses:** The Greeks knew marjoram as "joy of the mountains" and used it as a remedy for sadness. Herbalists have prescribed marjoram to treat asthma, increase sweating, lower fevers, encourage menstruation, and, especially, relieve indigestion. European singers preserved their voices with marjoram tea sweetened with honey. The herb has antioxidant and antifungal properties. Recent studies show marjoram inhibits several viruses, including the herpesvirus. Marjoram gargles and steam treatments relieve sinus congestion and hay fever. A massage oil made from marjoram helps relieve muscle and menstrual cramps. The diluted essential oil can be rubbed into sore gums, in place of clove oil. Aromatherapists use the scent to relax the mind, induce sleep, and even relieve grief.

Marjoram tastes like a mild oregano with a hint of balsam. Add leaves to salads, beef, veal, lamb, roasted poultry, fish, patés, and vegetables such as carrots, cauliflower, eggplant, mushrooms, parsnips, potatoes, squash, and tomatoes. The herb also complements stews, sautés, marinades, dressings, butters, oils, vinegars, and cheese spreads. Its antioxidant properties are so potent they have been shown to be excellent food preservatives.

An infusion added to the bath helps relieve aches, pains, and congestion. Marjoram's antiseptic properties make it a good facial cleanser, and it has been used in cosmetic facial waters. Marjoram freshens linen drawers, and you can add it to potpourri and sachets. Dried flowers may be used in crafts and arrangements. The herb dyes wool shades of green and purple, but the color is not long-lasting.

**Part Used:** Leaves

**Preservation:** Snip fresh leaves as needed. Harvest leaves just before flowering and hang them to dry.

**Precautions:** Moderate use is recommended during pregnancy.

**Medicinal Use:** Marjoram can be made into tea, but by far, the most common way to use it is in cooking. It is also available as an essential oil that can be diluted in vegetable oil and applied to the skin. A couple drops of essential oil can be added to a bath or steam.

# Marshmallow

**Perennial**

**Botanical Name:**
*Althea officinalis*

**Family:** Malvaceae

**Height:** 4 ft.

**Spread:** 2 ft.

**Description:** Marshmallow produces a tapering, woody taproot and woolly stems with several spreading, leafy branches. Flowers, pink to pale blue, appear from July through September. Marshmallow is native to Europe and naturalized in eastern North America. It's found in moist woods, salt marshes, and damp land near the sea.

**Ease of Care:** Easy

**Cultivation:** All mallows like full sun to partial shade and moist to wet, light, neutral soil. Mallows are hardy plants that will tolerate hot, dry summers and cold winters.

**Propagation:** Sow seeds in the fall in moderate climates. Seedlings grow rapidly the first year and should produce blooms by the summer of the second year. Take cuttings or divide in autumn.

**Uses:** Yes, those popular campfire confections originated with these lovely plants. The Greeks used marshmallow to treat wounds, toothaches, coughing, and insect stings. The Romans valued marshmallow roots and leaves for their laxative properties. And during the Renaissance, marshmallow was used extensively to treat sore throats, stomach problems, and even venereal diseases. Marshmallow is a wonderful demulcent that soothes digestive tract inflammations and irritations; it helps heals stomach ulcers. It is also used in formulas to treat urinary and prostate infections and inflammations. It enhances immunity by stimulating white blood cells. Applied as a poultice, it helps to heal cuts and bruises. The roots are sometimes used in salves and poultices.

In the kitchen, add uncooked young tops and tender leaves to spring salads, or fry roots with butter and onions.

**Part Used:** Leaves, flowers, roots

**Preservation:** Gather flowers after they bloom. Collect taproots in autumn from plants at least two years old. Remove lateral rootlets, wash, peel off corky bark, and dry in slices.

**Precautions:** None. Marshmallow is safe and nourishing.

**Medicinal Use:** Use roots for teas, pills, or tinctures. Drink 1 or more cups of tea or take up to 2 teaspoons (8 droppers full) of tincture per day of marshmallow. It is usually mixed with other herbs such as saw palmetto, hydrangea, nettle root, and horsetail to treat an enlarged prostate or with uva ursi, horsetail, plantain, and hydrangea to treat urinary infection. For coughs and sore throats, marshmallow is mixed with herbs such as elecampane, licorice, and mullein. To make a marshmallow poultice, mash or blend the fresh root and add enough cold water to form a gooey gel with a paste-like consistency. Apply the mixture directly to the skin.

# Meadowsweet

**Perennial**

**Botanical Name:**
*Filipendula ulmaria*

**Family:** Rosaceae

**Height:** To 6 ft., in flower

**Spread:** 2 ft.

**Description:** Meadowsweet produces elmlike leaves and large clusters of small white flowers, which bloom throughout summer and smell faintly of almonds. Also known as queen of the meadow, the herb grows wild in Europe and Asia and has been naturalized in North America, from Newfoundland to Ohio. You will find it growing in marshes, along stream banks, and in forests and meadows.

**Ease of Care:** Easy

**Cultivation:** Meadowsweet prefers rich, moist, well-drained soil and partial shade.

**Propagation:** Grow from seed or divide the roots of older plants in the spring or fall. It needs plenty of water to bloom.

**Uses:** The next time you take an aspirin, you can thank meadowsweet. It was from this former strewing herb that 19th-century German chemists developed the popular over-the-counter remedy. Meadowsweet's flower buds contain the pain-reliever salicin, from which researchers derived salicylic acid, aspirin's main component. Meadowsweet's ability to reduce pain is not as marked as aspirin's concentrated compounds, but the plant does not produce aspirin's main side effect: upset stomach. The herb is even used to ease the discomfort of stomach ulcers. It prevents excess acid in the stomach and is one of the best herbal treatments for heartburn.

Meadowsweet has been prescribed to treat headache, arthritis, menstrual cramps, stomach cramps and gas, low-grade fever, and inflammation. It also contains a chemical that fights diarrhea-causing bacteria. Meadowsweet promotes excretion of uric acid, so it is used to treat gout (a condition of excess uric acid) and some types of kidney stones. As an antiseptic diuretic, it is used for urinary tract infections. New research shows that meadowsweet may help prevent blood clots that can trigger heart attacks. Other studies indicate that the salicin in meadowsweet reduces blood sugar levels and may have use in managing diabetes.

**Part Used:** Flowers

**Preservation:** Harvest flower tops when the plant is in bloom. Dry or tincture.

**Precautions:** There are no known contraindications for meadowsweet; however, aspirin has been associated with birth defects and may trigger the fatal Reye syndrome if given to children with colds, flu, or chicken pox, so avoid giving meadowsweet to sick youngsters, until it is proved a safe alternative to aspirin.

**Medicinal Use:** Drink meadowsweet tea up to three times a day. Take ½ to 1 teaspoon tincture up to three times daily. Meadowsweet is often mixed with other gentle pain relievers or digestive aids such as licorice and slippery elm.

# Milk Thistle

**Annual or Biennial**

**Botanical Name:**
*Silybum marianum*

**Family:** Asteraceae
(Compositae)

**Height:** To 3 ft., in flower

**Spread:** To 3 ft.

**Description:** Milk thistle leaves are large, shiny, and spiny. Violet-purple flowers appear from late summer to early autumn. Milk thistle is native to central and western Europe and has become naturalized elsewhere. It is often found on dry, rocky or stony soils in wastelands and fields, and along roads.

**Ease of Care:** Easy

**Cultivation:** Milk thistle prefers sun and well-drained soil.

**Propagation:** The herb grows easily from seed.

**Uses:** Legend has it that milk thistle sprang from the milk of the Virgin Mary, and for centuries, herbalists have recommended it for increasing milk in nursing mothers. But the herb's pri-

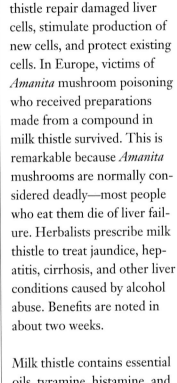

mary use in modern times is in detoxifying and nourishing the liver. The flavonoids in milk thistle repair damaged liver cells, stimulate production of new cells, and protect existing cells. In Europe, victims of *Amanita* mushroom poisoning who received preparations made from a compound in milk thistle survived. This is remarkable because *Amanita* mushrooms are normally considered deadly—most people who eat them die of liver failure. Herbalists prescribe milk thistle to treat jaundice, hepatitis, cirrhosis, and other liver conditions caused by alcohol abuse. Benefits are noted in about two weeks.

Milk thistle contains essential oils, tyramine, histamine, and a flavonoid called silymarine. Milk thistle has antioxidant properties and counteracts some of the detrimental effects of environmental toxins. A bitter tonic, the leaves stimulate bile production—it has been prescribed to improve appetite and assist digestion. Once cultivated widely as a nutritious culinary herb, young milk thistle leaves may be eaten as a

salad or potherb. To eat the leaves, cut off their sharp edges with scissors and steam. Serve as you would spinach.

**Part Used:** Seeds, leaves, and shoots

**Preservation:** Gather shoots and leaves in spring, seeds in late summer when ripe. Dry or tincture the seeds.

**Precautions:** None

**Medicinal Use:** Drink a milk thistle tea up to three times a day. Take up to ½ teaspoon (2 droppers full) of tincture up to three times a day, or take milk thistle in pill form. Grind milk thistle seeds in a coffee grinder and sprinkle on food.

# Motherwort

**Perennial**

**Botanical Name:**
*Leonurus cardiaca*

**Family:** Lamiaceae (Labiatae)

**Height:** 4 ft.

**Spread:** 1 ft.; may become invasive

**Description:** Motherwort has stout, square stems tinged with red or violet. Lower leaves are lobed, like those of maple. Upper leaves are narrow and toothed. The plant produces whorls of small, white, pink, or red blooms in summer.

**Ease of Care:** Easy

**Cultivation:** Motherwort prefers average, well-drained soil and full sun but will tolerate most conditions.

**Propagation:** Sow seed in the spring; thin seedlings to 12 inches.

**Uses:** As its name implies, motherwort is useful for treating conditions associated with childbirth. The herb contains a chemical called leonurine, which encourages uterine contractions. Motherwort is used as a uterine tonic before and after childbirth. It has also been used for centuries to regulate the menstrual cycle, to promote the flow of mother's milk, and to treat menopausal complaints.

Motherwort is a mild relaxing agent often recommended by herbalists to reduce anxiety and depression and treat nervousness, insomnia, heart palpitations, and rapid heart rate. Russian studies show that motherwort is good for hypertension because it relaxes blood vessels and calms nerves. Motherwort injections have been shown to prevent formation of blood clots, which improves blood flow and reduces risk of heart attack, stroke, and other diseases. Motherwort is also useful for headache, insomnia, vertigo, and delirium from fever. It is sometimes used to relieve asthma, bronchitis, and other lung problems, usually mixed with mullein and other lung herbs.

**Part Used:** Leaves

**Preservation:** Harvest leaves after flowers bloom; dry or tincture.

**Precautions:** Don't use motherwort if you have clotting problems or take medication to thin your blood. Avoid motherwort if you are pregnant, unless a health professional recommends its use. Some people may develop a rash after handling motherwort.

**Medicinal Use:** Drink up to 4 cups of motherwort tea a day. It is bitter; you may wish to mix it with other herbs. It is often taken with other women's tonics such as red raspberry or heart tonics such as hawthorn. Take up to 1 teaspoon (4 droppers full) of tincture a day.

# Mullein

**Biennial**

**Botanical Name:**

*Verbascum thapsus*

**Family:** Scrophulariaceae

**Height:** To 7 ft. in full flower; the leaves, to 8 in.

**Spread:** 2–3 ft.

**Description:** Mullein is a common plant, often found along roads and in untended fields. The herb's leaves have soft, fine hairs, which irritate the mucous membranes of animals that attempt to eat them. The woolly leaves also protect the herb from moisture loss and insects. Mullein's round, fibrous stem is sturdy and downy and produces bright yellow flowers from midsummer to early autumn. Dried, the flowers exude a very faint, honey-like scent.

**Ease of Care:** Easy

**Cultivation:** Don't try to grow mullein indoors. It prefers open spaces. Mullein likes rich soil but will grow in poor soil in dry wastelands. Thin or transplant to 3 feet.

**Propagation:** Sow seeds in spring or summer. Mullein readily self-seeds.

**Uses:** According to Homer, mullein was given to Ulysses to protect him from Circe's sorcery. For centuries, mullein was considered an amulet against witches and evil spirits. Also called Aaron's rod, candlewick plant, hag's taper, and velvet dock, the plant has many uses—from medicinal to household. Citing just one example, the dried stems were dipped in suet and burned as torches.

For centuries, mullein's leaves have been used to heal lung conditions. Herbalists once even recommended that patients with lung diseases smoke dried, crumbled mullein leaves. Ayurvedic physicians prescribed mullein to treat coughs. And colonists considered mullein so valuable they brought it with them to America, where Indians eventually adopted it for treating coughs, bronchitis, and asthma.

Contemporary herbalists still recommend internal use of mullein leaves to treat colds, sore throat, and coughs. The flowers and leaves reduce inflammation in the urinary and digestive tract and treat colitis, intestinal bleeding, and diarrhea. The fresh flower infused alone or with garlic in olive oil makes an ear oil for pain and inflammation associated with an earache.

The leaves make good tinder, and the dried tops can be used in flower arrangements. Flower infusions are employed in creams, facial steams, and shampoos to soothe skin and brighten fair hair.

**Part Used:** Flowers, leaves

**Preservation:** Harvest leaves during mullein's first growing season and flowers as soon as they open. The flower stalk appears the second year. To preserve mullein, remove the green parts from the flowers, then dry the flowers gently without artificial heat. Be careful not to lose the yellow color, which is part of the healing substance. Leaves may be dried as well.

**Precautions:** The fine hairs on the leaves irritate some people's skin and cause a rash.

**Medicinal Use:** You can take mullein leaves in pill, tincture, or tea form. Use up to a few cups of tea or a teaspoon of tincture (4 droppers full) a day. Mullein is often combined with other herbs that treat lung conditions, such as elecampane.

# Mustard

**Annual**

**Botanical Name:** *Brassica alba*

**Family:** Cruciferae

**Height:** To 2 ft.

**Spread:** 1 ft.

**Description:** You'll recognize species of the large mustard family by their strong smell and four-petaled flowers. Mustard flowers are small and yellow, and the petals resemble a Maltese cross. Lower leaves are pinnately lobed or coarsely toothed; upper leaves are not as lobed. The plant flowers in early summer. Mustards grow just about everywhere. These are hardy plants, and their seeds remain plantable for years. *Brassica alba*, white mustard, grows wild throughout the world and has many cousins, including cabbage, broccoli, and turnips.

**Ease of Care:** Easy

**Cultivation:** Plant mustard seeds ⅛ inch deep in a sunny spot, where the soil is average to poor and well drained. Yellow mustard tolerates heavy soil conditions better than black mustard. Thin seedlings to about 9 inches apart. Mustard prefers heavy feeding: Regularly add well-rotted manure or compost to the soil. Mustard supposedly stimulates growth of beans, grapes, and fruit trees. It is said to keep flea beetles away from collards. Mustard also releases a chemical in the soil that inhibits cyst nematodes and prevents root rot and also many other plants from growing near it.

**Propagation:** To grow mustard for its leaves, sow seeds at several intervals from spring through early fall. If you're growing mustard for its seeds, sow in spring or late summer. Once established, it will easily self-sow; it can even become a garden pest.

**Uses:** You haven't really tasted mustard until you've made it yourself. To make mustard from seeds, boil ⅓ cup cider vinegar, ⅔ cup cider, 2 tablespoons honey, ⅛ tablespoon turmeric, and up to 1 teaspoon salt. While hot, combine with ¼ cup ground mustard seeds. Blend in a food processor. After the mixture is smooth, add 1 tablespoon olive oil. This recipe makes 1¼ cups of mustard.

Mustard has many medicinal uses, too. If you're old enough, you may remember getting a mustard plaster when you had a cold. Mustard seeds warm the skin and open the lungs to make breathing easier. Mustard plasters may also relieve rheumatism, toothache, sore muscles, and arthritis. Its chief constituent, mustard oil, gives it its heat and flavor. These constituents also make mustard an appetite stimulate and a powerful irritant. Mustard in small doses improves digestion. Young leaves are vitamin-rich additions to salads, or they can be boiled with onions and salt pork.

**Part Used:** Leaves, seeds

**Preservation:** Harvest leaves for salads when they are young and tender. Harvest seeds when pods have turned brown but before they split open. Spread plants on a tray. Within a couple of weeks the seeds should ripen. Winnow seeds from pods by rubbing them in the palm of your hand. Store whole or ground mustard seed in tightly covered jars.

**Precautions:** Consuming large quantities of mustard seed may cause vomiting. Don't leave mustard plasters on too long or they may blister skin.

**Medicinal Use:** To make a poultice, mix powdered seeds with an equal amount of flour and enough water to form a paste. Spread mustard plaster on a cloth and place the cloth, poultice side down, on the skin. Leave on about 20 minutes. Remove if the poultice becomes uncomfortable. Wash affected area.

# Nasturtium

**Annual**

**Botanical Name:**
*Tropaeolum majus*

**Family:** Tropaeolaceae

**Height:** 1 ft., bush; 5–10 ft., vines

**Spread:** 1½ ft., bush; vines ramble

**Description:** Nasturtiums produce distinctive, blue-green circular leaves on fleshy stems. The plants come in a variety of types, ranging from compact bushes to spreading vines. They produce large, attractive blooms that range from pale yellow, pink, and apricot to deep, rich gold, orange, and burgundy. Nasturtiums are native to South America and widely cultivated elsewhere.

**Ease of Care:** Easy

**Cultivation:** Nasturtiums like full sun to partial shade in average to poor, moist soil. They are said to repel whiteflies, cabbage pests, and squash bugs. But they attract aphids, so be on the lookout for these insects. The plant flowers throughout summer until the first frost. Beautiful ornamental plants, nasturtiums make an eye-catching addition to any garden. Vines are great in hanging planters, in window boxes, or on trellises and fences.

**Propagation:** Seeds are large. Sow them in late spring in any spot that can use bright color and where vines have a place to climb.

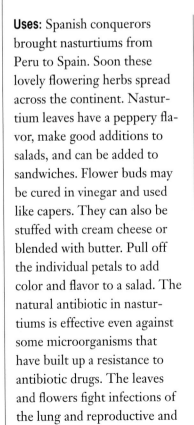

**Uses:** Spanish conquerors brought nasturtiums from Peru to Spain. Soon these lovely flowering herbs spread across the continent. Nasturtium leaves have a peppery flavor, make good additions to salads, and can be added to sandwiches. Flower buds may be cured in vinegar and used like capers. They can also be stuffed with cream cheese or blended with butter. Pull off the individual petals to add color and flavor to a salad. The natural antibiotic in nasturtiums is effective even against some microorganisms that have built up a resistance to antibiotic drugs. The leaves and flowers fight infections of the lung and reproductive and urinary tracts. To relieve itching skin, try rubbing the juice of the fresh plant on the skin.

**Part Used:** Leaves, flowers

**Preservation:** Harvest fresh leaves and flowers as needed. Pickle unripe seeds in vinegar and use them in salads.

**Precautions:** Large amounts of the seeds act as a strong laxative (purgative).

**Medicinal Use:** Nasturtiums are medicinal when eaten. You can use them as a tincture; however, they are seldom used in this form. Sometimes the leaves are added to herb teas. One tasty way to use nasturtium is to make an herbal vinegar to use on salads.

# Nettle

**Perennial**

**Botanical Name:** *Urtica dioica*

**Family:** Urticaceae

**Height:** 3–6 ft.

**Spread:** 1–2 ft.

**Description:** Brush against a bushy nettle plant and you'll feel as if you've been stung by bees. The herb's single stalk forms dark-green, saw-toothed leaves, which are covered with "hairs" containing formic acid, a substance that causes pain if it comes in contact with your skin. Nettle's small, greenish flowers appear in clusters from July through September. The herb is native to Europe and Asia and widely naturalized. In North America it ranges from Newfoundland to Ontario, west to Colorado, and south to the Carolinas. You'll find nettle in weedy places, often near water.

**Ease of Care:** Easy

**Cultivation:** Nettle prefers average to rich, moist soil and full sun to partial shade. Gardeners like it in their gardens because nettle may stimulate growth and production of essential oils in companion plants. Nettle also hosts several beneficial insects that prey on harmful pests. But it can be very invasive. To prevent this, cut it way back when harvesting before it goes to seed. You may need to do this several times every summer.

**Propagation:** Nettle grows from seeds dispersed in spring, or you can produce new plants by dividing in spring or fall.

**Uses:** The Anglo-Saxons named nettle after their word for "needle." During the Bronze Age, fabric was woven from nettle. As recently as World War I, Germans wove nettle fabric when cotton supplies were low.

Nettle was once used to reduce arthritic pains and uric acid in joints and tissues (excess uric acid causes gout, a painful inflammatory condition). Nettle improves circulation and treats asthma. It is a light laxative; nettle tea has also been prescribed for intestinal weakness, diarrhea, and malnutrition. Nettle is a diuretic useful for treating bladder problems. Several studies demonstrated that the root successfully reduces prostate inflammation. Nettle treats eczema and skin rashes, increases mother's milk, slightly lowers blood sugar, and decreases profuse menstruation.

Nettle is so versatile that it has been used for centuries as a spring tonic to improve general health. The herb is rich in anti-inflammatory flavonoids and vital nutrients, including vitamins D, C, and A as well as minerals, such as iron, calcium, phosphorus, and magnesium. Thus, nettle has been used to treat malnutrition, anemia, and rickets. Hair shampoos and conditioners often include nettle because it is said to benefit the scalp and encourage hair growth.

Nettle loses its sting when cooked, dried, or ground. It is a healthy and tasty addition to scrambled eggs, pasta dishes, casseroles, and soups. Young shoots may be steamed then tossed in salads or eaten like kale or spinach. You also may juice nettle and drink it alone or combine it with other fruit or vegetable juices. Nettle leaves dye wool shades of yellow and green.

**Part Used:** Root, leaves

**Preservation:** Tincture fresh or dried nettle.

**Precautions:** Wear gloves to pick nettles. Ingesting large amounts of older nettle plants may irritate the kidneys.

**Medicinal Use:** Drink 2 to 6 cups a day. Take 1 to 2 teaspoons (4 to 8 droppers full) of tincture per day. Drink 1 to 2 ounces of juice per day, or eat nettle as a vegetable. Nettle is often mixed with different herbs in a variety of medicinal preparations.

# Oats

**Annual**

**Botanical Name:** *Avena sativa*

**Family:** Gramineae

**Height:** 2–4 ft.

**Spread:** 1 in.

**Description:** The grass produces a fibrous root and a hollow jointed stem with narrow, flat, pale-green leaves. The grain is "hairy" and grooved. Oats are native to southern Europe and eastern Asia. They are widely cultivated as a food.

**Ease of Care:** Easy

**Cultivation:** Widely cultivated for their nourishing grain, oats can also be grown in an herb garden.

**Propagation:** Sow seed in spring.

**Uses:** The oat seed is used in two different phases of its growth: in its fresh, milky stage and as a grain once the seed is ripe and dried. Is there anyone who has not eaten oatmeal? This ubiquitous and nourishing cereal contains starches, proteins, vitamins, minerals, and dietary fiber nutritionists recommend we consume each day. Several clinical trials have found that regular consumption of oat bran reduces blood cholesterol levels in just one month. High-fiber diets may also reduce risk of colon and rectal cancer. Oats contain the alkaloid gramine, which has been credited with mild sedative properties. In its milky stage, oat tincture has been prescribed for nerve disorders and as a uterine tonic. Researchers found that fresh oats have some value in treating addiction and reducing nicotine craving. Fresh, green oats ease the anxiety that often accompanies drug withdrawal. Oat straw is sometimes made into a high-mineral tea.

Oatmeal has been used topically to heal wounds and various skin rashes. With their demulcent and soothing qualities, oats are found in soaps and bath and body products. Oatmeal baths and poultices are wonderful for soothing dry, flaky skin or alleviating itching from poison oak and chicken pox. Used in the bath, oatmeal makes a good facial scrub and helps clear up skin problems.

**Part Used:** Grain, fresh berry, and shaft (oat straw)

**Preservation:** Gather fresh oats and oat straw in the spring and the oat berry in the late summer. Oat straw and whole dried oat groats may be dried. The fresh oat seed must be fresh-tinctured—once it is dried, it loses some of its medicinal properties.

**Precautions:** Most people tolerate oats well, but some people, especially those with bowel disorders, may experience discomfort after suddenly increasing fiber consumption. Always drink plenty of liquids after eating fibrous foods. If you have an intolerance to gluten-containing grains, don't eat oats.

**Medicinal Use:** Take ¼ to ¾ teaspoon (1 to 3 droppers full) a day of a tincture of fresh oats. Make a paste by adding water to ground oats. You can easily grind them in a coffee grinder or a food processor. For a bath, put fine-ground oats in a porous bag and place in bath water. This bag can be used to scrub the body in place of soap for people who are sensitive to soap. Oat straw tea is often combined with other high-mineral herbs, such as nettles. The fresh oats are used with other nervous system herbs, such as St. John's wort.

# Oregon Grape

**Perennial**

**Botanical Name:**
*Berberis aquifolium*

**Family:** Berberidaceae

**Height:** 3–6 ft.

**Spread:** To 4 ft.

**Description:** An evergreen shrub, Oregon grape produces dense, oblong leaves with prickly edges similar to those of holly. The dark green leaves turn bronze, crimson, or purple in fall. Tiny flowers are bright yellow in spring; the inner bark of the rhizome is also bright yellow. The tree produces deep purple berries. Oregon grape is found in coniferous forests throughout the American Northwest and Canada.

**Ease of Care:** Easy

**Cultivation:** Oregon grape prefers well-drained, humusy soil and full sun. The plant hosts wheat rust fungus but is immune to the disease. Oregon grape may suffer from leaf spot and powdery mildew.

**Propagation:** Take cuttings in midsummer and set out new plants the following spring. Collect berries in fall and plant seeds in spring.

**Uses:** Oregon grape's prime constituent, the alkaloid berberine, improves blood flow to the liver and stimulates bile to aid digestion. Thus, Oregon grape root may be used to boost liver function and treat jaundice, hepatitis, poor intestinal tone and function, and gastrointestinal debility. Berberine effectively kills *Giardia* and *Candida* organisms and several other intestinal parasites, which are responsible for intestinal up-

sets and vaginal yeast infections. Oregon grape root is useful to treat serious cases of diarrhea and digestive tract infection.

Oregon grape is also useful for treating colds, flu, and numerous other infections. In the laboratory, it's been shown to kill or suppress the growth of several disease-causing microbes. Oregon grape's berberine content makes it a good eye wash, douche, or skin cleanser for infections. The tincture is used to treat eczema, acne, herpes, and psoriasis.

High in vitamin C, the berries may be eaten raw or cooked in jam. Berries are also used to flavor jelly, wine, and soups. They have been used in folk medicine and seem to have some of the same medicinal properties as the root, but they

are probably not as potent. Oregon grape root and bark dye wool yellow and tan; fruits impart a purplish blue color.

**Part Used:** Root (the medicine is in the yellow area under the outer root bark), berries

**Preservation:** Dig roots in fall, and dry in a paper bag.

**Precautions:** Oregon grape stimulates liver function, so if you have liver disease, use only under the care of a health practitioner. Avoid it if you are pregnant. Otherwise, use the herb for two to three weeks, abstain for several weeks, and resume if necessary.

**Medicinal Use:** You can drink up to 3 cups of tea a day, although due to the bitter taste, you will probably want to mix it with other herbs or take the herb as a tincture. Take ½ to 1 teaspoon of the tincture (2 to 4 droppers full) up to three times a day. For an eye wash, make a strong tea (2 teaspoons of Oregon grape per cup of water) and strain carefully through a coffee filter before using in an eye cup.

# Parsley

**Biennial** (often grown as an **Annual**)

**Botanical Name:**
*Petroselinum crispum*

**Family:** Apiaceae (Umbelliferae)

**Height:** 2–3 ft., in flower

**Spread:** 8 in.

**Description:** Parsley is often grown as an annual to obtain fresh-tasting leaves. The herb's attractive, rich-green, dense leaves form a rosette base, and the plant produces tiny, greenish-yellow flowers in early summer. Parsley comes in two forms: curly and Italian. The latter has flat leaves and is stronger-flavored than the curly variety. Curly parsley makes a nice edging plant, and both varieties can be grown in pots indoors. Parsley grows wild in many parts of the world and is cultivated throughout the temperate world.

**Ease of Care:** Easy

**Cultivation:** Parsley prefers full sun or partial shade in a moist, rich soil. Parsley is said to repel asparagus beetles.

**Propagation:** Soak seeds in warm water for several hours to speed germination. Sow seeds in the garden once the soil is warm in spring. The seeds often take many weeks to germinate. Parsley is difficult to transplant unless small.

**Uses:** You may think of parsley as a "throw-away" herb. It is universally used as a garnish that generally goes uneaten. But if you discard this natural breath sweetener, you'll be wasting a powerhouse of vitamins and minerals. Parsley contains vitamins A and C (more than an orange), and small amounts of several B vitamins, calcium, and iron. The leaves and root have diuretic properties and are used to treat bladder infections. Parsley's strong odor derives from its essential oils, one of which,

apiol, has been extracted for medicinal uses. It is used in pharmaceutical drugs to treat some kidney ailments. Parsley seeds, or a compound in them, is used in some pharmaceutical preparations to treat urinary tract disorders. Another of parsley's compounds reduces inflammation and is a free-radical scavenger, eliminating these destructive elements. It also stimulates the appetite and increases circulation to the digestive organs. The root has more medicinal properties than the leaves.

Parsley's clean flavor blends with most foods and is often found in ethnic cuisines, including those of the Middle East, France, Belgium, Switzerland, Japan, Spain, and England. Parsley complements most meats and poultry and is a good addition to vegetable dishes, soups, and stews. It is always an ingredient in the famous bouquet garni used by cooks throughout the Western world. To make white sauce, the stems are used instead of the leaves to impart less color.

**Part Used:** Leaves, stems, seeds, root

**Preservation:** Snip leaves as needed and use fresh. Hang-dry parsley or freeze. To prepare the roots, wash and cut them into small pieces while they are fresh and pliable. Dry on a screen in a warm place.

**Precautions:** Avoid the root, seeds, and large amounts of the leaves if you're pregnant. Also avoid the root and seeds if you have kidney problems. Parsley is fine to eat in foods, however.

**Medicinal Use:** Add parsley to foods to obtain its benefits. Parsley can also be taken in tea, tincture, and pill form. Take the root or leaves in tea or ¼ teaspoon (1 dropper full) of tincture a day. Commercially, parsley root is used mostly for its diuretic properties and is almost always mixed with other herbs. Occasionally, parsley is added to herbal teas for the treatment of urinary tract problems.

# Passion Flower

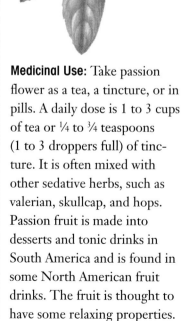

**Perennial**

**Botanical Name:**
*Passiflora incarnata*

**Family:** Passifloraceae

**Height:** 25–30 ft.

**Spread:** Creeping vine

**Description:** Passion flower produces coiling tendrils and showy, colorful blossoms with white or lavender petals and a brilliant pink or purple corona. Flowers appear from early to late summer. The plant produces three to five toothed, lobed leaves and a berry with thin yellow skin and a sweet, succulent pulp. Passion flower is native from Florida to Texas and may be found as far north as Missouri. The herb also is abundant in South America. Passion flower grows in full sun to partially shaded, dry areas, in thickets, along fences, and at the edge of wooded areas.

**Ease of Care:** Moderate

**Cultivation:** Passion flower prefers deep, well-drained soil, plenty of water, and some shade. Revitalize the soil each spring, replacing the top layer with new topsoil, but don't overfertilize since very rich soil results in fewer flowers. Prune old branches in late winter and early spring to get better blossoms. The herb is susceptible to thrips and mealybugs. You can also grow passion flower indoors in a large pot, although it won't reach its normal height.

**Propagation:** Sow seeds in the spring, although they can take years to germinate. Take cuttings in spring or fall. Plants are sold in most nurseries.

**Uses:** Few herbs have as many religious connections as passion flower. When Spanish explorers discovered the vine growing in South America, they were struck by its elaborate blossoms. Passion flower's five petals and five sepals, they reasoned, represented the 10 faithful apostles. The flower's dramatic corona looked to them like Jesus's crown of thorns. And the herb's five stamens symbolized Christ's five wounds. Curling tendrils reminded them of the cords used to whip Jesus, and the leaves were seen as the hands of his persecutors.

Passion flower's chief medicinal value is as a sedative. The Aztecs used it to promote sleep and relieve pain. Today the flowers are used in numerous pharmaceutical drugs in Europe to treat nervous disorders, heart palpitations, anxiety, and high blood pressure. It has also been prescribed for tension, fatigue, insomnia, and muscle and lung spasms. Unlike most sedative drugs, it has been shown to be nonaddictive, although it is not a strong pain reliever.

**Part Used:** Flowers, fruit

**Preservation:** Gather flowers after they bloom, and dry or tincture.

**Precautions:** Used in moderation, passion flower is considered safe. Don't use its close relative blue passion flower, which is commonly grown because it is one of the more hardy species.

**Medicinal Use:** Take passion flower as a tea, a tincture, or in pills. A daily dose is 1 to 3 cups of tea or ¼ to ¾ teaspoons (1 to 3 droppers full) of tincture. It is often mixed with other sedative herbs, such as valerian, skullcap, and hops. Passion fruit is made into desserts and tonic drinks in South America and is found in some North American fruit drinks. The fruit is thought to have some relaxing properties.

# Peppermint

**Perennial**

**Botanical Name:**
*Mentha piperita*

**Family:** Lamiaceae
(Labiatae)

**Height:** 2–2½ ft.

**Spread:** 1 ft.

**Description:** Peppermint produces dark-green, spear-shaped leaves on stems that arise from an underground network of spreading stems. Though peppermint and spearmint are close relatives, spearmint *(M. spicata)* has green, pointed, somewhat hairy leaves and has a milder, cooler taste. Both plants can become invasive, so plant them in an isolated location, or contain the herbs in a pot. The herb flowers in July and August. Mints are native to Europe and Asia; some varieties are found in South Africa, America, and Australia. They have become naturalized throughout North America, from Canada to Mexico.

**Ease of Care:** Easy

**Cultivation:** Peppermint likes full sun to partial shade and average, moist soil. Mints are said to repel aphids, flea beetles, and cabbage pests.

**Propagation:** Take cuttings in midsummer; divide at any time during the growing season.

**Uses:** You may enjoy peppermint candies, especially after a meal, but this useful plant isn't found just in confections. A carminative and gastric stimulant, promoting the flow of bile to the stomach and aiding digestion, peppermint has been prescribed to treat indigestion, flatulence, colic, and nausea. An antispasmodic, peppermint calms muscles in the digestive tract, reduces colon spasms, and is recommended as a treatment for irritable bowel syndrome and colitis. It also reduces the inflammation of stomach ulcers and colitis. The herb—even its fragrance—eases the pain of headaches. Peppermint's main compound, menthol, is very antiseptic, killing bacteria,

viruses, fungi, and parasites, while balancing intestinal flora. Menthol is found in most heating balms, vapor balms, and liniments because of its heating properties.

Experiment with peppermint in the kitchen. Use it in jellies, sauces, salads, vegetable dishes, and beverages. Peppermint is used to flavor candy, gum, and even dental products and toothpicks. Peppermint makes a

good addition to sachets and potpourri. Sniffing peppermint helps clear the sinuses, so it is often used in inhalers. Studies also show that inhaling peppermint stimulates brain waves, increases concentration, and helps keep you awake. Steeped in rosemary vinegar, peppermint helps to control dandruff.

**Part Used:** Leaves

**Preservation:** Pick shoots in early to middle summer. Hang-dry or freeze.

**Precautions:** The essential oil is very hot so always dilute it. Peppermint is safe to use in moderation. If you have a hiatal hernia, gastroesophageal reflux disease, or chronic heartburn, peppermint could worsen the symptoms.

**Medicinal Use:** Drink the tasty tea freely. In tinctures, peppermint is most often mixed with other herbs that aid digestion or are relaxing. Take the tea or a few drops of peppermint extract to ease digestion or motion sickness. Use the essential oil in liniments or a vapor balm.

# Plantain

**Perennial**

**Botanical Name:**
*Plantago major*

**Family:** Plantaginaceae

**Height:** ½–1½ ft.

**Spread:** To 7 in.

**Description:** Plantain is native to Europe, but it's probably growing in your own backyard. Hardy and adaptable, plantain has made itself at home throughout the world. American Indians, in fact, called it "white man's foot" because it seemed to follow the European colonists wherever they went. Often you'll see plantain growing along roads, in meadows and, to the chagrin of homeowners, in lawns. *Plantago major* has thick, broad, and oval leaves that form a compact rosette. The even more common *P. lanceolata* has similar leaves, but they are much more narrow. The herb's flowers are very tiny and yellowish-green, appearing from June through September.

**Ease of Care:** Easy

**Cultivation:** Extremely hardy, plantain thrives in average, well-drained soil in full sun to shade.

**Propagation:** Sow seed in early spring or fall. The plant grows quickly and self-seeds readily. But before you plant seeds, check your lawn. Chances are plantain already grows there.

**Uses:** Don't consider this ubiquitous plant a nuisance. Plantain is a powerful healer and has been used for centuries to treat a variety of ailments. The ancient Saxons, in fact, regarded plantain as one of the essential herbs.

If a bee stings you, apply crushed, fresh plantain leaves to the welt, which will soon disappear. And if you stumble into a patch of poison ivy, you needn't scratch and suffer. Apply a poultice of plantain leaves to relieve your discomfort. Some people, moreover, have been known to chew plantain root to stop the pain of a toothache. A diuretic, the herb is useful for treating urinary problems. Lung disorders, such as asthma and bronchitis, also respond to plantain. Research from India shows that it reduces the symptoms of colds and coughs and relieves the pain and wheezing associated with bronchial problems.

In the kitchen, steam tender young plantain leaves as you would spinach, or eat small amounts fresh in salads, although they are too fibrous for most people's tastes. The seeds are edible. Add small amounts to other grains to increase protein. The species *P. psyllium* is a popular laxative; it is used, as is *P. ovata*, in products such as Metamucil. As with other foods that provide bulk, it has been shown to reduce cholesterol levels. Applied externally, the plant stimulates and cleanses the

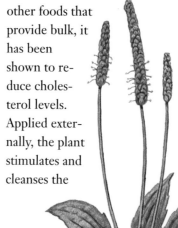

skin and encourages wounds to heal faster. Plantain has also been used to dye wool a dull gold or camel color.

**Part Used:** Leaves, root, seed

**Preservation:** Harvest fresh leaves any time. You can preserve the properties of plantain leaves and roots in lotions and salves. Dig the root in fall and use fresh or dried. Harvest seeds when ripe, shake and blow off the shaft, and grind them.

**Precautions:** None

**Medicinal Use:** Use fresh plantain leaves for poultices. Chew the fresh root for toothache. You can make the leaves into a tincture, tea, or pills. For urinary tract problems, they are often mixed with dandelion root, and for infection, they are mixed with uva ursi. To make an herbal combination for coughs and bronchial congestion, mix plantain with elecampane and mullein. Add fresh leaves and fresh or dried roots to any all-purpose skin salve.

# Raspberry

**Perennial**

**Botanical Name:** *Rubus idaeus*

**Family:** Rosaceae

**Height:** 4 ft.

**Spread:** 3 ft.

**Description:** Native to North America and Europe, this shrubby, thorny plant, also known as hindberry and bramble, quickly spread around the world. You'll find raspberry thickets along the edges of woods and in untended fields. The raspberry plant produces a prickly stem. Its flowers are white and appear in the spring and summer of its second year. Berries ripen in June and July. Each fruit is composed of lots of little fruits, or drupelets, which give it its familiar shape. The plant produces erect shoots or canes that, in time, flop over and reproduce. Raspberry leaves are pale green above, gray-white beneath, and serrated with a rounded base.

**Ease of Care:** Easy

**Cultivation:** The plant prefers full sun in loose, rich, well-drained soil, with manure or compost.

**Propagation:** Divide roots or plant ½-inch cuttings in a few inches of soil. But be careful that your raspberry bushes do not take over your garden. Once rooted, the plant is prolific, sending up new shoots with frequency.

**Uses:** Long revered for its healing properties, raspberry is an astringent, stimulant, and tonic. Seventeenth-century English herbalist Nicholas Culpepper recommended raspberry for a number of ailments, including "fevers, ulcers, putrid sores of the mouth and secret parts...spitting blood...piles...stones of the kidney...and too much flowing of women's courses." American Indians used raspberry as a treatment for wounds. And contemporary herbalists prescribe raspberry for diarrhea, nausea, vomiting, and morning sickness. In addition, raspberry leaves are thought to tone uterine muscles and, thus, have long been used by pregnant women to prevent miscarriage and reduce labor pains. They can be used throughout pregnancy. They relieve menstrual cramps if taken as a tonic over a period of time. Raspberry leaves are

also good for women with uterine problems such as fibroids, endometriosis, or excessive menstrual bleeding.

The fruit is a tonic and may be good for the blood. Fresh raspberries can have a mild laxative effect, but a tea from the leaves is a cure for diarrhea and dysentery. Fresh or frozen raspberries have many uses in the kitchen.

**Part Used:** Fruit, leaves

**Preservation:** Harvest berries in summer. Harvest leaves any time, but the best time is before the plant bears fruit; use fresh or dried.

**Precautions:** None

**Medicinal Use:** The leaves of raspberry make a tasty hot or iced tea. During pregnancy, mix them with other gentle herbs such as lemon grass or chamomile for some variety. To prevent miscarriage, use equal parts raspberry leaf, false unicorn root, and cramp bark; drink 2 to 3 cups a day. If using tincture of raspberry, take ¼ to ½ teaspoon (1 to 2 droppers full) a day, as needed. Use raspberry tea externally as a wash for sores, ulcers, and raw skin surfaces. Eat the fruit fresh, or freeze or preserve in vinegar or liquor.

# Red Clover

**Perennial**

**Botanical Name:**
*Trifolium pratense*

**Family:** Fabaceae (Leguminosae)

**Height:** To 2 ft.

**Spread:** 8 in.; invasive

**Description:** This wide-ranging legume produces leaves in groups of three and fragrant red or purple ball-shaped flowers. Like its relatives, beans and peas, red clover adds nitrogen to the soil. Sufficient nitrogen is important to produce healthy plants. As a result, red clover is a popular winter and early spring cover crop to enrich the soil, but because it is a tenacious perennial that spreads by means of runners, it must be well chopped before you replant the garden. You'll find it growing in fields and vacant lots. The plant is widely cultivated.

**Ease of Care:** Easy

**Cultivation:** Red clover thrives in moist, well-drained soil with full sun.

**Propagation:** Sow seeds in the spring or fall.

**Uses:** Red clover, a favorite of honey bees, is one of the world's oldest agricultural crops. This ubiquitous field flower has been used as a medicine for millennia, revered by Greeks, Romans, and Celts. But it's in the last 100 years that red clover has gained prominence as the source of a possible cancer treatment. Researchers have isolated several antitumor compounds such as biochanin A in red clover, which they think may help prevent cancer. The herb also contains antioxidants and a form of vitamin E. There is some evidence that it helps prevent breast tumors.

Some of red clover's constituents are thought to stimulate the immune system. Another constituent, coumarin, has blood-thinning properties. Its hormonelike effect makes red clover a potential treatment for some types of infertility and

symptoms of menopause. A diuretic, sedative, and anti-inflammatory herb, red clover has been recommended for the skin conditions eczema and psoriasis. It also has some antibacterial properties.

You may pick flowers and add them to salads throughout the summer. Tiny florets are a delightful addition to iced tea. Eat red clover's nutritious leaves cooked since they are not digestible raw.

**Part Used:** Flowers, leaves

**Preservation:** Gather leaves and flowers in early summer when tops are in bloom.

**Precautions:** Avoid red clover if you're pregnant or have a history of bleeding easily. Also, because it is a blood thinner, avoid it just before surgery.

**Medicinal Use:** It makes a pleasant-tasting tea, hot or iced. Drink 1 cup up to three times a day. Take 1 to 2 teaspoons (4 to 8 droppers full) of tincture up to three times a day.

# Rosemary

**Perennial**

**Botanical Name:**
*Rosmarinus officinalis*

**Family:** Lamiaceae
(Labiatae)

**Height:** 4–6 ft.

**Spread:** 2–4 ft.

**Description:** Rosemary makes a stunning addition to any garden. An attractive, spreading evergreen, its gray-green, needle-shaped leaves may be pruned to form a low hedge. A low-growing variety of rosemary provides a wonderful ground cover. The herb produces pale blue flowers from December through spring. Rosemary is found on hills along the Mediterranean, in Portugal, and in northwestern Spain. The herb is cultivated widely elsewhere.

**Ease of Care:** Moderate

**Cultivation:** Rosemary likes sandy, alkaline soil and full sun but will grow in partial sun. Grow rosemary as a potted plant in cold climates, or protect it from winter winds.

**Propagation:** Sow seed; take cuttings or layer in spring.

**Uses:** Before the advent of refrigeration, cooks wrapped meat in rosemary leaves to preserve it. The herb's strong piney aroma has prevented commercial use as a preservative, but efforts are underway to create a preservative without the scent. Modern studies show that rosemary has potent antioxidant properties. It is an astringent, expectorant, and diaphoretic (induces sweating). It promotes digestion and stimulates the activity of the liver and gallbladder to aid both in digestion of fats and the detoxification of the body. It also inhibits formation of kidney stones. The herb has been prescribed to treat muscle spasms. Rosemary oil helps reduce the pain of rheumatism when used as a liniment. An antiseptic, it can be applied to eczema and wounds. It strengthens blood vessels and improves circulation, so it is useful to treat varicose veins and other problems related to poor circulation. For this reason, it can also relieve some headaches. A foot bath containing rosemary is good for swollen ankles and feet that tend to be numb or cold often—both signs of poor circulation. It makes a good gargle for sore throats, gum problems, and canker sores. New studies indicate that compounds in rosemary may help to prevent cancer.

In the kitchen, rosemary's pungent taste—something like mint and ginger—complements poultry, fish, lamb, beef, veal, pork, game, cheese, and eggs, as well as many vegetables, including potatoes, tomatoes, spinach, peas, and mushrooms. Rosemary essential oil is found in soaps, creams, lotions, and perfumes. The oil and herb are added to cosmetics to improve skin tone. The herb makes a fragrant, refreshing bath additive and hair rinse. It stimulates the scalp and helps control dandruff. And dried branches make good arrangements and wreaths.

**Part Used:** Leaves; branches in decorations

**Preservation:** Pick rosemary leaves when needed and use fresh. Hang-dry stems or freeze 3- to 4-inch growth tips.

**Precautions:** None

**Medicinal Use:** Rosemary is most often found in the kitchen where it lends its healing properties to food. Also add rosemary to lotions, cream, and salves for its skin-healing properties. It is often combined with lavender in aromatherapy products to sweeten its pungent aroma. To improve circulation, use a rosemary liniment, or add a few drops of the essential oil to a bath or to a pan of water for soaking feet or hands.

# Rue

**Perennial**

**Botanical Name:**
*Ruta graveolens*

**Family:** Rutaceae

**Height:** 3 ft.

**Spread:** 2 ft.

**Description:** Rue produces blue-green, teardrop-shaped leaves in clusters. It is an attractive and unusual plant to use as a focal point in a garden design, producing yellow to yellow-green flowers from June through August. Rue is native to southern Europe. The plant is no longer found in the wild but is cultivated widely in Europe and America.

**Ease of Care:** Easy

**Cultivation:** Rue prefers full or partial sun in poor, sandy, alkaline soil in a location protected from the wind. It may be grown easily as a potted plant. Some gardeners advise that you don't plant rue near basil, sage, or cabbage, but rue is said to enhance growth of figs and roses.

**Propagation:** Sow seed outdoors in spring, or start indoors a few weeks before the last frost and transplant once the soil has warmed. Take cuttings in midsummer.

**Uses:** The Greeks believed that rue cured nervous indigestion, improved eyesight, was an antidote to poison, and treated insect bites. Today, rue is more popular as a medicine in several countries other than the United States. The exception is the Latino community in the United States who uses *Ruta* to relieve menstrual cramps and to regulate menstruation. Throughout Latin America, people use rue tea to treat colds and rue compresses applied to the chest to treat congestion. Rue is also used topically as a liniment to relieve the pain of rheumatoid arthritis and sore muscles. In traditional Chinese medicine, rue is used to decrease the inflammation of sprains, strains, and bites. Rue contains rutin, which strengthens fragile blood vessels, so the herb helps diminish varicose veins and reduces bruising when used internally or topically. Rue eardrops decrease the pain and inflammation of an earache.

Taken internally, rue relaxes muscles and nervous indigestion and improves circulation in the digestive tract. People in the Middle East use it to kill intestinal parasites, and in India, they say it improves mental clarity, which is possible because of its action on circulation.

Although it is bitter, minute amounts are used to flavor some baked goods. The Italians use rue as a bitter digestive, eating small amounts with other bitter greens and using it in a liqueur, *grappa con ruta*.

Dried rue seed heads add interest and texture to arrangements.

**Part Used:** Leaves, seed heads

**Preservation:** Pick leaves just before the flowers open, and hang them to dry. Collect the seed heads when they begin to dry.

**Precautions:** Use rue internally with extreme caution: It may cause gastrointestinal pains. Large amounts cause vomiting, mental confusion, and convulsions. And in rare cases, exposure to sunlight after ingesting rue causes severe sunburn. The entire plant is covered in glands that produce an essential oil, which irritates the skin of some people. If you are one of these people, wear gloves when handling rue. It is a uterine stimulant, so do not use during pregnancy.

**Medicinal Use:** Rue tea is extremely bitter—and potent—so is best combined with other herbs. Take no more than 1 cup of tea or ¼ teaspoon (1 dropper full) of tincture a day of pure rue. For a liniment, combine it with rosemary and heating herbs such as cayenne and peppermint in an alcohol base. Apply the tincture directly to bruises, varicose veins, and any inflammation.

# Sage

**Perennial**

**Botanical Name:**
*Salvia officinalis*

**Family:** Lamiaceae (Labiatae)

**Height:** 3 ft.

**Spread:** 2 ft.

**Description:** Sage produces long, oval, gray-green, slightly textured leaves; it comes in variegated and purple-leaved varieties. Sage is a good edging plant, attractive in any garden. In June, the herb produces whorls of pink, purple, blue, or white flowers. Sage is native to the Mediterranean. A hardy plant, it has become naturalized elsewhere and is cultivated as far north as Canada.

**Ease of Care:** Easy

**Cultivation:** Sage prefers full sun in a well-drained, sandy, alkaline soil. Protect it from the wind. Sage is said to enhance growth of cabbages, carrots, strawberries, and tomatoes, but some gardeners recommend that you keep it away from onions.

**Propagation:** Sow seed, take cuttings, divide, or layer in spring.

**Uses:** You may associate sage with Thanksgiving. The herb is often used to flavor poultry dressings. The Arabs associated sage with immortality, and the Greeks considered it an herb that promotes wisdom. Appropriately enough, a constituent in sage was recently discovered to inhibit an enzyme that produces memory loss and plays a role in Alzheimer disease. However, it's unlikely that use of the herb alone will benefit these conditions. Sage's essential oils have antiseptic properties, and the tannins are astringent. It has been used for centuries as a gargle for sore throat and inflamed gums. The herb is useful in treating mouth sores, cuts, and bruises. Sweating is decreased about two hours after ingesting sage; in fact, it is used in some deodorants and a German antiperspirant. It is also useful to prevent hot flashes, and it has some estrogenic properties. It decreases mother's milk so is useful while weaning children. It decreases saliva flow in the mouth and has successfully been used by people who have overactive salivary glands. It is a strong antioxidant and may prove useful against cell degeneration in the body. As a hair conditioner, a sage infusion reduces overactive glands in the scalp, which are sometimes responsible for causing dandruff. It also gives gloss to dark hair.

Sage's sharp, almost camphor-like taste complements salads, egg dishes, soups, breads, marinades, sausage, beef, pork, veal, fish, lamb, duck, goose, and a variety of vegetables, including tomatoes, asparagus, beans, and onions.

Sage is sometimes found in perfumes and cosmetics. Dried leaves on the branches make a good ornamental that complements arrangements and wreaths. Sage dyes wool shades of yellow or green-gray.

**Part Used:** Leaves

**Preservation:** Harvest sage and use fresh as needed. Hang leaves to dry or lay on a screen, or freeze.

**Precautions:** In large amounts, thujone, a constituent of sage, may cause a variety of symptoms, culminating in convulsions, but it is safe in the small amounts found in sage leaves.

**Medicinal Use:** Use sage in food or tea; however, as tea, sage is best mixed with other herbs that are not as pungent-tasting, such as mint.

# St. John's Wort

**Perennial**

**Botanical Name:**
*Hypericum perforatum*

**Family:** Hypericaceae

**Height:** To 3 ft.

**Spread:** 1 ft.

**Description:** The bright yellow flowers of this erect herb appear from June to July. Green leaves are small and oblong and appear to have "pores" when held up to the light. Native to Europe, St. John's wort has become naturalized throughout North America in woods and meadows. St. John's wort received its name perhaps because it blooms around June 24, the day celebrated as the birthday of Christ's cousin, John the Baptist. The herb exudes a reddish oil from its glands when a leaf is crushed.

**Ease of Care:** Easy

**Cultivation:** St. John's wort is a wild herb that may be transplanted to a garden. A hardy herb, it will grow in most soils.

**Propagation:** Sow seed in spring.

**Uses:** St. John's wort has been used as a medicine for centuries. Early European and Slavic herbals mention it. It has long been used as an anti-inflammatory for bruises, varicose veins, hemorrhoids, strains, sprains, and contusions. It is used internally and topically (in tincture, oil, or salve form) for these conditions. The plant, especially its flowers, is high in flavonoid compounds that reduce inflammation.

Studies show that St. John's wort relieves anxiety and is an antidepressant. Some researchers believe that one of its constituents, hypericin, interferes with the body's production of a depression-related chemical called monoamine oxidase (MAO). In one study, it relieved depression in menopausal women in four to six weeks.

The herb has also been used to treat skin problems, urinary conditions such as bed-wetting, painful nerve conditions such as carpal tunnel syndrome, and symptoms of nerve destruction. The tannin and oil in the plant have antibacterial properties. Scientists investigating the potential of one of its constituents as a treatment for AIDS discovered it also fights viral infection. It is also effective against flu. The National Cancer Institute has conducted several preliminary studies showing that constituents in St. John's wort also may have potential as a cancer-fighting drug. The herb dyes wool shades of yellow and red.

**Part Used:** Leaves, flowers

**Preservation:** Gather leaves and flowers after the plant has bloomed. Tincture or infuse in oil when fresh—the herb loses much of its medicinal proper-ties when dried. Store oil in a dark container; it should keep for two years.

**Precautions:** After consuming large quantities of the herb, cattle develop severe sunburn and become disoriented; however, there are no documented reports of humans having this reaction. Recent testing among AIDS patients showed that St. John's wort is nontoxic. Avoid St. John's wort if you take an MAO inhibitor drug.

**Medicinal Use:** Take ½ to 1 teaspoon (2 to 4 droppers full) of tincture up to three times a day. To make St. John's wort oil, soak puréed leaves and flowers in olive oil. Keep in a warm place for 4 to 6 days. Strain and apply topically. St. John's wort must be used fresh to acquire its active ingredients, so make your own oil or tincture, or purchase only products made from the fresh plant. You can take St. John's wort pills, but be sure they are made from either freeze-dried herbs or a dried extract since the herb loses most of its medicinal properties when air-dried.

# Santolina

**Perennial**

**Botanical Name:**
*Santolina chamaecyparissus*

**Family:** Asteraceae
(Compositae)

**Height:** 1–2 ft.

**Spread:** 1 ft., spreads

**Description:** This spreading evergreen produces light silver-gray, cottony leaves with an interesting knobby look. The herb makes a great edging or low hedge and was once popular in knot gardens. Santolina is a member of the daisy family, and its bright-yellow, button-like flowers appear in June and July. Santolina, also known as grey santolina, is native to the Mediterranean region and cultivated widely.

**Ease of Care:** Easy

**Cultivation:** Santolina likes full sun and average, sandy, preferably alkaline soil. In severely cold climates, protect your plants, or grow them in pots and bring them inside when temperatures drop.

**Propagation:** Sow seed in the spring; cut, divide, or layer in early summer.

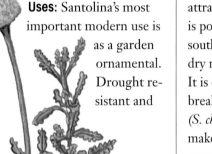

**Uses:** Santolina's most important modern use is as a garden ornamental. Drought resistant and

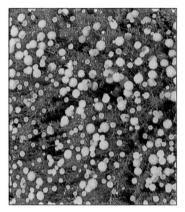

attractive as a ground cover, it is popular for landscaping in southern California and other dry regions of the Southwest. It is often planted as a fire break. A dwarf santolina (*S. chamaecyparissus* 'Nana') makes a low, tight-growing ground cover. Other members of the family are the cultivar "Plumosus" with its feathery leaves, and a green santolina (*S. virens*).

Once used to expel parasitic worms, this astringent herb is rarely prescribed for medicinal purposes in the West, but it is an antiseptic for bacterial and fungal skin infections. It can be rubbed into sore muscles as a liniment. Small quantities of this herb taken internally act as a digestive bitter that stimulates appetite and digestion. Santolina has a musky fragrance that enhances potpourri and sachets. The essential oil is sometimes used in perfumes. Fresh branches are used to make herbal wreaths, although you must work with them when they are still fresh; they become quite brittle when they dry. The plant dyes wool shades of gold and yellow. Speaking of wool, the strong scent of the leaves also repels wool moths. Place a sachet containing the leaves in among sweaters and blankets in drawers, closets, or storage boxes.

**Part Used:** Leaves; branches for decoration

**Preservation:** Harvest leaves and branches in late summer. Hang-dry.

**Precautions:** Ingesting large amounts of santolina can cause digestive upsets, rather than cure them.

**Medicinal Use:** Infuse in vegetable oil for a liniment. You can take a few tablespoons of tea to aid digestion, but be forewarned—it is very bitter!

# Savory, Summer

**Annual**

**Botanical Name:**
*Satureja hortensis*

**Family:** Lamiaceae (Labiatae)

**Height:** 1–1½ ft.

**Spread:** 8–12 in.

**Description:** This attractive annual has soft, flat, gray-green, narrow leaves. The plant has a light, airy appearance. Winter savory *(S. montana)* is a hardy perennial. Summer savory is tastier but has a shorter growing season than winter savory: It flowers from midsummer to the first frost. Both savories are native to the Mediterranean region; summer savory has become naturalized in North America, Asia, and Africa.

**Ease of Care:** Easy

**Cultivation:** Summer savory likes full sun in a light, average, sandy soil. The herb does not like to be transplanted. It grows easily in containers.

**Propagation:** Sow seed in spring after the soil is warm.

**Uses:** The Romans believed savory was sacred to satyrs, mythical man-goats who were said to roam the forests. The Romans also planted it near beehives to increase honey production. They used savory to flavor vinegars and introduced the herb to England, where the Saxons adopted and named it for its spicy taste. Winter savory was said to curb sexual appetite; summer savory, to increase it. Guess which variety was most popular? Summer savory has antiseptic and astringent properties, so it has been used to treat diarrhea and mild sore throats. Like many culinary herbs, it aids digestion, stimulates appetite, and relieves a minor upset stomach and eliminates gas—probably one reason it is so popular to flavor bean dishes. It also kills several types of intestinal worms.

In the kitchen, summer savory's flavor, reminiscent of thyme, brings out the best in butters, vinegars, beans, soups, eggs, peas, eggplant, asparagus, onions, and cabbage. It is one of the flavorings in salami and other commercial foods. If you are unfamiliar with the herb, try using it in recipes that call for parsley or chervil. It is often considered a lighter substitute for sage or thyme.

**Part Used:** Leaves

**Preservation:** Harvest leaves when the plant begins to flower; hang or dry on screens.

**Precautions:** None

**Medicinal Use:** To receive savory's medicinal properties, use it in foods. If you find the essential oil, use it to make antiseptic skin salves.

# Saw Palmetto

**Perennial**

**Botanical Name:**
*Serenoa repens*

**Family:** Palmaceae

**Height:** To 6 ft.

**Spread:** Sprawls

**Description:** Saw palmetto is a low, shrubby plant with a creeping trunk. It produces palmlike, deeply divided leaves. Olive-shaped berries are dark purple to black and grow in bunches, ripening from October to December. The herb is found in dense stands along the Atlantic coasts of Georgia and Florida.

**Ease of Care:** Moderate

**Cultivation:** Saw palmetto is a wild plant that thrives in swampy, well-drained soils. It needs hot weather and temperatures that do not dip below freezing to survive.

**Propagation:** Transplant plants. It can also be grown from seed, but this is more difficult.

**Uses:** Saw palmetto has long been considered an aphrodisiac, sexual rejuvenator, and treatment for impotence. The action of saw palmetto has been well studied, and the herb is popular for treating prostate enlargement. In one study, study participants experienced significant improvement in

prostate enlargement in only 45 days, with almost no side effects, and certainly none of the serious side effects seen with the drugs normally prescribed. Saw palmetto is recommended for weakening of urinary organs and resulting incontinence.

Saw palmetto also has been touted as a steroid substitute for athletes who wish to increase muscle mass, although no documentation supports this claim. Herbalists agree, however, that saw palmetto may benefit cases of tissue wasting, weakness, and debility. It was prescribed by Eclectic physicians in the early 19th century for frail people or those who were weak from chronic illness to make them stronger. This may be because saw palmetto improves digestion and absorption of nutrients. The herb is a diuretic, expectorant, and tonic, making it useful for treating colds, asthma, and bronchitis.

**Part Used:** Berries

**Preservation:** Gather the fruit after berries turn black. Dry or tincture.

**Precautions:** None

**Medicinal Use:** Drink up to 2 cups of tea a day. Take ¼ to 1 teaspoon (1 to 4 droppers full) of tincture up to twice a day. Saw palmetto is often combined in preparations with other prostate herbs, such as nettle root and the African herb pygeum.

# Shepherd's Purse

**Annual or Biennial**

**Botanical Name:**
*Capsella bursa-pastoris*

**Family:** Cruciferae

**Height:** 1 ft.

**Spread:** 6 in.; may become invasive

**Description:** This herb's name alludes to the shape of its fruits, which resemble the purses that Europeans once hung from their belts. Smooth, slightly hairy stems arise from a basal rosette of leaves. The herb produces white flowers throughout the year, followed by triangular-shaped fruits. Shepherd's purse is found frequently in gravelly, sandy, or loamy soil. It grows just about everywhere, including Greenland, where it was introduced by Vikings more than a thousand years ago.

**Ease of Care:** Easy

**Cultivation:** Shepherd's purse is not often cultivated, perhaps because it grows so readily as a garden weed; you can also find it readily in the wild. The herb tolerates most soils but prefers well-drained, sandy loam and full sun to partial shade. The plant can become invasive.

**Propagation:** Shepherd's purse grows easily from seeds sown in spring.

**Uses:** The Greeks and Romans used the seeds of shepherd's purse as a laxative. By the 16th century, the herb was prescribed to stop bleeding

and eliminate blood in urine. Colonists introduced shepherd's purse to America, where it quickly became a common weed.

Shepherd's purse contains substances that hasten coagulation of blood—thus it has long been prescribed for treating excessive menstrual flow. During World War I, wounded soldiers were given shepherd's purse tea. The herb also may benefit those with ulcers, colitis, and Crohn dis-

ease. Used topically, shepherd's purse heals lacerations and other skin injuries. Some herbalists have prescribed it for treating eczema and skin rashes. The herb's peppery-tasting young leaves may be added to soups and stews or eaten like spinach.

**Part Used:** Leaves and the flower tops

**Preservation:** Harvest leaves and flower tops as flowers open. Dry or tincture. The fresh plant is more potent than the dried plant.

**Precautions:** Because shepherd's purse constricts blood vessels and appears to induce clotting, people with a history of hypertension, heart disease, or stroke should avoid it.

**Medicinal Use:** For excessive menstrual bleeding, take a few days to a week before the period and during the period. Drink up to 1 cup, several times a day. The tea is bitter tasting, so you may want to mix it with another herb. Take ½ teaspoon (2 droppers full) of tincture twice a day.

# Shiitake Mushroom

**Annual**

**Botanical Name:** *Lentinus edodes*

**Family:** Tricholomataceae

**Height:** To 6 in.

**Spread:** To 6 in.

**Description:** The shiitake mushroom is a fungus that grows on dead tree trunks in the wild.

**Ease of Care:** Moderate

**Cultivation:**

Shiitakes and other mushrooms are cultivated commercially and found in the wild. Years ago, few people would have tried to grow their own shiitake mushrooms, but the popularity of the mushroom due to its flavor and medicinal qualities has led to a great interest among growers. The traditional method of growing shiitakes is to use hardwood logs as a host in which to place the spawn—the material used to propagate mushrooms. Shiitake mushrooms require moisture and darkness to grow. When you purchase a kit to grow these (or any) mushrooms, you will receive detailed instructions on how to grow them.

**Propagation:** Mushrooms reproduce by spores.

**Uses:**

Shiitake mushrooms have long been a staple of Chinese cuisine. Now research has found that lentinan, a chemical in shiitake mushrooms, slows the growth of cancerous tumors in animals. Scientists hope that lentinan may one day be used to enhance the human immune system and help people fight off cancer and infections.

In China and Japan, shiitake mushrooms have been used for hundreds of years as a medicine to lower blood cholesterol as well as to fight cancer. Shiitake mushrooms also contain cortinelin, a strong antibacterial agent, which kills a wide range of disease-causing germs. A sulfide compound extracted from shiitake mushrooms has also been found to have antibiotic properties. Shiitakes have been used to treat depressed immune-system disorders, including AIDS.

Shiitake mushrooms are a nutritious food source, packed with protein and full of vitamins $B_1$, $B_2$, $B_{12}$, niacin, and pantothenic acid.

**Part Used:** Mushroom caps

**Preservation:** Dry for teas and tinctures.

**Precautions:** None

**Medicinal Use:** Shiitake mushrooms can be eaten fresh or dried and reconstituted. To reconstitute, cover a handful of dried shiitakes with water and soak 10 to 30 minutes. Use in foods such as soups, stews, and noodle dishes. Chinese physicians recommend eating 2 to 4 ounces of shiitake mushrooms two to three times a week to prevent cancer. Shiitake is also available in pills or as a tincture. Take the amounts suggested on the manufacturer's package.

# Skullcap

**Perennial**

**Botanical Name:**
*Scutellaria lateriflora*

**Family:** Lamiaceae (Labiatae)

**Height:** 1–2 ft.

**Spread:** 8 in., spreading

**Description:** Skullcap is a slender, branching, square-stemmed plant with opposite, serrated leaves. Its blue flowers, which have two "lips," resemble the skull-caps worn in medieval times, hence, the herb's name. Several species of skullcap grow in Europe and Asia. Also known as mad dog weed and Virginia skullcap, the herb is found throughout the United States and southern Canada.

**Ease of Care:** Moderate

**Cultivation:** Skullcap prefers well-drained, moist soil and partial shade. Once rooted, the herb requires little care.

**Propagation:** Sow seeds or divide roots in early spring. Thin seedlings to 6 inches.

**Uses:** Skullcap received its common name, mad dog weed, in the 18th century, when the herb was widely prescribed as a cure for rabies, although no scientific evidence supports its use for that disease. The herb is a sedative often recommended for treating insomnia, nervousness, nervous twitches, and anxiety. Russian researchers have found that skullcap helps stabilize stress-related heart disease. Herbalists have also employed skullcap to treat symptoms of premenstrual syndrome (PMS). Skullcap has been found to have anti-inflammatory properties. The herb inhibits release of acetylcholine and histamine, two substances released by cells that cause inflammation and symptoms of allergic reactions. Japanese studies indicate that skullcap increases levels of HDL (high-density lipoprotein, or "good" cholesterol).

And Chinese researchers report that the Chinese species, *S. baicalensis*, is useful in treating hepatitis, improving liver function, reducing swelling, and increasing appetite. It is also a strong immune system herb.

**Part Used:** Leaves

**Preservation:** Gather leaves after flowers bloom in summer; dry or tincture.

**Precautions:** Used in moderation, skullcap is safe. Large amounts of tincture may cause confusion, giddiness, or convulsions.

**Medicinal Use:** Take skullcap as a tea, a tincture, or in pills. The taste is slightly bitter, so most people mix it with peppermint or chamomile when they drink it as a tea. In formulas to ease nervous system problems, it is mixed with herbs such as valerian, passion flower, and chamomile. Take up to 2 cups of tea or ½ teaspoon (2 droppers full) of tincture a day.

Unfortunately, what most manufacturers of commercial products claim is skullcap is really the much less expensive germander—this is especially true for the tea. Your best bet is to grow your own or buy skullcap products from a reputable herb company.

# Slippery Elm

**Perennial**

**Botanical Name:**
*Ulmus rubra*
(previously *U. fulva*)

**Family:** Ulmaceae

**Height:** To 60 ft.

**Spread:** 25 ft.

**Description:** The trunk bark of this stately tree is brown, but branch bark is whitish. Slippery elm leaves are broad, rough, hairy, and toothed. The tree is native to North America from southern Canada to Florida. In the 18th and 19th centuries, American forests were covered with elms, but most succumbed to Dutch elm disease. Today slippery elm is found in far fewer numbers in moist woodlands and along streams.

**Ease of Care:**
Moderate

**Cultivation:** Slippery elm prefers average soil and requires sun and moisture. You can grow it in a yard, provided you have enough space.

**Propagation:** Purchase seedlings to plant.

**Uses:** American colonists learned from Indians how to employ the herb as a food and medicine. In the days before refrigerators, Americans wrapped foods in slippery elm to retard spoilage: The powdered bark contains cells that expand into a spongy mass to form a protective covering. They also used moistened slippery elm powder to form bandages, make casts for broken bones, coat pills, and make a nourishing gruel for invalids. In the last century, you would have been hard-pressed to find a home in America that did not contain slippery elm lozenges.

Slippery elm is used to treat sore throats, coughs, colds, and gastrointestinal disorders—in a word, anything that needs to be soothed. Mucilage, the most abundant constituent of slippery elm bark, has a moistening, soothing action. The tannins are astringent. This combination makes slippery elm ideal for soothing inflammations, reducing swelling, and healing damaged tissues.

The powder is a healing food. Stir slippery elm powder into oatmeal or applesauce for an oatmeal-like gruel that soothes an inflamed stomach or ulcer. It is often recommended as a restorative herb for people who suffer from prolonged flu, stomach upset, chronic indigestion, and malnutrition stemming from these conditions.

**Part Used:** Inner bark

**Preservation:** Powder the bark.

**Precautions:** None

**Medicinal Use:** Strips of bark are best prepared by soaking in cold water for several hours. Stir 2 to 3 tablespoons of the powdered bark in juice, puréed fruit, oatmeal, or other foods. You may also mix slippery elm powder with hot water, bananas, and applesauce. In treating sore throat and coughs, slippery elm is most effective made into lozenges or syrup. (See instructions for making lozenges and syrup in Chapter 3.) Today, due to the increasing scarcity of slippery elm, herbalists often use alternative herbs such as comfrey for topical use and marshmallow for internal use.

# Sweet Woodruff

**Perennial**

**Botanical Name:** *Galium odoratum* (previously *Asperula odoratum*)

**Family:** Rubiaceae

**Height:** 6–8 in.

**Spread:** 6 in.

**Description:** Sweet woodruff produces small, knife-shaped leaves that circle in tiers around the stemlike wheel spokes. This rich green perennial spreads by means of underground stems to make a lovely ground cover. Its white, funnel-shaped flowers appear in May and June. Native to Europe, North Africa, and Asia, the herb is often found deep in forests.

**Ease of Care:** Easy

**Cultivation:** Sweet woodruff insists on average, moist soil in woodland shade.

**Propagation:** Sow seed in fall to sprout in spring; divide after the plant flowers, allowing several months for the roots to re-establish themselves before the first frost.

**Uses:** Herbalists consider sweet woodruff a diuretic, diaphoretic, antispasmodic, and light sedative. It is especially useful to treat nervous indigestion. The herb has been used historically to treat kidney stones, nervousness, and wounds. It is also an anticoagulant, thereby reducing the risk of blood clots. Sweet woodruff has been used to flavor Scandinavian cordials, and it imparts a sort of vanilla-like bouquet to white wine. It is the flavoring in Europe's traditional May wine and other alcoholic beverages. (The FDA approves its use for alcoholic beverages.) The herb is used in potpourri and perfumes; its scent, described as like that of new-mown hay, is due to coumarin, which is also found in hay and clover. Branches dye wool tan; roots yield a red dye.

**Part Used:** Leaves

**Preservation:** Pick fresh sweet woodruff and use as needed. The scent increases as it dries. Hang to dry or lay on screens.

**Precautions:** Very large doses of sweet woodruff may cause vomiting and dizziness. Test animals suffered liver damage, among other effects, when fed coumarin, a constituent of sweet woodruff, but you would have to eat massive amounts daily to reach an equivalent amount.

**Medicinal Use:** Sweet woodruff can be made into tea but is a more popular remedy infused in wine. To make May wine, add a handful of the chopped fresh or dried herbs to a liter of white wine. Let sit four weeks, then strain and serve. Apply mashed, fresh leaves to wounds.

# Tarragon, French

**Perennial**

**Botanical Name:**
*Artemisia dracunculus*

**Family:** Asteraceae
(Compositae)

**Height:** 2 ft.

**Spread:** 1 ft.

**Description:** This perennial has long, narrow, pointed leaves, but its flowers rarely appear. Be sure to get the French rather than the Russian variety of tarragon. The Russian variety looks much the same but has somewhat narrower, lighter green leaves, and it flowers and produces seed. But Russian tarragon has less of the sweetly aromatic flavor of its French cousin. Test the plant by crushing, smelling, and tasting a few leaves. Tarragon is probably native to the Caspian Sea area and possibly Siberia and Europe. It is cultivated in Europe, Asia, and the United States.

**Ease of Care:** Moderate

**Cultivation:** Tarragon prefers full sun to partial shade in a sandy, average, well-drained alkaline soil. It may also be grown successfully as a potted plant. Cut tarragon back in the fall or early spring. Protect it with mulch during winter. Tarragon is said to enhance the growth of most companion vegetables.

**Propagation:** Since it produces no seeds, buy your first plant, then take cuttings in summer and fall; divide or layer in early spring.

**Uses:** Thomas Jefferson was one

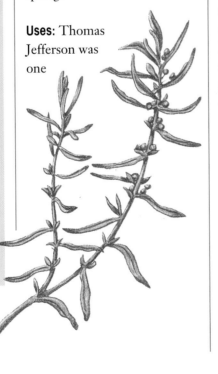

of the first Americans to grow this lovely and useful plant. Tarragon stimulates appetite, relieves gas and colic, and makes a good local anesthetic for toothaches. Tarragon has antifungal and antioxidant properties and has been used to preserve foods. It's also found in perfumes, soaps, cosmetics, condiments, and liqueurs. One of the French *fines herbes*, tarragon has a strong flavor that may overpower foods, so use it sparingly in salads and sauces, including remoulade, tartar, and bearnaise sauces. Tarragon enhances fish, pork, beef, lamb, game, poultry, patés, rice, barley, vinegars, mayonnaise, and butter. It also goes well with a number of vegetables, including potatoes, tomatoes, carrots, onions, beets, asparagus, mushrooms, cauliflower, and broccoli.

**Part Used:** Leaves

**Preservation:** Pick leaves or 3- to 4-inch growth tips at any time for fresh use. Cut the stems and hang to dry. Don't dry tarragon too long or it will lose its flavor. Store immedi-

ately in an airtight container. You can also capture tarragon's flavor in vinegar or oil.

**Precautions:** For culinary use, tarragon is considered safe. Although the plant contains estragole, which produces tumors in mice, it has not been associated with human cancer.

**Medicinal Use:** Use tarragon in cooking. Chew the fresh leaves to relieve a toothache.

# Thyme

**Perennial**

**Botanical Name:**
*Thymus vulgaris*

**Family:** Lamiaceae
(Labiatae)

**Height:** 10–12 in.

**Spread:** 1–1½ ft.

**Description:** These tiny-leaved, wide-spreading perennials make a good inexpensive ground cover that can be clipped and mowed regularly. Thyme's profuse lilac to pink blooms appear in June and July and are especially attractive to bees. Native to the western Mediterranean region, thyme is cultivated widely. There are many species and varieties of thyme with self-descriptive names, including woolly thyme, silver thyme, lemon thyme, and golden thyme.

**Ease of Care:** Easy

**Cultivation:** Thyme does well in full sun in poor to average, well-drained soil. Trim it back each spring to encourage abundant new growth. It also may be grown as a potted plant. Some gardeners believe that thyme enhances growth of eggplant, potatoes, and tomatoes. It is said to repel cabbage worms and whiteflies.

**Propagation:** Sow seed or divide in spring or fall; take cuttings or layer in early summer.

**Uses:** You may have noticed thyme's distinctive flavor in cough medicines. Thymol, a prime constituent, is found in a number of them. Thymol is also used commercially to make colognes, aftershaves, lotions, soaps, detergents, and cosmetics. Thyme also was used as an antiseptic to treat wounds as recently as World War I. In fact, it is one of the most potent antiseptics of all the herbs. Thymol is found in many mouthwashes and gargles for sore throats and mouth and gum infections. It is one of the

main ingredients in Listerine, along with compounds from eucalyptus and peppermint. This commercial mouthwash was found to cause 34 percent less gum inflammation than other brands and decrease plaque formation on the teeth. Vapor balms, used to rub on the chest to relieve congestion, also contain thymol. Thyme

destroys fungal infections. Its antispasmodic qualities make it useful for treating asthma, whooping cough, stomach cramps, gas, colic, and headache. It also reduces compounds in the body that produce menstrual cramps.

Thyme preparations increase circulation in the area where applied.

One of the French *fines herbes*, thyme complements salads, veal, lamb, beef, poultry, fish, stuffing, patés, sausage, stews, soups, bread, butters, mayonnaise, vinegars, mustard, eggs, cheese, and many vegetables, including tomatoes, onions, eggplant, leeks, mushrooms, asparagus, and green beans.

**Part Used:** Leaves

**Preservation:** Harvest leaves any time for fresh use. Pick before and during flowering, and hang-dry.

**Precautions:** In moderate amounts, thyme causes no problems, but use the essential oil carefully: It can burn the skin.

**Medicinal Use:** Thyme is used medicinally in foods. Sometimes it is used in tinctures for digestive problems, but more often, it is in liniments, salves, skin antiseptics, cough syrup and drops, mouthwashes, and vapor balms.

# Uva Ursi

**Perennial**

**Botanical Name:**

*Arctostaphylos uva ursi*

**Family:** Ericaceae

**Height:** 6 in.

**Spread:** 3 in.

**Description:** Uva ursi's pink-red berries are a favorite food of bears, hence the herb's common name, bearberry. Because uva ursi leaves were often used as tobacco, the plant also is known as kinnikinnick, a Native American word that means smoking mixture. Uva ursi is a delicate ground cover with fibrous roots and leathery, oblong leaves. The herb produces white, red-tinged flowers in April and May. Uva ursi is found throughout the northern hemisphere, especially in dry, rocky areas.

**Ease of Care:** Easy

**Cultivation:** Uva ursi can sometimes be purchased at nurseries as a ground cover. Sow seeds in the fall or spring. The herb likes peaty soil and full sun. Uva ursi needs little care, except for watering. The herb is generally free of pests and disease.

**Propagation:** Sow seeds in the spring; take cuttings or layer in spring.

**Uses:** Uva ursi leaves contain up to 40 percent tannic acid, enough to make them once useful in tanning leather. Tannins and the glycoside arbutin give uva ursi its astringent and antiseptic properties.

Herbalists suggest uva ursi primarily to treat bladder infections. Uva ursi is particularly indicated for illnesses caused by *Escherichia coli (E. coli)*, a bacterium that lives in the intestines and can invade the urinary tract. It works particularly well in the alkaline environment this bacteria produces. Externally, the herb has been used to treat sprains, swellings, and sore muscles.

Uva ursi dyes wool shades of camel to green.

**Part Used:** Leaves

**Preservation:** Gather leaves in spring or early summer. Tannin levels increase in fall, so gather only young leaves. Dry for infusions, or tincture.

**Precautions:** Because uva ursi may stimulate the uterus, don't take it if you're pregnant. Also

don't use it if you have an active kidney infection since it will be too irritating.

**Medicinal Use:** You must boil uva ursi leaves to extract the healing arbutin. Drink up to 3 cups of uva ursi tea a day. For a tea low in tannic acid, infuse the herb in cold water for 12 to 24 hours. Take ¼ to 1 teaspoon (1 to 4 droppers full) of tincture up to three times a day. Mix uva ursi with milder urinary herbs such as marshmallow and fennel seed.

# Valerian

**Perennial**

**Botanical Name:**
*Valeriana officinalis*

**Family:** Valerianaceae

**Height:** 3–5 ft., in flower

**Spread:** 1 ft.

**Description:** There are some 200 species of valerian, a plant with an erect, hollow, hairy stem that produces four to eight pairs of dark green leaves. Held on tall, thin stalks, valerian flowers are small and pink-tinged and appear in June through July. Various medicinal species of the herb are native to Europe and western Asia and grow wild in North America. There are also several native American species. You may find valerian in grasslands, damp meadows, and along streams.

**Ease of Care:** Easy

**Cultivation:** Valerian prefers rich, moist, humusy soil and full sun to partial shade.

**Propagation:** Divide roots in spring or fall. Seeds germinate poorly. Sow them in a cold frame in April and transplant in May. Divide valerian every three years to prevent over-crowding.

**Uses:** Ask most people what the smell of valerian reminds them of and they're likely to say old socks. Nonetheless, cats go wild over valerian and so do rats. Lore has it, in fact, that the Pied Piper used valerian to rid Hameln of rodents. In ancient times, valerian was widely used as a treatment for epilepsy. Today valerian finds its chief value in soothing anxiety and promoting sleep. Clinical studies have identified constituents in valerian known as valepotriates, which appear to affect the central nervous system but produce few, if any, side effects. Several studies show that valerian shortens the time needed to fall asleep and improves quality of sleep. Unlike commonly used sedatives, valerian does not cause a drugged or hung-over sensation or effect dream recall in most people. In one study, it even calmed hyperactive children.

The relaxing action of valerian also makes it useful for treatment of muscle cramps, menstrual cramps, and high blood pressure. Valerian relaxes vein and artery walls and is especially indicated for blood pressure elevations caused by stress and worry. Valerian is recommended for tension headaches as well as heart palpitations.

Valerian mildly stimulates the intestines, can help dispel gas and cramps in the digestive tract, and is weakly antimicrobial, particularly to bacteria. More than a hundred soothing valerian preparations are sold in Germany. Valerian improves stomach function and relieves gas and painful bowel spasms. The herb has been used commercially to flavor tobacco and some beverages.

**Part Used:** Root

**Preservation:** Gather roots in fall or spring, before shoots appear, and dry.

**Precautions:** Valerian occasionally has the opposite effect of that intended, stimulating instead of sedating. Reducing the dosage usually alleviates the problem. Valerian may cause headaches, dizziness, and heart palpitations when taken in large doses. Don't take valerian if you're pregnant.

**Medicinal Use:** Valerian has a disagreeable taste, so mix it with other herbs such as peppermint if you drink it as tea. Take a cup of tea or 2 capsules of the powdered root an hour before bed. Or take ½ to 1 teaspoon (2 to 4 droppers full) of tincture up to three times a day. It is often combined with other sedative herbs such as skullcap, chamomile, and lemon balm.

# Willow

**Perennial**

**Botanical Name:** *Salix spp.*

**Family:** Salicaceae

**Height:** 35–75 ft.

**Spread:** To 5 ft.

**Description:** The ubiquitous willow is found throughout temperate regions of the Northern hemisphere. Its long leaves on flexible branches are narrow and lance-shaped, lending the tree a graceful appearance. Willows have tiny flowers in cylindrical catkins and blossom in midspring. The tree's bark is rough and grayish brown.

**Ease of Care:** Moderate

**Cultivation:** Often found along river banks, willow likes soggy soil but will grow well in any moist garden bed. The tree prefers full sun.

**Propagation:** Willow cuttings root easily. In moist soil, root young, leafless branches several feet long. In spring, take hardwood cuttings 9 to 12 inches long and root in water. Even leafy summer cuttings will root. The problem is that rooted cuttings are sometimes difficult to transplant. When you succeed in getting new plants to grow, stand back: Cuttings grow quickly and must be pruned back diligently. Don't worry about pruning. The tree will come back bushier than ever.

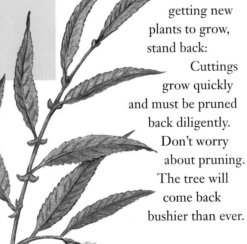

**Uses:** Although their long billowing branches bring to mind "weeping," willows were considered a symbol of joy by the ancient Egyptians, who prized the trees that grew along the banks of the Nile. And well they should have. This attractive shade tree is also a potent healer.

The various species of willow contain salicin, from which salicylic acid, the main ingredient of aspirin, is derived, and herbalists often recommend the plant to relieve pain. The Chinese have been putting it to this purpose since 500 B.C. It's also a useful herb for women with painful periods. Willow contains enough salicylate to suppress chemicals known as prostaglandins, one cause of painful menstrual cramps.

Willow is also used to treat fever, headache, hay fever, neuralgia, and inflammation of joints. The inner bark is an astringent and antiseptic: Decoctions of white willow bark are valued in facial lotions and baths for their astringent properties.

Willow's lovely foliage enhances decorative arrangements. Willow wood is extremely supple and has long been used to make baskets.

**Part Used:** Bark, shoots, wood

**Preservation:** Harvest bark and wood any time. Gather shoots in the spring. Use willow fresh or dried.

**Precautions:** In animal studies, aspirin has been associated with increased risk of birth defects, thus, avoid willow if you are pregnant. Also, the use of aspirin in children has been linked to Reye syndrome, a rare but potentially fatal disease. Although willow has not been associated with Reye syndrome, it's still best not to give willow to children with colds, flu, or chicken pox.

**Medicinal Use:** Take willow as tincture, tea, or pills. The tea is bitter so most people prefer to get their medicinal dose of willow in tincture or pill form. Pills are sold both as capsules and tablets and can be used in place of aspirin. Take up to 4 cups of tea, 1 teaspoon (4 droppers full) of tincture, or 6 pills a day.

# Witch Hazel

**Perennial**

**Botanical Name:**

*Hamamelis virginiana*

**Family:** Hamamelidaceae

**Height:** 8–15 ft

**Spread:** 15 ft.

**Description:** Witch hazel is a small, deciduous tree, with twisting stems and long, forked branches. The herb's smooth bark may be gray or brown, its leaves oval. Bright-yellow flowers are threadlike and appear in September and October. Some species bloom in winter. The plant is indigenous to North America, from Quebec south to Florida and west to Minnesota and Texas. You're likely to encounter witch hazel in moist, light woods or along rocky streams.

**Ease of Care:** Moderate

**Cultivation:** Witch hazel prefers moist, rich, neutral to acid soil, and full sun to partial shade.

**Propagation:** To germinate seeds, expose them to temperatures of 40 degrees Fahrenheit for three months. You can also propagate witch hazel by taking cuttings or by layering.

**Uses:** Witch hazel has long been prized as an astringent cosmetic and medicinal herb. Its leaves, twigs, and bark contain tannic and gallic acids and essential oils. Witch hazel dries weeping, raw tissues. A cloth soaked in strong witch hazel tea and applied to the skin reduces the swelling and pain of hemorrhoids, bruises, wounds, and sprains and promotes speedy healing. It can also tighten and soothe aching varicose veins and reduce inflammation associated with blood clots (phlebitis) in the legs.

Witch hazel lotions are useful on rough, swollen hands. And the herb is a popular skin cleanser and body lotion; it is also effective in treating insect bites, sunburns, and poison oak and ivy rashes and is an ingredient in aftershaves. The herb is also used as a mouthwash, gargle, and douche.

**Part Used:** Leaves, twigs, bark

**Preservation:** Gather leaves, twigs, and bark in early fall before the tree flowers; dry or tincture.

**Precautions:** The tannins in witch hazel may produce nausea if consumed in large quantities. Pay attention to the label of any witch hazel prepation you purchase. While you can ingest the tincture made with grain alcohol, many preparations are made from the poisonous rubbing (isopropyl) alcohol.

**Medicinal Use:** Drink a cup of witch hazel tea up to three times a day. Take up to ½ teaspoon (2 droppers full) of tincture, two to six times a day. Limit use to a few weeks.

To make witch hazel lotion, place twigs and bark in a blender with enough vodka to cover. Chop as fine as possible, and transfer to a glass jar. Shake the mixture vigorously once a day and strain after two weeks. Blend 1 ounce of witch hazel liquid with ½ ounce aloe vera gel and ½ ounce vitamin E oil. Store in a tightly stoppered bottle.

A tincture made from witch hazel, goldenseal (or Oregon grape root), and calendula and applied to the outer ear is useful to treat swimmer's ear. This same combination in an infusion makes an effective douche for vaginal infections. A gargle of 8 ounces of witch hazel tea and a couple drops of the essential oils of myrrh and clove bud reduces the pain of a sore throat, or, as a mouth rinse, treats swollen, infected gums. Also use this as a pain- and inflammation-relieving gum rub for teething babies. A tea made from witch hazel, chamomile, mint, and thyme is effective for diarrhea.

# Wormwood

**Perennial**

**Botanical Name:** *Artemisia absinthium*

**Family:** Asteraceae (Compositae)

**Height:** 3–4 ft.

**Spread:** 2 ft.

**Description:** Wormwood produces handsome, fine, silver-green leaves. The plant flowers in July and August and is at the height of its glory in autumn. It is a hardy herb, unharmed by frost. Wormwood is native to the Mediterranean region and has become naturalized throughout the temperate world. It is cultivated widely.

**Ease of Care:** Easy

**Cultivation:** Like the other popular species of *Artemisia*, southernwood (*A. abrotanum*), wormwood likes full sun in almost any kind of soil, as long as it's alkaline. Add lime if soil is naturally acidic.

**Propagation:** Sow seed or take cuttings in summer; divide in spring or fall.

**Uses:** Wormwood is steeped in mystique. It is said to have grown up in the trail left by the serpent as it slithered from the Garden of Eden. The herb is a prime ingredient of an addictive alcoholic drink called absinthe, which is illegal in most countries, including the United States. Wormwood got its name because it expels intestinal worms. The plant also is an antiseptic, antispasmodic, and carminative, and it increases bile production. It has been used to treat fever, colds, jaundice, and gallstones.

Compresses soaked in the tea are said to be good for irritations, bruises, and sprains. Wormwood oil has been used as a liniment to relieve the pain of rheumatism, neuralgia, and arthritis. The plant is also an anti-

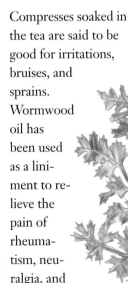

fungal and antibacterial, and new research indicates that compounds in one of the species of wormwood, *A. annua*, could be a cure for malaria. Wormwood is also a flea and moth repellant. Although it is brittle when dried, it makes a beautiful foundation for a wreath or swag.

**Part Used:**
Leaves; branches in arrangements

**Preservation:**
Harvest leaves after the plant

flowers. Hang to dry. Store in airtight containers.

**Precautions:** In large doses, wormwood's active constituent, thujone, is a convulsant, poison, and narcotic. The herb is not very water-soluble, but tinctures are high in thujone, so don't use tinctures internally. Topical use is generally considered safe, but wormwood may cause dermatitis in some people. Do not use wormwood internally for more than a couple days unless you are under the supervision of a physician or qualified herbalist and not at all if you are pregnant.

**Medicinal Use:** Take a teaspoon of the tea at a time, up to ½ cup a day.

# Yarrow

**Perennial**

**Botanical Name:**
*Achillea millefolium*

**Family:** Asteraceae
(Compositae)

**Height:** To 3 ft.

**Spread:** To 1 ft.

**Description:** Yarrow's Latin name means "a thousand leaves," a reference to the herb's fine, feathery foliage. Erect and covered with silky "hairs," yarrow produces white flower heads from June through September. The herb is native to Europe but has become naturalized throughout North America. You'll find yarrow growing along roads and in fields and waste places.

**Ease of Care:** Easy

**Cultivation:** Yarrow likes full sun and well-drained soil. The herb will adapt to almost any type of garden except those with soggy soil. Creeping species of yarrow, which may be mowed, will rot unless the soil is well drained. Occasionally, yarrow falls prey to powdery mildew, rust, or stem rot. Yarrow may benefit companion plants by attracting helpful insects, such as wasps and lady bugs.

**Propagation:** Sow seed in the spring; divide in spring or fall.

**Uses:** In the epic *Iliad*, Homer reports that legendary warrior Achilles used yarrow leaves to treat the wounds of his fallen comrades. Studies show that yarrow is a fine herb indeed for accelerating healing of cuts and bruises. The Greeks used the herb to stop hemorrhages. Gerard's famous herbal cited yarrow's benefits in 1597. And after colonists brought the plant to America, Indians used it to treat bleeding, wounds, infections, headaches, indigestion, and sore throat.

Clinical studies have supported the longstanding use of yarrow to cleanse wounds and make blood clot faster. Yarrow treats bleeding stomach ulcers, heavy menstrual periods, and bleeding from the bowels. An essential oil known as azulene is responsible for yarrow's ability to reduce inflammation. Traditional Chinese medicine credits yarrow with the ability to nurture the spleen, liver, kidney, and bladder. Several studies have shown that yarrow improves uterine tone and reduces uterine spasms in animals. Apigenin and flavonoid constituents are credited with yarrow's antispasmodic properties.

The herb also contains salicylic acid, aspirin's main constituent, making it useful for relieving pain. Chewing the leaves or root is an old toothache remedy. Yarrow fights bacteria and dries up congestion in sinus and other respiratory infections and allergies. The plant has long been a standby herb for promoting sweating to bring down fevers in cases of colds and influenza. It also relieves bladder infections.

Because of its astringent and cleansing properties, yarrow is sometimes added to skin lotions. Flowers and stalks dry well, making attractive decorations. The flowers dye wool shades of yellow to olive.

**Part Used:** Flowers, leaves, roots

**Preservation:** Gather flowers in late spring or early summer, when the plant is in full bloom. Dig roots in fall. Dry for teas or preserve in tinctures.

**Precautions:** Some people are sensitive to yarrow. The most common indicators of sensitivity are sneezing, headache, or nausea.

**Medicinal Use:** Chew fresh yarrow root for relief of toothache. Press mashed fresh leaves or powdered dried leaves or flower tops over cuts to stop bleeding. Soak a cloth in yarrow tea and apply this compress to wounds and bruises. Take ½ to 2 teaspoons (2 to 8 droppers full) of tincture or several cups of tea up to three times a day. A popular tea to reduce fever is made with equal parts of yarrow, elderberry flowers, and peppermint. Drink it hot and it reduces a fever; the cold tea is a diuretic.

# Yellow Dock

**Perennial**

**Botanical Name:**

*Rumex crispus*

**Family:** Polygonaceae

**Height:** To 3 ft.

**Spread:** 1 ft.

**Description:** Yellow dock produces a yellow taproot, leaves that taper to a point, and whorls of greenish flowers that appear on tall stems in midsummer. The herb is native to Eurasia and grows as a weed throughout temperate and subtropical regions.

**Ease of Care:** Easy

**Cultivation:** Yellow dock is a wild plant that likes poor to average soil in weedy places.

**Propagation:** Plants grow from seed in spring.

**Uses:** Yellow dock root stimulates intestinal secretions and promotes bile flow, which aids fat digestion and has a light laxative action. The root is also used to treat anemia and can dramatically increase iron levels in the blood in only a few weeks. Long considered a blood purifier, yellow dock may also be effective in treating a number of conditions that stem from liver dysfunction, including skin eruptions, headaches, and unhealthy hair and nails. An astringent and tonic, yellow dock has been used to treat ringworm, laryngitis, and gingivitis.

Steam or sauté very young leaves as you would greens. The tall flower stalks are used in dried flower arrangements and are prized by flower arrangers because they retain their attractive rusty-red color when dried.

**Part Used:** Root, leaves; flower stalks for dried arrangements

**Preservation:** Gather roots in the fall; dry or tincture. Gather young leaves in early spring and eat fresh.

**Precautions:** Although it is unlikely that anyone would want to do so, eating several bowls of dock salad could cause gas, cramping, and diarrhea. The

leaves contain oxalic acid, which may contribute to some types of kidney stones. The root should be avoided by people with a history of gallbladder attacks.

**Medicinal Use:** You can drink up to 3 to 4 cups a day of yellow dock tea. However, yellow dock is bitter, so add herbs such as peppermint or lemon balm to improve the flavor. Take up to ½ teaspoon (2 droppers full) of the tincture a day.

# Ashwaganda

*Withania somnifera*

**Uses:** As Ayurvedic medicine becomes more popular in North America, so does one of its most important herbs. Considered a miracle herb, ashwaganda has been revered in India for thousands of years. The herb is classified as a rejuvenative tonic and an adaptogen, meaning it may increase the body's resistance to disease. It is prescribed for treating conditions caused or aggravated by stress. In a study of people with anxiety disorders, ashwaganda improved the mental condition of almost all who took it. It is used in India to treat asthma, bronchitis, cancer, *Candida* infections, fever, inflammation, nausea, and rheumatism. In addition, studies indicate the herb may reduce serum cholesterol levels and help treat osteoarthritis.

**Precautions:** Seeds are poisonous; use the roots and leaves.

**Medicinal Use:** Drink up to 3 cups, four times a day, or take up to 1 teaspoon of tincture. It is also available in pills. Ashwaganda is most often blended with other herbs.

# Cascara Sagrada

*Rhamnus purshiana*

**Uses:** Cascara sagrada is often recommended by herbalists for chronic constipation. It is regarded as a tonic to the large intestine, and of all the strong laxatives, its actions are the gentlest. It is also recommended to treat hemorrhoids.

**Precautions:** The fresh herb contains chemicals that can cause intestinal cramps, so purchase dried, aged bark. Don't use cascara sagrada for more than two weeks, or you may become dependent on it as you would any laxative. Avoid the herb if you are pregnant or have ulcers, ulcerative colitis, irritable bowel syndrome, or hemorrhoids.

**Medicinal Use:** You can drink 1 to 2 cups of infusion a day, but it tastes very bitter. Take ½ teaspoon of tincture; follow package directions for the pills or syrup. Cascara takes hours to produce a laxative effect, so take only one dose and wait for results. If you make your own preparation, add a carminative such as ginger, cinnamon, or fennel to prevent gas and muscle spasms.

# Cranberry

*Vaccinium macrocarpon*

**Uses:** Cranberry is excellent for treating bladder infections. One way that cranberry works is by acidifying the urine and making an inhospitable environment for the alkaline-loving bacteria. Recently, researchers also discovered that cranberry contains potent bacteria-fighting components. The delicious, tart berry is also rich in nutrients.

**Precautions:** Cranberry is safe to use in moderation, but avoid using any herb that stimulates the kidneys if you have kidney disease.

**Medicinal Use:** One way to enjoy cranberries is to use cranberry extract, available in natural food stores. (Avoid the cranberry juice cocktail sold in grocery stores; it contains sugar, which can help an infection linger.) Add sparkling mineral water for an effervescent treat. Cranberry is also available as pills, or make your own remedy with fresh berries. Cranberry can be mixed with urinary tract tonics such as marshmallow or fennel, but most often it is used alone.

# Devil's Claw

*Harpagophytum procumbens*

**Uses:** Although this herb gets its name from its clawlike fruit, the plant's tuber is used medicinally. Devil's claw has been prescribed for arthritis, rheumatism, and other types of pain caused by inflammation. Two of its active components, harpagoside and betasitosterol, have been shown to have anti-inflammatory properties. Studies have compared it favorably with the anti-inflammatory drugs cortisone and phenylbutazone but without their harmful side effects. The herb is also used to reduce fevers, and an ointment made from the herb may be applied to ulcers, sores, and boils. It is a diuretic, it stimulates the liver, gallbladder, and the lymph system, and it lowers blood sugar.

**Precautions:** Because it may stimulate uterine muscles, do not use devil's claw preparations during pregnancy.

**Medicinal Use:** It is used alone or with other anti-inflammatories. It is most often sold in pill form but is occasionally available as a tincture.

# Kava

*Piper methysticum*

**Uses:** Kava has been revered by Polynesian islanders for thousands of years for its sedative and tonic diaphoretic properties. A substance in the plant produces mildly sedative and tranquilizing effects. One of several studies with kava showed it helped reduce depression and anxiety after only one week of use. German researchers found kava as powerful a remedy as the benzodiazepine family of tranquilizers. Unlike tranquilizers, kava is nonaddictive and does not dull the senses. The herb has some antiseptic and anticonvulsant properties. One of its most important uses is for urinary tract disorders. As an antiseptic and anti-inflammatory, it is good for treating cystitis and problems due to an enlarged prostate. It is also used to ease the pain and inflammation of rheumatism and gout internally as a tea or tincture and topically as a liniment.

**Precautions:** Excessive use has caused a yellow skin rash.

**Medicinal Use:** Take kava as a tea, a tincture, or in pills. It is sometimes blended with other herbs that relax the muscles or nervous system. Take up to 4 cups of tea or 1 teaspoon of tincture a day.

# Kelp

*Fucus vesiculosus*

**Uses:** A good source of iodine, kelp has been used to treat goiter (an enlarged thyroid gland) and overactive thyroid disease. It was the original source of iodine discovered in 1812. It has long been recognized to help in weight reduction; this action may be due to its effect on the thyroid. Kelp also appears to reduce cholesterol and blood pressure and may be used to prevent infection. A rich source of minerals, it is a staple of Japanese diets. Kelp is added to many herbal salt substitutes; although it is salty, kelp contains much less sodium than salt, and it is loaded with potassium. Powdered kelp also stops bleeding when applied topically to a wound. During World War II, British medics relied on this treatment when medical supplies became scarce.

**Precautions:** Kelp is generally considered safe.

**Medicinal Use:** If you gather your own kelp, be sure you don't collect it from polluted sources. Purchase dried kelp from health food stores; add it to salads, soups, stews, and Japanese dishes. Sprinkle powdered kelp on foods. Take kelp capsules as directed on the package.

# Ma Huang, Ephedra

*Ephedra sinica*

**Uses:** Ma huang contains the powerful decongestant alkaloid ephedrine. (The U.S. species, Mormon tea, contains none of the highly stimulating alkaloids.) The plant is a tonic and diuretic. Useful for treating respiratory problems, it has been prescribed for colds, fever, and influenza. When used appropriately, ma huang is effective in alleviating constriction in the chest, diminishing allergic reactivity, and reducing asthma symptoms.

Ma huang is sold as an herbal medication in Germany and Sweden and has been used in China for at least 5,000 years. The U.S. Food and Drug Administration has approved for sale ephedrine as a decongestant and bronchodilating agent. Because of ephedrine's stimulating effects, ma huang has found its way into numerous formulas for weight loss and increasing energy. But its use for these effects can be dangerous.

**Precautions:** Ma huang may elevate blood pressure, so avoid it if you have hypertension. In large amounts, ma huang may cause heart palpitations, nervousness, sweating, and insomnia. Don't use the herb if you are pregnant or nursing. If you have diabetes, an enlarged prostate, or thyroid disease, seek professional advice before using ma huang. If you take MAO inhibitors or beta blockers, stay away from any products containing ephedrine.

**Medicinal Use:** Drink up to ½ cup of tea twice a day. Take ¼ to 1 teaspoon tincture up to three times a day. Ma huang is usually combined with other herbs in formulas for sinus and respiratory congestion.

# Pau d'Arco

*Tabebuia altissima*

**Uses:** Pau d'arco holds promise in the treatment of

cancers, such as leukemia; *Candida* and other infection-causing organisms; and debilitating diseases, such as arthritis. Studies are now underway to back up reports of its successful use in South American clinics in the treatment of such disorders. In one study, it reduced most of the symptoms, especially the pain, in people with various types of cancer. The only side effect was a few cases of nausea. South American Indians have used pau d'arco for centuries: Its use may predate the Incas. It has laxative and antioxidant properties and may be a potent immune-system stimulant. Used internally, the bark relieves pain and increases urine flow. Used topically or internally, it treats skin conditions caused by bacteria, fungi, or parasites and may also help psoriasis and eczema.

**Precautions:** Pau d'arco may cause nausea or produce a severe laxative effect in very high doses.

**Medicinal Use:** Take ½ teaspoon of the tincture and as many as 2 to 4 cups a day of tea. Pau d'arco is often combined with other herbs that bolster the immune system.

# Psyllium

*Plantago ovata*

**Uses:** Psyllium was used by Indian, Persian, and Arab physicians in the Middle Ages as an emollient and lubricating agent. Psyllium seeds are full of mucilage and swell when added to water, so they are useful in treating diarrhea, constipation, and irritable bowel syndrome. Psyllium is a popular drugstore laxative, used in products such as Metamucil. Bulk laxatives such as psyllium are much easier on the intestines than irritating laxatives such as senna, aloe, or cascara sagrada; they can be used by the very young and very old, pregnant women, or frail individuals. They also don't cause the problem with dependency so common with most laxatives. Psyllium seeds may also help lower cholesterol. In addition, the seed is a good ingredient for cosmetic facial masks.

**Precautions:** Drink plenty of water when you use psyllium seeds to prevent bloating and cramps. Psyllium is one of the safest laxatives, but consult with your health care practitioner if you are pregnant.

**Medicinal Use:** Take 1 teaspoon of psyllium seeds with at least 8 ounces of water up to three times a day.

# Schisandra

*Schisandra chinensis*

**Uses:** An adaptogen, schisandra may increase the body's resistance to disease. It is useful in protecting the liver and neutralizing liver toxins. The Chinese have developed it into a drug to treat liver disorders such as hepatitis. It stimulates the nervous system without producing side effects associated with caffeine or amphetamine use. The herb also has antibacterial, antitoxic, and antiallergenic properties. One of its most common uses is to treat lung disorders. In China, the herb is often used to combat fatigue. Studies show it makes people more alert and also relieves headaches, insomnia, and dizziness. In traditional Chinese medicine, it is given as a sexual tonic.

**Precautions:** None

**Medicinal Use:** Take in pills, tea, or tincture. Schisandra is often mixed with other herbs that improve immune function

and treat the lungs. Take up to 4 cups of tea or 1 teaspoon of tincture daily.

# Tea Tree

*Melaleuca alternifolia*

**Uses:** Tea tree is one of the best herbs for treating skin problems. In one Australian study, it worked as well as the standard treatment of benzoyl peroxide to treat acne, although its action was slower. Antiseptic and antifungal, tea tree infusions and oils are useful in many types of infections, including those caused by the herpesvirus and *Candida* organisms. It treats shingles, acne, diaper rash, gum infections, sore throat, vaginal infections, burns, cuts, abrasions, and infected wounds. Studies show tea tree also stimulates immune-system functions. A tea tree oil salve protects the skin from burns caused by radiation cancer therapy.

**Precautions:** Always dilute tea tree essential oil before using.

**Medicinal Use:** Tea tree is available almost exclusively as an essential oil. Use topically in salves, ointments, and hair care preparations. To treat wounds, apply a compress or salve of tea tree oil. Use tea tree throat lozenges. Tea tree also makes an excellent gargle, although it's not very tasty. Add 1 drop of the essential oil to ½ cup warm water and ½ teaspoon salt; gargle as needed. Add a few drops to steaming water and inhale to reduce lung and sinus congestion.

# Turmeric

*Curcuma longa*

**Uses:** A prime ingredient of Indian curries and garam masala, this bright-yellow member of the ginger family is also useful for treating wounds. Turmeric root aids digestion, kills parasites, protects the liver, and may help treat arthritis. It reduces prostaglandins in the body, which are responsible for causing inflammation and menstrual cramps. In some clinical studies, a compound in turmeric, curcumin, was as effective in decreasing inflammation as cortisone and phenylbutazone. Like cayenne, turmeric stops the neurotransmitter, substance P, from sending pain signals to the brain. It also holds potential as a drug for heart disease, and scientists are investigating turmeric's anti-cancer properties and its restorative action on the liver. Traditional Chinese medicine uses turmeric to treat pain, menstrual cramps, and digestive upsets.

**Precautions:** Turmeric has anti-clotting properties and should be avoided by people with clotting disorders. Large amounts of turmeric may cause digestive system upset.

**Medicinal Use:** Sprinkle turmeric powder on wounds. For a traditional Ayurvedic medicine, steep 1 teaspoon powder in 1 cup of warm milk for 15 minutes; drink up to three times a day. Turmeric is usually combined with other herbs in pills or tinctures. Add it to lentils, rice, and vegetables. It is an inexpensive substitute for saffron.

# Wild Yam

*Dioscorea villosa*

**Uses:** As an antispasmodic, wild yam is used by herbalists to treat colic, stomach pain, and cramps. Wild yam is also appropriate for flatulence and dysentery with cramps, especially if the conditions are caused or aggravated by excess stomach acid. It also lessens the pain of gallstones and kidney stones, relieves spasms in the urinary tract, and promotes the flow of bile. Due to its pain-relieving and antispasmodic properties, wild yam can, in some cases, relieve the pain of rheumatoid arthritis. It is used to prevent menstrual cramps and miscarriage. Reports that wild yam contains a form of natural progesterone are not true, and its popular use in "hormone" creams is questionable. A compound in yam, called diosgenin, is used as the basis for synthesizing several steroids, including progesterone and estrogen; however, this complicated process can be performed only in a laboratory, not in the body. The herb is also a diuretic and expectorant.

**Precautions:** None

**Medicinal Use:** Drink up to 6 cups, three times a day. Take ½ to 2 teaspoons of tincture up to three times a day. For menstrual pain, use wild yam with other uterine pain relievers such as cramp bark; for arthritis, mix it with devil's claw; and for urinary tract problems, mix with fennel and marshmallow.

# Yucca

*Yucca* spp.

**Uses:** American Indians used yucca as a cleansing herb. Navajo warriors used yucca for food on long journeys. And the roots were once crushed and used for soap. Research indicates that yucca contains chemicals that may be useful in treating arthritis. In one study, people with arthritis were given a compound from yucca; others received a placebo. Three times the number of study participants who took yucca experienced relief from swelling, pain, and stiffness than those who received the placebo. Some of these people felt better in only a few days; others took a few weeks to notice improvement.

**Precautions:** None

**Medicinal Use:** Drink up to 2 cups of yucca infusion a day—although it tastes bitter and unpleasant—or take ½ teaspoon (2 droppers full) of tincture. The most common way to purchase yucca is in pill form. This herb is often mixed with other anti-inflammatory herbs, such as turmeric, licorice, and bupleurum.

# Chapter Five

# Herbs in the Kitchen

**S**age stuffing alongside a roasted turkey. Cinnamon-spiced apple pie in the oven. Many of our most cherished memories involve food. Herbs look beautiful growing in the garden. But it's in the kitchen that they really work their magic.

Herbs impart a wide range of flavors, from subtle to robust. And many cuisines derive their signature tastes from the herbs that flavor them. Cayenne packs a punch in East Indian, Thai, Cajun, and Creole dishes. Thyme lends its savory aroma to French cuisine. Dill is a staple of Scandinavian cookery. And Mexican food relies heavily on cilantro. Can you imagine pizza without oregano? Spaghetti sauce without basil? Perish the Oriental stir-fry that lacks ginger and garlic.

When we add herbs to food, we add much more than just seasoning. Did you know meat dishes once were wrapped in rosemary to retard mold? Preservation is no longer rosemary's prime function, but the herb remains a staple in kitchens all over the world. In fact, before the advent of refrigeration and packaged foods, herbs were used as much for their preservative and digestive properties as for flavoring. Many culinary herbs contain essential oils and other substances that prevent foods from spoiling in hot climates as well as soothe stomach muscles and enhance digestion. Marjoram, cinnamon, and coriander are good examples of herbs

*Sprigs of oregano from this herb garden may soon add distinctive flavor to sauces, meats, pasta, or vegetables.*

## Uses for Culinary Herbs

**Anise:** sauces, desserts

**Basil:** pesto, tomatoes, Mediterranean and Thai cuisine

**Burnet:** salads, vinegars

**Caraway:** bread, cakes, biscuits, soups, casseroles, cabbage, German cuisines

**Cayenne:** eggs, cheese, Middle Eastern and Creole cuisines

**Chives:** salads, soups, cheese, eggs, baked potatoes

**Cinnamon:** mulled drinks, desserts, baked goods, poached fruit

**Cloves:** stocks, poached meats, pot roasts, baked ham, apples, mulled drinks

**Coriander:** curries, pickles, ratatouille, rice

**Dill:** fish, bread, casseroles, soups, pickles

**Fennel:** fish, lentils, baked goods, sausage, Indian and German cuisines

**Garlic:** dressings, casseroles, sauces, butters, dips, patés, soups, breads, stir-fries, Italian and Oriental cuisine

**Ginger:** stir-fries, curries, pickles, mulled drinks, Thai cuisine

**Horseradish:** sauces, vinegars, beef, poultry, fish

**Juniper:** meats, game, patés

**Lemon balm:** wines, custards, fish, mushrooms, cheese

**Lovage:** broths, soups, casseroles, chicken, ham, fish

**Marjoram:** savory meat, vegetable dishes, sauces

**Mustard:** pickles, marinades, sautés, sauces, salad dressings

**Nasturtium:** salads

**Nutmeg:** desserts, fruits, sauces, vegetables, eggs

**Oregano:** sauces, meats, vegetables, pasta

**Parsley:** garnish, butters, sauces, salads

**Rosemary:** lamb, poultry, fruit, wine, Middle Eastern cuisine

**Sage:** meats, stuffings, sauces, sausages, cheeses

**Summer savory:** beans, cabbage, cauliflower, meats, eggs

**Tarragon:** salads, eggs, chicken, lamb, fish, vinegars, sauces

**Thyme:** savory dishes, French cuisine

**Turmeric:** curries, rice, fish, pickles, Indian and Thai cuisines

that aid digestion. Bitter herbs stimulate our appetites, while herbs such as angelica, fennel, and savory can prevent gas and bloating in the event we overeat. And parsley, mint, anise, and cardamom sweeten the breath after we push ourselves away from the table.

Herbs are packed with vitamins, minerals, and other nutrients. Rose hips contain 20 times more vitamin C than oranges; dandelion leaves have nearly twice the vitamin A of spinach; and parsley and kelp are sources of calcium and other minerals. Herbs can even help us wean ourselves from excessive use of sugar and salt.

## Classic Herb Combinations

### Fines Herbes

*Chervil*
*Parsley*
*Chives*
*Tarragon*

Mince equal amounts of fresh or frozen herbs together, and use to flavor egg and cheese dishes, soups, and sauces. To retain full flavor, add the herbs at the last minute of cooking.

Other popular additions to the basic *fines herbes* recipe are basil, burnet, marjoram, savory, thyme, and watercress.

### Bouquet Garni

*3 sprigs parsley or chervil or both*
*1/2 bay leaf*
*2 sprigs thyme*

Sometimes called a herb bouquet, this herb mixture flavors broths, soups, and stews.

Tie fresh or frozen herbs together and add directly to the pot or, for clear stock, enclose in a cheesecloth bag and remove from the liquid at the end of cooking time.

When using dried ingredients, mix the following: 1 tsp dried parsley, 1/8 teaspoon thyme, 1/8 teaspoon marjoram, 1/4 bay leaf.

## Cajun Seasoning Mix

Cajun seasoning mix, fish fillets such as red snapper, and a heavy skillet are all you need to make blackened seafood for dinner tonight.

*2 Tbsp salt*
*1 Tbsp paprika*
*1 1/2 tsp garlic powder*
*1 tsp onion powder*
*1 tsp ground red pepper*
*1/2 tsp ground white pepper*
*1/2 tsp black pepper*
*1/2 tsp dried thyme leaves, crushed*
*1/2 tsp dried oregano leaves, crushed*

Combine all ingredients. Sprinkle on fish and cook over high heat in a large, heavy skillet, turning once.

Part of the pleasure of cooking with herbs comes from the fun of experimenting with them. So don't be afraid to add a pinch of dried herbs here and some fresh chopped herbs there. It's practically impossible to ruin a dish by adding herbs. Of course, this is not to suggest you should overwhelm your foods with seasonings. Be judicious in your use of herbs. Potatoes should taste like potatoes, not chives. Fish should taste like fish, not tarragon. And don't blitz a dish with three or four herbs when you're learning about the flavors herbs impart. It's best to try one at a time. Savor its distinct aroma and enjoy its flavor.

*If you like your food hot and spicy, this is the herb for you. It may look innocent, but cayenne pepper packs a punch!*

# Mixed Grain Tabbouleh

½ **cup uncooked bulgur**

3 **cups canned chicken broth, divided**

1 **cup uncooked long grain brown rice**

2 **ripe tomatoes, seeds removed**

¼ **cup fresh mint leaves, chopped**

¼ **cup fresh basil, chopped**

¼ **cup fresh oregano, chopped**

½ **cup green onions with tops, minced**

3 **Tbsp fresh lemon juice**

3 **Tbsp olive oil**

½ **tsp salt**

½ **tsp black pepper**

1. Combine bulgur and 1 cup chicken broth in 1-quart saucepan. Bring to a boil over medium-high heat. Reduce heat to low. Simmer, covered, 15 minutes or until broth is absorbed and bulgur is fluffy. Set aside.

2. Combine brown rice and remaining 2 cups chicken broth in 2-quart saucepan. Bring to a boil over medium-high heat. Reduce heat to low. Simmer, covered, about 45 minutes or until broth is absorbed and rice is tender. Set aside.

3. To seed tomatoes, cut each tomato crosswise in half. Hold tomato halves over bowl, cut sides down, and squeeze to remove seeds; discard. Chop tomatoes to measure 1 cup.

4. Combine tomatoes, chopped herbs, green onions, lemon juice, oil, salt, and pepper in large bowl. Stir in bulgur and rice. Allow to cool to room temperature. Garnish with lemon wedges and mint leaves, if desired.

*Makes 6 (1-cup) servings*

# Spicy Lentil and Chickpea Soup

*Inspired by a traditional Moroccan sauce called harissa, this flavorful soup is a great source of fiber and iron.*

½ **cup dried chickpeas (garbanzo beans)**

4 **cans (14 ounces each) ⅓-less-salt chicken broth**

1 **cup dried lentils**

1 **large onion, chopped**

1 **rib celery, chopped**

1 **tsp ground turmeric**

½ **tsp salt**

½ **tsp ground cinnamon**

½ **tsp black pepper**

¼ **tsp ground ginger**

¼ **tsp ground red pepper**

¼ **cup uncooked rice**

3 **cups chopped ripe tomatoes**

¼ **cup chopped fresh parsley**

2 **Tbsp chopped fresh cilantro**

6 **lemon wedges**

1. Sort and rinse chickpeas. Place in large saucepan, cover with water, and let soak overnight. Drain chickpeas and return to saucepan. Add chicken broth to saucepan; bring to a boil over high heat. Reduce heat to low; cover and simmer 1 hour.

2. Sort and rinse lentils; add to chickpeas with onion, celery, turmeric, salt, cinnamon, black pepper, ginger, and ground red pepper. Cover and simmer 45 minutes or until lentils are tender.

3. Stir in rice and tomatoes; bring to a boil over medium-high heat. Reduce heat to low; cover and simmer 20 to 25 minutes or until rice is tender.

4. Stir in parsley and cilantro; simmer 5 minutes. Serve with lemon wedges; garnish with additional fresh cilantro, if desired.

*Makes 6 servings*

# Chicken-Barley Soup

1½ **pounds chicken thighs**

2 **medium ribs celery, sliced**

2 **medium carrots, peeled, thin sliced**

1 **small leek, sliced**

6 **cups cold water**

1½ **tsp salt**

½ **tsp dried marjoram leaves, crushed**

¼ **tsp ground black pepper**

¼ **tsp dried summer savory leaves, crushed**

**Bouquet garni***

¼ **small red bell pepper**

⅓ **cup quick-cooking barley**

3 **cups fresh spinach (loosely packed), chopped**

**Salt and ground black pepper to taste**

**Celery leaves for garnish**

*Sometimes called an herb bouquet, bouquet garni is a bundle of seasonings tied with a string or wrapped in cheesecloth and added to soups and stocks to boost flavor. See page 146 for the traditional bouquet garni ingredients.*

1. Rinse chicken thighs; remove and discard skin. Place chicken in 5-quart Dutch oven.

2. Add celery, carrots, leek, water, salt, marjoram, black pepper, savory, and bouquet garni to Dutch oven. Bring to a boil over high heat. Reduce heat to medium-low; simmer, uncovered, 45 minutes or until chicken is tender.

3. Cut red pepper into 1-inch long narrow strips. Set aside.

4. Remove chicken from soup and let cool slightly. Remove bouquet garni; discard. Skim off foam and as much fat from soup as possible. (Or refrigerate soup several hours and remove fat that rises to surface. Refrigerate chicken while chilling soup.)

5. Add barley to soup. Bring to a boil over high heat. Reduce heat to medium-low; simmer, uncovered, 10 minutes or until barley is almost tender.

6. Meanwhile, remove chicken meat from bones; discard bones. Cut chicken into bite-size pieces.

7. Stir chicken, spinach, and bell pepper into soup. Simmer 5 minutes or until spinach is wilted, chicken is heated, and bell pepper is tender. Season with additional salt and black pepper to taste. Ladle into bowls. Garnish, if desired.

*Makes 6 servings*

# Fresh Tomato Pasta Soup

1 Tbsp olive oil

½ cup onion, chopped

1 clove garlic, minced

3 pounds fresh tomatoes, coarsely chopped

3 cups ⅓-less-salt chicken broth

1 Tbsp fresh basil, minced

1 Tbsp fresh marjoram, minced

1 Tbsp fresh oregano, minced

1 tsp fennel seed

½ tsp ground black pepper

¾ cup uncooked rosamarina or other small pasta

½ cup (2 ounces) shredded part-skim mozzarella cheese

Marjoram sprigs for garnish

1. Heat oil in large saucepan over medium heat. Add onion and garlic; cook and stir until onion is tender. Add tomatoes, broth, basil, marjoram, oregano, fennel seed, and black pepper.

2. Bring to a boil; reduce heat. Cover; simmer 25 minutes. Remove from heat; cool slightly.

3. Purée tomato mixture in food processor or blender in batches. Return to saucepan; bring to a boil. Add pasta; cook 7 to 9 minutes or until tender. Transfer to serving bowls. Sprinkle with mozzarella. Garnish with marjoram sprigs, if desired.

*Makes 8 (¾-cup) servings*

# Garden Vegetable Bulgur Stew

2 fresh medium tomatoes

4 ounces fresh green beans

2 medium green onions

1 Tbsp vegetable oil

1 large onion, chopped

2 medium carrots, thinly sliced

1 small zucchini (4 ounces), sliced

¾ cup canned garbanzo beans, drained (½ of 15-ounce can)

1 can (12 ounces) tomato juice (1½ cups)

1 cup water

⅓ cup bulgur wheat

1 Tbsp dried mint leaves, crushed

1 tsp dried summer savory leaves, crushed

½ tsp salt

Dash ground black pepper

Sour cream for garnish

Fresh mint for garnish

1. Remove skin from tomatoes. To loosen skin, place tomatoes in small saucepan of boiling water for 30 to 45 seconds. Rinse immediately under cold running water. Peel and chop tomatoes.

2. Wash green beans and discard tips; cut beans into 1-inch pieces.

3. Discard root ends of green onions; slice green tops.

4. Heat oil in 5-quart Dutch oven over medium heat. Cook and stir onion until tender.

5. Stir tomatoes, carrots, green beans, green onions, garbanzo beans, tomato juice, water, bulgur, mint, savory, salt, and pepper into Dutch oven. Bring to a boil over high heat. Reduce heat to medium-low; simmer, uncovered, about 20 minutes or until beans and carrots are slightly tender.

6. Add zucchini to vegetable mixture. Bring to a boil over high heat. Reduce heat to medium-low; simmer, uncovered, about 4 minutes or until zucchini is slightly tender.

7. Serve in bowls and garnish with dollops of sour cream and fresh mint, if desired.

*Makes 4 servings*

# Herbed Angel Hair Mushroom Wedge

**4 cups cooked angel hair pasta**

**¾ cup cholesterol-free egg substitute**

**½ cup grated Parmesan cheese**

**2 green onions with tops, chopped**

**1 Tbsp fresh basil, chopped**

**1 Tbsp fresh sage, chopped**

**1 Tbsp fresh mint, chopped**

**⅛ tsp ground black pepper**

**1 Tbsp olive oil**

**2 cups fresh mushrooms, sliced**

**1 cup Tomato-Sage Sauce (recipe follows)**

1. Preheat oven to 375°F.

2. Combine pasta with egg substitute, Parmesan cheese, onions, basil, sage, mint, and black pepper in large bowl. Mix well. Set aside.

3. Heat oil in medium non-stick skillet over low heat. Add mushrooms; cook and stir 2 to 3 minutes or until tender. Add mushrooms to pasta mixture.

4. Spray 9-inch square baking pan with nonstick cooking spray. Pour pasta mixture into pan, pressing firmly until packed down. Bake 25 to 30 minutes or until crisp and lightly browned and center is firm to touch. Remove from oven; cool slightly.

5. Prepare Tomato-Sage Sauce; set aside.

6. Loosen pasta mixture from edges and bottom with spatula. Invert to remove from pan. Cut into wedges. Serve with Tomato-Sage Sauce.

*Makes 8 servings*

## Tomato-Sage Sauce

**2 cans (10 ounces each) no-salt-added whole tomatoes, with juice**

**1 tsp olive oil**

**3 cloves garlic, minced**

**¼ cup fresh parsley, chopped**

**2 Tbsp fresh sage, chopped**

**2 tsp sugar**

**¼ tsp ground black pepper**

1. Place tomatoes in food processor or blender; process until chopped fine. Set aside.

2. Heat oil in medium saucepan over low heat. Add tomatoes, garlic, parsley, sage, sugar, and black pepper. Cook over medium heat 30 minutes or until thickened.

*Makes 8 (¼-cup) servings*

# Ratatouille

½ pound eggplant, cut into ½-inch cubes

1 small onion, sliced and separated into rings

1 small zucchini, thinly sliced

½ medium green bell pepper, chopped

1 tomato, cut into wedges

1 Tbsp grated Parmesan cheese

1 stalk celery, chopped

¼ tsp salt (optional)

¼ tsp dried chervil, crushed

¼ tsp dried oregano leaves, crushed

¼ tsp garlic, minced

⅛ tsp dried thyme, crushed

Dash ground pepper

Combine all ingredients in 2-quart microwavable casserole; cover. Microwave at HIGH (100% power) 7 to 10 minutes or until eggplant is translucent, stirring every 3 minutes.

*Makes 6 servings*

# Herbed Scallops and Shrimp

¼ cup fresh parsley, chopped

¼ cup lime juice

2 Tbsp fresh mint, chopped

2 Tbsp fresh rosemary, chopped

1 Tbsp honey

1 Tbsp olive oil

2 cloves garlic, minced

¼ tsp ground black pepper

½ pound raw jumbo shrimp, peeled and deveined

½ pound bay or halved sea scallops

1. Combine parsley, lime juice, mint, rosemary, honey, oil, garlic, and black pepper in medium bowl; blend well. Add shrimp and scallops. Cover; refrigerate 1 hour.

2. Preheat broiler. Put shrimp and scallops on skewers. Brush with marinade. Broil 5 minutes or until shrimp are opaque and scallops are lightly browned. Serve immediately.

*Makes 4 servings*

# Lemon-Ginger Chicken with Puffed Rice Noodles

**Vegetable oil for frying**

**4 ounces rice noodles, broken in half**

**1 stalk lemon grass***

**3 boneless, skinless chicken breast halves**

**3 cloves garlic, minced**

**1 tsp fresh ginger, chopped fine**

**¼ tsp black pepper**

**¼ tsp ground red pepper**

**¼ cup water**

**1 Tbsp cornstarch**

**2 Tbsp peanut oil**

**6 ounces fresh snow peas (Chinese pea pods), ends trimmed**

**1 can (8¾ ounces) baby corn, drained, rinsed, and cut lengthwise into halves**

**¼ cup cilantro, chopped**

**2 Tbsp packed brown sugar**

**2 Tbsp fish sauce**

**1 Tbsp light soy sauce**

*\*Or substitute 1½ tsp grated lemon peel.*

**1.** Heat 3 inches vegetable oil in wok or Dutch oven until oil registers 375°F on deep-fry thermometer. Fry noodles in small batches 20 seconds or until puffy, holding down noodles in oil with slotted spoon to fry evenly. Drain on paper towels; set aside.

**2.** Cut lemon grass into 1-inch pieces, discarding outer leaves and roots.

**3.** Cut chicken breasts into 2½×1-inch strips.

**4.** Combine chicken, lemon grass, garlic, ginger, black pepper, and red pepper in medium bowl; toss to coat. Combine water and cornstarch in cup; set aside.

**5.** Heat wok over high heat 1 minute or until hot. Drizzle 2 Tbsp peanut oil into wok and heat 30 seconds. Add chicken mixture; stir-fry 3 minutes or until no longer pink.

**6.** Add pea pods and baby corn; stir-fry 1 to 2 minutes.

Stir cornstarch mixture; add to wok. Cook 1 minute or until thickened.

**7.** Add cilantro, brown sugar, fish sauce, and soy sauce; cook until heated through. Discard lemon grass. Serve over reserved rice noodles.

*Makes 4 servings*

# Roasted Rosemary-Lemon Chicken

**1 whole chicken
(3¼ pounds)**

**½ tsp ground black
pepper**

**1 lemon, cut into eighths**

**¼ cup fresh parsley**

**4 sprigs fresh rosemary**

**3 fresh sage leaves**

**2 sprigs fresh thyme**

**1 can (14 ounces) ⅓-less-
sodium chicken broth**

**1 cup onions, sliced**

**4 cloves garlic**

**1 cup carrots, thin sliced**

**1 cup zucchini, thin
sliced**

**¼ cup water**

**Rosemary and lemon
for garnish**

1. Preheat oven to 350°F. Trim fat from chicken, leaving skin on. Rinse chicken and pat dry with paper towels. Fill cavity of chicken with black pepper, lemon, parsley, rosemary, sage, and thyme. Close cavity with skewers.

2. Combine broth, onions, and garlic in heavy roasting pan. Place chicken over broth.

Bake 1½ hours or until juices run clear when pierced with fork. Remove chicken to serving plate.

3. Combine carrots and zucchini in small saucepan with tight-fitting lid. Add ¼ cup water; bring to a boil over high heat. Reduce heat to medium. Cover and steam 4 minutes or until vegetables are crisp-tender. Transfer vegetables to colander; drain.

4. Remove skewers. Discard lemon and herbs from cavity of chicken. Remove skin from chicken. Cut chicken into pieces. Remove onions and garlic from pan with slotted spoon to medium serving bowl or plate. Add carrots and zucchini; mix well. Arrange vegetable mixture around chicken. Garnish with fresh rosemary and lemon, if desired.

*Makes 6 servings*

# Spinach Stuffed Manicotti

1 package (10 ounces) frozen spinach

8 manicotti shells

2 egg whites

1½ tsp olive oil

1 tsp dried rosemary leaves, crushed

1 tsp dried sage leaves, crushed

1 tsp dried oregano leaves, crushed

1 tsp dried thyme leaves, crushed

1 tsp garlic, chopped

1½ cups fresh or canned tomatoes, chopped

4 ounces ricotta cheese

1 slice whole wheat bread, torn into coarse crumbs

Yellow pepper rings and sage sprig for garnish

stir rosemary, sage, oregano, thyme, and garlic in hot oil about 1 minute. Do not let herbs turn brown. Add tomatoes; reduce heat to low. Simmer, uncovered, 10 minutes, stirring occasionally.

6. Combine spinach, cheese, and crumbs in bowl. Fold in egg whites. Fill shells with spinach mixture using a spoon.

7. Place one third of the tomato mixture on the bottom of a 13×9-inch baking pan. Arrange manicotti in pan. Pour tomato mixture over manicotti. Cover with foil.

8. Bake 30 minutes or until bubbly. Garnish, if desired.

*Makes 4 servings*

1. Cook spinach according to package directions. Place in colander to drain. Let stand until cool enough to handle. Squeeze spinach between hands to remove excess moisture. Set aside.

2. Cook pasta. Drain in colander. Rinse under warm running water; drain.

3. Separate egg whites from yolks. Beat the whites lightly with a fork. (Discard yolks or cover with cold water and refrigerate, tightly covered, for no more than 3 days.)

4. Preheat oven to 350°F.

5. Heat oil in small saucepan over medium heat. Cook and

# Glazed Pork Tenderloin

2 whole well-trimmed pork tenderloins (about 1½ pounds)
½ cup canned jellied cranberry sauce or currant jelly
1 Tbsp grated horseradish
½ cup chicken broth
¼ cup Rhine or other sweet white wine
Salt and pepper to taste (optional)

1. Preheat oven to 325°F.

2. Place tenderloins on meat rack in shallow roasting pan.

3. Combine jellied cranberry sauce and horseradish in small saucepan. Heat over low heat until cranberry sauce is melted; stir well.

4. Brush half of mixture over tenderloins.

5. Roast 30 minutes; turn tenderloins over. Brush with remaining cranberry mixture. Roast an additional 30 to 40 minutes, depending on thickness of tenderloins, or until thermometer registers 165°F.* Remove thermometer and check temperature of other tenderloin.

6. Transfer tenderloins to cutting board; tent with foil. Let stand 10 minutes.

7. Remove meat rack from roasting pan. To deglaze the pan, pour broth and wine into pan. Place over burners and cook over medium-high heat, stirring frequently and scraping up any browned bits, 4 to 5 minutes or until sauce is reduced to ½ cup.

8. Strain sauce through a fine-mesh strainer; season to taste with salt and pepper, if desired.

9. Carve tenderloins into thin slices with carving knife. Serve with sauce.

*Makes 6 servings*

*The most accurate way to measure internal temperature of thin pork tenderloins is with an instant read thermometer, which has a narrower stem than a standard meat thermometer. Insert thermometer into thickest part of tenderloin. Do not leave the thermometer in the tenderloin during roasting since the thermometer is not ovenproof.*

# Ruffled Tuna Kabobs

1 tuna steak, 1 inch thick (about ¾ pound)

⅓ cup low sodium soy sauce

3 Tbsp red wine vinegar

1 Tbsp vegetable oil

1 Tbsp packed dark brown sugar

1 Tbsp ground coriander

1 tsp ground ginger

⅛ tsp ground red pepper

1 clove garlic, minced

12 (8-inch) bamboo skewers

1. Rinse tuna and pat dry with paper towels.

2. For ease in slicing, wrap fish in plastic wrap; freeze about 1 hour or until firm but not frozen.

3. Slice fish across the grain into 12 (¼-inch-thick) slices.

4. To make marinade, combine soy sauce, vinegar, oil, sugar, coriander, ginger, pepper, and garlic in casserole

dish. Place fish slices in marinade, stirring to coat; cover. Marinate in refrigerator 1 to 6 hours, turning slices once or twice.

5. Cover skewers with cold water; soak 20 minutes to prevent them from burning. Remove skewers from water. Weave 1 fish slice accordion style onto each skewer.

6. Brush fish with marinade. You can use remaining marinade as a dipping sauce for kabobs: Place marinade in small saucepan and bring to a full boil.

7. Preheat broiler. Place skewers crosswise on broiler pan rack. Broil 4 inches beneath heat 1 to 2 minutes or until fish is opaque and flakes easily when tested with fork. Serve immediately.

*Makes 12 kabobs*

# Chicken with Lime Butter

**3 whole chicken breasts, split, skinned, and boned**
**½ tsp salt**
**½ tsp pepper**
**⅓ cup vegetable oil**
**Juice of 1 lime**
**½ cup butter, softened**
**1 tsp fresh chives, minced**
**½ tsp dried dill weed, crushed**
**Lime slices, quartered cherry tomatoes, and dill sprigs for garnish**

1. Sprinkle chicken with salt and pepper.

2. Heat oil in large skillet over medium heat. Add chicken to skillet in single layer. Cook 6 minutes or until chicken is light brown, turning once. Cover; reduce heat to low. Cook 10 minutes or until chicken is tender and no longer pink in center. Remove chicken to serving platter; keep warm.

3. Drain oil from skillet.

4. Simmer lime juice over low heat 1 minute or until juice begins to bubble.

5. Stir in butter, 1 tablespoon at a time, until sauce thickens. Remove sauce from heat; stir in chives and dill weed.

6. Spoon sauce over chicken. Garnish, if desired.

*Makes 6 servings*

# Sauerbraten with Gingersnap Gravy

3 cups water

1 cup cider vinegar

1 onion, thinly sliced

3 Tbsp brown sugar

1½ tsp salt

1 tsp ground ginger

1 tsp whole allspice

1 tsp whole cloves

½ tsp juniper berries

2 cloves garlic, crushed

1 beef rump roast (about 4 pounds)

2 Tbsp vegetable oil

2 Tbsp all-purpose flour

¼ cup crushed ginger-snaps

1. To prepare marinade, bring water and vinegar to a boil in large saucepan over high heat. Remove from heat; add onion, sugar, salt, ginger, allspice, cloves, juniper berries, and garlic. Cool slightly.

2. Place roast in large bowl or plastic food storage bag; pour marinade over roast. Cover and refrigerate for at least 8 hours, turning occasionally.

3. Remove roast from marinade, reserving marinade. Pat dry with paper towels. Heat oil in Dutch oven over medium-high heat until hot. Brown roast on all sides.

4. To braise roast, add marinade to Dutch oven. Reduce heat to low. Cook, covered, 2½ to 3 hours or until fork-tender. Remove roast from Dutch oven; set aside. Strain braising liquid through fine-meshed sieve into large bowl; discard spices and onion.

5. Skim fat from braising liquid and discard. Measure 2 cups braising liquid; discard remaining liquid. Place 1½ cups liquid in Dutch oven.

6. Place flour in small bowl; gradually whisk ½ cup braising liquid into flour. Stir mixture into liquid in Dutch oven. Add gingersnaps; mix well. Bring to a boil.

7. Return roast to Dutch oven. Reduce heat to low; cook, covered, 15 to 20 minutes.

*Makes 6 to 8 servings*

# Mogul-Style Fried Chicken

**1 tsp Garam Masala, divided (recipe follows)**
**½ cup unsalted butter**
**4 boneless, skinless chicken breast halves or thighs (1 pound)**
**1 egg, beaten**
**3 cloves garlic, minced, divided**
**2 tsp fresh ginger, minced, divided**
**½ tsp turmeric, divided**
**½ tsp salt, divided**
**½ cup onion, chopped**
**2 Tbsp shredded unsweetened coconut***
**¾ cup plain yogurt**
**¼ cup whipping cream**
**¼ cup whole cashews for garnish**

*\*Or substitute sweetened coconut rinsed with boiling water.*

1. Prepare Garam Masala. Set aside.

2. To prepare clarified butter, or ghee, melt butter in small skillet over low heat. Remove from heat. Skim off and discard white foam that forms on top. Skim off clear clarified butter and reserve. Discard white milk solids.

3. Gently pound chicken to ¼-inch thickness.

4. Blend egg, ½ tsp garlic, 1½ tsp ginger, ½ tsp Garam Masala, ¼ tsp turmeric, and ¼ tsp salt in shallow bowl. Dip chicken in mixture; turn to coat.

5. Heat clarified butter in large skillet over medium-high heat. Add chicken. Cook 4 to 5 minutes per side or until golden brown and no longer pink in center. Remove chicken; drain on paper towels.

6. To prepare sauce, pour off all but 2 Tbsp clarified butter from skillet. Reduce heat to medium. Add onion. Cook and stir 3 to 5 minutes or until soft and golden.

7. Add coconut, remaining garlic, remaining ½ tsp ginger, ½ tsp Garam Masala, ¼ tsp turmeric, and ¼ tsp salt. Cook and stir 30 seconds.

8. Remove skillet from heat. Place yogurt in small bowl. Stir several spoonfuls hot mixture into yogurt. Stir yogurt mixture into sauce.

9. Add chicken; turn to coat. Heat over low heat until heated through. Remove chicken to serving dish.

10. Stir cream into sauce. Do not boil. Spoon sauce over chicken. Garnish, if desired.

*Makes 4 servings*

## Garam Masala

**2 tsp cumin seeds**
**2 tsp whole black peppercorns**
**1½ tsp coriander seeds**
**1 tsp fennel seeds**
**¾ tsp whole cloves**
**½ tsp whole cardamom seeds (pods removed)**
**1 cinnamon stick, broken**

Preheat oven to 250°F. Combine spices on cookie sheet; bake 30 minutes, stirring occasionally. Powder warm spices in clean coffee or spice grinder, or use mortar and pestle. Store in covered glass jar.

*Note: Garam masala is also available at specialty stores or Indian markets.*

# Koftas (Lamb Meatballs in Spicy Gravy)

2 tsp Garam Masala (page 161)

1½ pounds ground lamb or ground round

2 eggs

1½ cups onions, chopped fine, divided

½ cup cilantro, chopped

2 cloves garlic, minced

1 tsp fresh ginger, minced

1½ tsp salt, divided

24 whole blanched almonds

1 Tbsp peanut oil

1 tsp ground coriander

1 tsp ground cumin

1 tsp chili powder

½ tsp turmeric

2 tomatoes, peeled, seeded, and chopped

½ cup water

1 cup plain yogurt

Fresh cilantro and chilies for garnish

1. Prepare Garam Masala. Place 2 tsp in medium bowl. Add lamb, eggs, ½ cup onion, cilantro, garlic, ginger, and ½ tsp salt; mix well. Cover and refrigerate at least 1 hour or overnight.

2. Divide mixture into 24 portions. Shape into ovals or balls; insert 1 almond into each meatball.

3. Heat oil in large skillet over medium-high heat until

hot. Add half the meatballs; cook 8 minutes or until brown, turning frequently. Remove meatballs from skillet. Repeat with remaining meatballs.

4. Reduce heat to medium. Add remaining 1 cup onion. Cook and stir 6 to 8 minutes or until browned. Stir in remaining 1 tsp salt, coriander, cumin, chili powder, and turmeric. Add tomatoes. Cook 5 minutes or until tomatoes are tender.

5. Add water; bring mixture to a boil over high heat. Add meatballs. Reduce heat to medium-low. Simmer 15 minutes or until thoroughly cooked. Remove meatballs from skillet to serving platter; keep warm.

6. Remove skillet from heat; place yogurt in small bowl. Stir in several spoonfuls hot mixture. Stir yogurt mixture into sauce in skillet. Cook over medium-low heat until sauce thickens. Do not boil. Pour sauce over meatballs. Garnish, if desired.

*Makes 6 servings*

# Crisp Fish Cakes

**Ginger Dipping Sauce (recipe follows)**
1 pound boneless catfish, halibut, or cod fillets
1 Tbsp fish sauce
3 cloves garlic, minced
1 Tbsp cilantro, chopped
2 tsp grated lemon peel
1 tsp fresh ginger, chopped fine
⅛ tsp ground red pepper
Peanut oil for frying
1 head curly leaf lettuce
1 medium green or red apple, cut into thin strips, or 1 ripe mango, diced
½ cup cilantro leaves
⅓ cup fresh mint leaves

1. Prepare Ginger Dipping Sauce; set aside.

2. Rinse fish and pat dry with paper towels. Trim grayish-white fat layer from skin side of catfish fillet; discard. Cut fish into 1-inch pieces.

3. Process fish pieces in food processor 10 to 20 seconds or just until coarsely chopped. (Do not purée.) Add fish sauce, garlic, cilantro, lemon peel, ginger, and red pepper; process 5 seconds or until combined.

4. Rub cutting board with 1 to 2 tsp oil. Place fish mixture on board; pat evenly into 7-inch square. Cut into 16 squares with sharp knife; shape each square into 2-inch patty.

5. Heat 1 to 1½ inches oil in large skillet over medium-high heat until oil registers 360° to 375°F on deep-fry thermometer. Use slotted spoon to lower 4 patties into hot oil.

6. Fry patties 2 to 3 minutes or until golden and fish is white in center. (Overcooking will dry fish and cause patties to shrink.) Remove patties; drain on paper towels; repeat with remaining patties.

7. Pile fish cakes on serving platter with lettuce leaves, apple, cilantro leaves, mint, and Ginger Dipping Sauce. To eat, stack 1 fish cake, apple strips, cilantro, and mint in center of lettuce leaf. Drizzle with sauce; enclose filling in lettuce leaf and eat out of hand.

*Makes 6 to 8 servings*

## Ginger Dipping Sauce

¼ cup rice vinegar
2 Tbsp water
1 tsp sugar
1 tsp fresh ginger, minced
½ tsp red pepper flakes
½ tsp fish sauce

Mix all ingredients in small bowl until sugar dissolves.

# Roasted Herb & Garlic Tenderloin

1 well-trimmed beef
   tenderloin roast (3 to
   4 pounds)
1 Tbsp black pepper-
   corns
2 Tbsp fresh basil,
   chopped, or 2 tsp dried
   basil, crushed
1½ Tbsp fresh thyme,
   chopped, or 1½ tsp
   dried thyme leaves,
   crushed
1 Tbsp fresh rosemary,
   chopped, or 1 tsp dried
   rosemary, crushed
1 Tbsp garlic, minced
   Salt and black pepper
   (optional)

1. Preheat oven to 425°F.

2. Tie roast with cotton string at 1½-inch intervals to hold its shape.

3. Place peppercorns in small, heavy, resealable plastic food storage bag. Seal bag tightly. Pound peppercorns with meat mallet or rolling pin until cracked.

4. Place roast on meat rack in shallow roasting pan. Combine cracked peppercorns, basil, thyme, rosemary, and garlic in small bowl; rub over top surface of roast.

5. Insert meat thermometer into thickest part of roast.

6. Roast in oven 40 to 50 minutes until thermometer registers 125° to 130°F for rare or 135° to 145°F for medium-rare, depending on thickness of roast.

7. Transfer roast to carving board; tent with foil. Let stand 10 minutes before carving. Remove string; discard.

8. To serve, carve crosswise into ½-inch thick slices with large carving knife. Season with salt and pepper, if desired.

*Makes 10 to 12 servings*

# Marinated Grilled Lamb Chops

8 well-trimmed lamb loin chops, cut 1 inch thick (about 2¼ pounds)

3 cloves garlic, minced

2 Tbsp fresh rosemary, chopped, or 2 tsp dried rosemary, crushed

2 Tbsp fresh mint leaves, chopped, or 2 tsp dried mint leaves, crushed

¾ cup dry red wine

⅓ cup butter or margarine, softened

¼ tsp salt

¼ tsp freshly ground black pepper

Fresh mint leaves for garnish

1. To marinate, place chops in large, resealable plastic food storage bag. Combine garlic, rosemary, and mint in small bowl. Combine ½ of garlic mixture and wine. Pour wine mixture over chops in bag. Close bag securely; turn to coat. Marinate chops in refrigerator 2 to 4 hours, turning occasionally.

2. Add butter, salt, and pepper to remaining garlic mixture; mix well. Spoon onto center of sheet of plastic wrap. Using plastic wrap as a guide, shape butter mixture into 4×1½-inch log. Wrap securely in plastic wrap; refrigerate until ready to serve.

3. Prepare grill.

4. Drain chops, discarding marinade. Grill, covered, over medium coals about 9 minutes or to desired doneness, turning once.

5. Cut butter log crosswise into 8 (½-inch) slices. Top each chop with slice of seasoned butter. Garnish, if desired.

*Makes 4 servings*

# Wild Rice, Mushroom, and Spinach Skillet

⅓ cup wild rice

⅓ cup brown rice

⅓ cup long-grain white rice

1½ cups water

1 can (10½ ounces) ⅓-less-salt chicken broth

2 Tbsp margarine

2 cups shiitake mushrooms, sliced

2 cups brown mushrooms, quartered

2 cups bok choy, chopped

2 cups spinach, shredded

¼ cup feta cheese, crumbled

Carrot curls and fresh herbs for garnish

1. Combine wild rice, brown rice, long-grain white rice, water, and chicken broth in medium saucepan. Bring to a boil over high heat; reduce heat to low. Simmer, covered, 45 minutes or until the rice is tender.

2. Melt margarine in large saucepan over medium heat. Add mushrooms; cook and stir 3 minutes. Add bok choy and spinach; cook and stir 3 minutes or until greens are wilted.

3. Add rice to greens in saucepan; stir until blended. Sprinkle with cheese just before serving. Garnish with carrot curls and fresh herbs, if desired.

*Makes 10 servings*

# Oven Roasted Potatoes with Herbs

- **3 pounds red potatoes, unpeeled, cut into 1½-inch cubes**
- **1 large sweet onion, cut into 1-inch cubes**
- **3 cloves garlic, minced**
- **3 Tbsp olive oil**
- **2 Tbsp butter, melted**
- **¾ tsp salt**
- **¾ tsp coarsely ground black pepper**
- **⅓ cup mixed herbs, such as basil, chives, parsley, oregano, rosemary, sage, tarragon, and thyme, chopped**
- **Fresh rosemary sprigs for garnish**

1. Preheat oven to 450°F. Arrange potatoes and onion in large shallow roasting pan.

2. Combine garlic, oil, butter, salt, and pepper in small bowl. Drizzle over potatoes and onion; toss well to combine.

3. Bake 30 minutes. Stir and bake 10 minutes more. Add herbs; toss well. Bake 10 minutes or until vegetables are tender and browned.

*Makes 6 servings*

# Crisp Zucchini Ribbons

- **3 small zucchini (about ¾ pound total)**
- **2 Tbsp olive oil**
- **1 Tbsp white wine vinegar**
- **2 tsp fresh basil, chopped, or ½ tsp dried basil, crushed**
- **½ tsp crushed red pepper flakes**
- **¼ tsp ground coriander Salt and black pepper**

1. Cut tip and stem ends from zucchini. With vegetable peeler, begin at stem end and make continuous ribbons down length of each zucchini.

2. Steam zucchini ribbons till crisp-tender. Transfer zucchini to warm serving dish.

3. Combine oil, vinegar, basil, red pepper, and coriander in small glass bowl, whisking until oil is thoroughly blended.

4. Pour dressing mixture over zucchini ribbons; toss gently to coat. Season with salt and pepper to taste. Serve immediately or refrigerate up to 2 days.

*Makes 4 side-dish servings*

# Green Beans and Shiitake Mushrooms

**10 to 12 dried shiitake
  mushrooms (about
  1 ounce)**

**⅓ cup fresh basil or
  cilantro**

**2 green onions, sliced
  diagonally**

**¾ to 1 pound fresh green
  beans, ends trimmed**

**¾ cup water, divided**

**3 Tbsp oyster sauce**

**1 Tbsp cornstarch**

**4 cloves garlic, minced**

**⅛ tsp red pepper flakes**

**1 Tbsp vegetable oil**

**⅓ cup roasted peanuts
  (optional)**

1. Place mushrooms in bowl; cover with hot water. Let stand 30 minutes or until caps are soft.

2. Break off and discard stems from basil. Rinse leaves; pat dry. Layer some of leaves on cutting board, then roll up jelly-roll fashion. Slice roll into ¼-inch thick slices; separate into strips. Repeat with remaining basil.

3. Drain mushrooms; squeeze out excess water. Remove and discard stems. Slice caps into thin strips.

4. Combine ¼ cup water, oyster sauce, cornstarch, garlic, and pepper flakes in small bowl; mix well. Set aside.

5. Heat wok or medium skillet over medium-high heat. Add oil and swirl to coat surface. Add mushrooms, beans, and remaining ½ cup water; cook and stir until water boils.

6. Reduce heat to medium-low; cover and cook 8 to 10 minutes or until beans are crisp-tender, stirring occasionally.

7. Stir cornstarch mixture; add to wok. Cook and stir until sauce thickens and coats beans. (If cooking water has evaporated, add enough water to form thick sauce.)

8. Stir in green onions, basil, and peanuts, if desired; mix well. Transfer to serving platter. Garnish as desired.

*Makes 4 to 6 servings*

# Garden Greens with Fennel Dressing

**Fennel Dressing**

- ½ **tsp unflavored gelatin**
- 2 **Tbsp cold water**
- ¼ **cup boiling water**
- ½ **tsp salt**
- ½ **tsp sugar**
- ¼ **tsp dry mustard**
- ⅛ **tsp black pepper**
- ¼ **tsp anise extract or ground fennel seeds**
- 1 **Tbsp fresh lemon juice**
- ¼ **cup raspberry or wine vinegar**
- 1¼ **tsp walnut or canola oil**

**Salad**

- 1 **head (10 ounces) Bibb lettuce, torn into bite-sized pieces**
- 1 **head (10 ounces) radicchio, torn into bite-sized pieces**
- 1 **bunch arugula (3 ounces), torn into bite-sized pieces**
- 1 **cup mache or spinach leaves, washed and torn into bite-sized pieces**
- 1 **fennel bulb (8 ounces), chopped fine (reserve fern for garnish)**
- 1 **Tbsp pine nuts, toasted**

**1.** To prepare dressing, sprinkle gelatin over cold water in small bowl; let stand 1 minute to soften. Add boiling water; stir 2 minutes or until gelatin dissolves. Add salt and sugar; stir until sugar completely dissolves. Add remaining dressing ingredients except oil; mix well. Slowly whisk in oil until well blended. Cover and refrigerate 2 hours or overnight. Shake well before using.

**2.** Place all salad ingredients except pine nuts in large bowl. Add dressing; toss until all leaves glisten. Divide salad among 6 chilled salad plates. Top each salad with ½ tsp pine nuts. Garnish with sprig of fennel fern.

*Makes 6 servings*

# Pesto

## Spinach Pesto

**1 bunch fresh spinach**
**1 cup fresh parsley leaves**
**⅔ cup grated Parmesan cheese**
**½ cup walnut pieces**
**6 cloves fresh garlic, crushed**
**4 flat anchovy filets**
**1 Tbsp dried tarragon leaves, crushed**
**1 tsp dried basil, crushed**
**1 tsp salt**
**½ tsp pepper**
**¼ tsp anise or fennel seed**
**1 cup olive oil**

1. Wash spinach thoroughly and remove stems. Pat dry with paper towels, and chop.

2. Place all ingredients except olive oil in covered food processor. Process until mixture is smooth.

3. With machine running, add oil in thin stream. Adjust seasonings, if desired.

4. Serve over pasta; toss gently to coat.

*Makes 2 cups*

## Olive-Basil Pesto

**¾ cup pine nuts or walnuts**
**1 cup kalamata olives, divided**
**1 cup packed fresh basil**
**1 clove garlic**
**½ cup Parmesan cheese**
**½ cup olive oil**
**2 Tbsp chopped pimiento**

1. To toast pine nuts, spread in single layer on baking sheet. Bake at 350°F for 8 to 10 minutes or until golden brown, stirring frequently. Remove pine nuts from sheet and cool.

2. Rinse olives and pat dry with paper towels. Slit open olives and remove pit.

3. Combine basil, ¾ cup olives, pine nuts, and garlic in food processor; process until smooth. Add cheese. With machine running, add oil, processing until well blended. Chop reserved ¼ cup olives. Stir olives and pimiento into mixture. This pesto is ideal with fish. Serve at room temperature.

*Makes about 1½ cups*

*Note: Store pesto in an airtight container in the refrigerator up to 2 weeks or freezer up to 3 months. Cover top of pesto with thin layer of olive oil before storing.*

# Salad Dressings

### Fresh Herb Dressing

½ **cup red wine vinegar**
2 **Tbsp olive oil**
1 **clove garlic, crushed**
1 **Tbsp fresh oregano, chopped**
1 **Tbsp fresh marjoram, chopped**
½ **tsp sugar**
⅛ **tsp black pepper**

Combine all ingredients in small bowl; mix well.

### Italian Salad Dressing

½ **cup extra virgin olive oil**
¼ **cup Basil-Garlic Champagne Vinegar (recipe follows)**
1 **tsp Dijon mustard**
½ **tsp salt**
½ **tsp sugar**
¼ **tsp black pepper**

1. Whisk oil, Basil-Garlic Champagne Vinegar, mustard, salt, sugar, and pepper in small bowl with wire whisk until well blended.

2. Place neck of funnel in a clean, dry decorative bottle.

Line funnel with double layer of cheesecloth or coffee filter.

3. Pour mixture into funnel; discard solids. Seal bottle. Store in refrigerator up to 1 month.

### Basil-Garlic Champagne Vinegar

¼ **cup fresh basil leaves**
4 **cloves garlic, crushed**
4 **dried hot red peppers**
1¼ **cups champagne sherry or aged sherry vinegar**

1. Place basil, garlic, and peppers in jar.

2. Place sherry in small saucepan. Bring just to a boil over medium-high heat. (Bubbles will begin to form on the surface of the sherry.) Remove saucepan from heat.

3. Pour sherry into jar; cover. Shake jar several times to distribute basil leaves. Store in cool, dark place at least 7 days, shaking occasionally.

4. Line funnel with double layer of cheesecloth or coffee filter.

5. Pour mixture into funnel. Add peppers and basil, if desired; cover. Store in cool, dark place up to 2 months.

# After-Dinner Treats

## Hot Mulled Cider

- 1 orange
- 1 lemon
- 12 whole cloves
- 6 cups apple cider
- ⅓ cup sugar
- 3 cinnamon sticks
- 12 whole allspice berries
  Additional cinnamon sticks and citrus strips for garnish

1. Pierce 6 evenly spaced holes around orange and lemon with point of wooden skewer. Insert whole cloves into the holes.

2. Cut a slice out of the orange to include all of the cloves. Cut the remainder of orange into thin slices. Repeat procedure with lemon.

3. Combine orange slices, lemon slices, cider, sugar, cinnamon sticks, and allspice in medium saucepan. Bring just to a simmer over medium heat. Do not boil. Reduce heat to low; cook 5 minutes.

4. Pour cider through a strainer into mugs. Discard fruit and seasonings. Garnish, if desired.

*Makes 6 (1-cup) servings*

## Fruit with Cranberry-Yogurt Sauce

- 6 cups baby greens
- 3 slices fresh pineapple, peeled and halved
- 2 kiwifruit
- 1 banana
- ½ cantaloupe
- 1 medium orange
- 1 medium apple
- 1 cup cranberries
- ¼ cup sugar
- 1½ cups vanilla low fat yogurt

1. Divide baby greens and pineapple evenly among salad plates. Peel and thinly slice kiwifruit and banana; add to salad plates. Remove rind from cantaloupe; slice cantaloupe and add to other fruits.

2. Remove peel from orange (avoid removing the bitter pith). Cut peel into 1-inch sections and place in food processor. Remove pith, cut peeled orange into quarters, and place in food processor. Peel, core, and slice apple. Add cranberries, apple, and sugar to food processor; process 10 seconds or until chopped fine, scraping side of bowl as needed. Add yogurt; process until blended. Pour sauce over fruits and greens. Serve immediately.

*Makes 6 servings*

# Gingerbread People

2¼ cups all-purpose flour
2 tsp cinnamon
2 tsp ground ginger
1 tsp baking powder
½ tsp salt
¼ tsp ground cloves
¼ tsp ground nutmeg
¾ cup butter, softened
½ cup packed light brown sugar
½ cup dark molasses
1 large egg
Red hot cinnamon candies
Icing (recipe follows)

1. Place flour, cinnamon, ginger, baking powder, salt, cloves, and nutmeg in large bowl; stir to combine.

2. Beat butter and brown sugar in large bowl at medium speed until light and fluffy, scraping side of bowl once. Beat in molasses and egg. Gradually add flour mixture. Beat at low speed until well blended, scraping side of bowl once.

3. Form dough into 3 disks. Wrap in plastic wrap; refrigerate 1 hour or until firm.

4. Preheat oven to 350°F. Work with 1 disk at a time. Roll out dough on lightly floured surface with lightly floured rolling pin to ³⁄₁₆ inch thickness.

5. Cut out gingerbread people with floured 5-inch cookie cutters, and place on ungreased cookie sheets. If desired, press cinnamon candies into dough for eyes or coat buttons.

6. Press dough trimmings together; reroll and cut out more cookies. (Rerolled dough produces slightly tougher cookies than first rolling.)

7. Bake about 12 minutes or until edges are golden brown. Let cookies stand on cookie sheets 1 minute, then cool on wire racks.

8. Prepare Icing. If desired, divide Icing into small bowls and tint with food coloring to use for decorative piping.

9. Spoon Icing into small resealable plastic freezer bag. Cut off tiny corner of one end of bag. Pipe Icing decoratively onto cooled cookies; press candies into icing. Let stand at room temperature 20 minutes or until set. Store tightly covered at room temperature or freeze up to 3 months.

*Makes about 16 large cookies*

## Icing*

1½ cups powdered sugar
2 Tbsp milk plus additional if needed
½ tsp vanilla

*\*Prepared creamy or gel-type frostings in tubes may be substituted for Icing, if desired.*

Place all ingredients in medium bowl; stir with spoon until thick, but spreadable. (If Icing is too thick, stir in 1 tsp additional milk.)

173

# Greek Lemon-Herb Cookies

2½ **cups all-purpose flour**
1 **tsp baking soda**
¼ **tsp salt**
1 **cup butter, softened**
1¼ **cups sugar, divided**
2 **egg yolks**
4 **tsp grated lemon peel, divided**
½ **tsp dried rosemary leaves, crushed**

1. Preheat oven to 375°F. Combine flour, baking soda, and salt in large bowl.

2. Beat butter and 1 cup sugar in large bowl at medium speed until light and fluffy, scraping side of bowl once. Beat in egg yolks, 3 tsp lemon peel, and rosemary.

3. Gradually add flour mixture. Beat at low speed until well blended, scraping side of bowl once.

4. Combine remaining ¼ cup sugar and 1 tsp lemon peel in small bowl.

5. Roll tablespoonfuls of dough into 1-inch balls; roll in sugar mixture to coat. Place balls 2 inches apart on ungreased cookie sheets. Press balls to ¼ inch thickness using flat bottom of drinking glass.

6. Bake 10 to 12 minutes or until edges are golden brown. Cool on wire racks. Store tightly covered at room temperature or freeze up to 3 months.

*Makes about 4 dozen cookies*

# Ginger-Baked Bananas with Cinnamon Cream

4 firm, ripe bananas, peeled

¼ cup butter or margarine, melted and divided

1 Tbsp lemon juice

¼ cup packed brown sugar

¼ cup quick or old-fashioned oats

¼ cup pecans or walnuts, chopped

1 Tbsp crystallized ginger, chopped fine

1 tsp granulated sugar

½ tsp ground cinnamon

½ cup whipping cream

1. Preheat oven to 375°F.

2. Place bananas in baking dish large enough to hold them in single layer.

3. Combine 2 Tbsp butter and lemon juice in small bowl; drizzle evenly over bananas.

4. Combine brown sugar, oats, pecans, ginger, and remaining 2 Tbsp butter; sprinkle evenly over bananas.

5. Bake 15 to 18 minutes or until topping is bubbly.

6. To prepare Cinnamon Cream, combine granulated sugar and cinnamon in cup.

7. Beat chilled whipping cream at high speed until soft peaks form. Gradually beat sugar mixture into whipped cream until stiff peaks form.

8. Serve bananas warm with Cinnamon Cream.

*Makes 4 servings*

# Fantasy in Berries

1 bag (12 ounces) frozen, unsweetened raspberries, thawed

¼ cup plus 2 Tbsp sugar, divided

1 Tbsp fresh lemon juice

2 cups fresh strawberries, sliced

1 cup fresh raspberries

1 cup fresh blueberries

1 cup low fat ricotta cheese

1 tsp vanilla extract

¼ tsp almond extract

1. To prepare raspberry sauce, place thawed raspberries, ¼ cup sugar, and lemon juice in blender or food processor; process until smooth. Pour through strainer to remove seeds. Spoon 3 Tbsp raspberry sauce on each of 8 plates. Tilt each plate, rotating to spread raspberry mixture over bottom of plate.

2. Arrange ¼ cup sliced strawberries, 2 Tbsp fresh raspberries, and 2 Tbsp blueberries on top of sauce in desired pattern on each plate.

3. Place cheese, remaining 2 Tbsp sugar, and vanilla and almond extracts in clean blender or food processor; process until smooth and satiny. Spoon cheese mixture into pastry bag and pipe the pastry "cream" onto the berries, using about 2 Tbsp on each serving. (Use star tip to make rosettes or various sizes of writing tips to drizzle "cream" over berries.) Before serving, garnish with mint sprigs and edible flowers, such as pansies, violets, or nasturtiums, if desired.

*Makes 8 servings*

# Chapter Six

# Decorating with Herbs

The splendor of your herb garden doesn't have to be confined to your yard. You can extend your enjoyment of the herbs you grow by preserving them in crafts that beautify your home.

From wall hangings to potted arrangements, herbal jewelry to potpourri, the choice of herbal crafts is limitless. Herbs reward you again and again with their diversity. The projects in this chapter cover a variety of crafts and several levels of difficulty. It may take some time and patience to develop the skills necessary to complete the different projects, but this is time well spent. So relax, pull up a chair, brew an herbal tea, and choose a project to begin your journey!

Using herbs in your decor adds fragrance, color, and a subtle, nostalgic touch to your home. Sprigs of herbs, whether fresh or dried, make aromatic and attractive additions to any decorating style. Arrange fresh or dried stems of one or more herb varieties in a vase, pitcher, or other decorative container. Use fresh herbs as a filler in fresh floral bouquets—mint, curly parsley, basil, rosemary, sage, and southernwood are all good choices. Tie several branches of dried herbs together with ribbon or cloth and hang them upside down as individual sprays or in groups in your kitchen, dining room, or pantry.

Herb flowers are as stunning in the house as they are in the garden. Calendulas have large daisylike blooms ranging from lemon-yellow to intense orange; borage produces brilliant blue,

*Hanging dried herbs creates a relaxing, comfortable atmosphere. Tie them individually or together, mixing assorted colors and aromas.*

star-shaped blossoms; tansy blooms are a strong-scented mass of small, bright-yellow buttons; and lavender provides abundant violet-blue spikes. Nasturtiums give the most outstanding display of all. They bloom abundantly right up until the first fall frost in a tremendous range of brilliant colors. And, of course, you can dry herb flowers to preserve their beauty.

Create a more formal presentation by making an herb wreath. Wood, wire, or plastic foam wreath forms are available at most craft stores and florist shops, or you can make your own with plywood or a wire coat hanger. You can also experiment with grape vines, rope, woven rattan, and straw rings to create unique wreath designs.

You can use additional herbs, clusters of dried flowers, pinecones, groups of whole spices such as nutmeg and cinnamon sticks, or bows to provide accents to your wreaths once you've completed the foliage base. You can even make a fresh herb wreath (ours appears on page 196).

Two of the most popular and simple ways to exhibit the beauty and aroma of herbs are to make potpourri and sachets. Potpourri is a mixture of sweet-scented petals, leaves, and spices that slowly release their perfume as an air freshener. Potpourri is quick and easy to make, since you simply stir together the herbs, petals, and spices. Place some in attractive containers around your house, storing the remainder in an airtight container. To revitalize a potpourri that is losing strength, simply drop two or three drops of essential oil into the container and leave it covered tightly for a few days.

Sachets are small packets of concentrated scent. Slip them into bureau drawers, a hope chest, or clothing and linen closets to delicately perfume these closed spaces. Make sachet bags from netting, silks, satins, and laces to add a feeling of opulent luxury and plain cottons or ginghams to complement a simple country theme. Fill them with basic blends of fragrant herbs, or use the potpourri mixes described in this chapter. If you slip stitch your sachets, you need only loosen the thread to add fresh ingredients.

## Herbs for the Floral Arts

Herbs used in traditional dried arrangements such as wreaths and swags need to be durable. Though herb foliage tends to be on the fragile side when dried, many are hardy enough to use. Among these are lamb's ears, sage, santolina, silver king artemisia, and sweet Annie. Herb flowers that are good choices in arrangements include catnip, echinacea, hyssop, lavender, oregano, rue, thyme, and yarrow.

### Herbs for Dried Arrangements

| HERB | PARTS USED |
|---|---|
| Angelica | seed heads |
| Caraway | seed heads |
| Catnip | flowering stems |
| Cayenne | peppers |
| Echinacea | seed heads and flowering stems |
| Fennel | seed heads |
| Garlic | seed heads and bulbs |
| Ginkgo | leaves |
| Hops | strobiles |
| Horehound | flowering stems |
| Hyssop | flowering stems |
| Mullein | flower stalks |
| Oats | seed heads |
| Oregon grape | branches and leaves |
| Rosemary | stems and leaves |
| Rue | seed heads |
| Sage | stems and leaves |
| Santolina | leaves |
| Silver king artemisia | stems and leaves |
| Sorrel, French | seed heads |
| St. John's wort | seed heads |
| Sweet Annie | stems and leaves |
| Thyme | flowering stems |
| Wormwood | stems and leaves |
| Yarrow | flowers |

Herbs lend themselves beautifully to fresh arrangements. Because they are so seldom used in this form, your arrangement will also become a conversation piece. One of the most striking aspects of herbs in fresh arrangements is the contrast you can create between the different herb foliage. Often, this contrast is so beautiful that you don't need to add flowers to the arrangement! Any nontoxic herb with stiff stems and attractive foliage or flowers is appropriate for fresh arrangements.

## Drying Herb Foliage and Flowers for Arrangements

When using herb foliage for arrangements, it is usually best to use fresh herbs. Sage, for example, retains a more natural look when used fresh in wreath making. If you dry it in bundles to use it later, it is not only more brittle, but it is more difficult to shape. Herb flowers, on the other hand, should be dried first. Hanging them upside down to dry helps them retain a stiff stem and prevents the flower heads from drooping. See pages 27–28 for complete drying instructions.

### Drying Tips

- Pick fresh material on a warm, dry day.
- Leave enough stem so the bundles can hang to dry.
- Bundle the material in small bunches of 12 stems each or fewer, and secure the ends with rubber bands or string.
- Hang on a line or on a nail in a warm, dark place with plenty of air circulation. If your drying area is not dark, remove the flowers once they are dry and store them in a box. Light can bleach the herbs' colors.

## Pressed Flowers

Use herbs that are too delicate for fresh or dried arrangements in the elegant and beautiful craft of pressed flowers. Pick herb flowers and foliage at their peak, then dry and press them in a flower press or between sheets of absorbent paper. Mount the resulting preserved botanical materials on beautiful paper or fabric, then frame them to make lovely, old-fashioned keepsakes of this year's garden. You can choose many flowers to create a garland or bouquet style "picture," or design a re-creation of the single herb you've pressed.

The beauty of this craft is multiplied by the fact that you can press and preserve nearly any plant. Combinations that work well in the garden or flower vase also work well in a pressed flower picture. See page 31 for instructions on making your own flower press.

*To preserve herbs, press them or hang-dry them on a drying rack.*

Pick flowers and foliage on a warm, dry day. Experience will tell you which flowers you prefer to work with, but flowers and foliage that have graceful arching stems lend themselves to the art. Make sure foliage and flowers are clean and free of debris.

To dry them, place the flowers and foliage in an old phone book or on sheets of absorbent paper (newspaper without print works well) in a flower press. The plants must be pressed in single layers. Take apart thick flowers such as carnations by carefully slicing them with a razor blade or X-acto knife, then put them back together in your picture. Cover each layer of flowers with several sheets of paper.

Place a piece of rigid cardboard over the paper, then apply weight, such as several books. You may stack several layers of flowers, paper, and cardboard. If you have a flower press, place clean paper on the flowers, then tighten the wing nuts firmly. It may take a

week to ten days before the flowers are ready for removal from the press. Check them to be sure they are completely dry.

# Herbs for Dyeing

In centuries past, before the invention of modern dyes, plant materials were used to apply color to cloth. The resulting colors were generally more subtle than what we're accustomed to today. The art of the dyer was a complicated one. Some colors required many bushels of plant material just to dye one pound of wool. The dyer had to know what part of the plant to use as some plants release dye from the roots, others from the leaves, flowers, or bark. Some plants had to be used fresh; others could be used when dried. Still other herbs required the addition of a mordant (an additive that brings out the color and sets the dye). Sometimes just extracting the dye was an all-day affair!

As many people rediscover the subtle beauty of natural dyes, the art form has been given new life. The easiest way to begin dyeing with herbs is to use those that do not require a mordant. These herbs include turmeric, elderberries, dandelion flowers, sage, onion (skins), and raspberries. These herbs release their dye when boiled gently on the stove. Untreated wool takes on color best, but you might also try untreated cotton.

# Herbs for Fragrance

Herbs have long been used for fragrance. Their myriad uses range from providing perfumery to warding off disease. You can dry

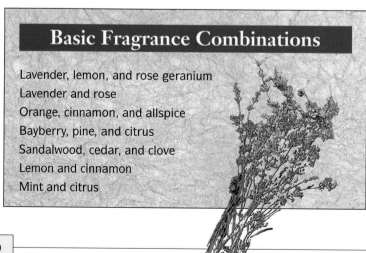

## Basic Fragrance Combinations

Lavender, lemon, and rose geranium
Lavender and rose
Orange, cinnamon, and allspice
Bayberry, pine, and citrus
Sandalwood, cedar, and clove
Lemon and cinnamon
Mint and citrus

## Say It with Herbs

Your crafts can speak for you if you know the language of plants. Follow this list of herbal sentiments:

| | |
|---|---|
| **Basil** | Love, good wishes, serious interest |
| **Bee balm** | Compassion, consolation |
| **Borage** | Roughness, rudeness |
| **Chamomile** | Humility, energy |
| **Cloves** | Dignity |
| **Cornflower (bachelor button)** | Delicacy |
| **Dianthus (carnations)** | Affection, maternal love |
| **Fennel** | Strength, flattery |
| **Horehound** | Health |
| **Lady's mantle** | Comfort, protection |
| **Lavender** | Devotion, suspicion, loyalty |
| **Marjoram** | Happiness, innocence |
| **Parsley** | Festivity, victory |
| **Rose geranium** | Preference |
| **Rue** | Virtue, understanding |
| **Sage** | Wisdom, domestic virtue, good health |
| **Tansy** | Resistance, immortal life |

The art of blending fragrances is difficult to master. It is always best to start with just two or three fragrances until you get to know what fragrances blend well with others. Listed on page 180 are some simple, basic combinations. With experience, you'll learn more complicated combinations.

*Lavender is one of the most popular decorative herbs because of its striking color and delightful fragrance. Place it in dried arrangements or simply tie it with ribbon to add a touch of color to any room.*

many fragrant herbs for use, whole or powdered, in sachets, potpourri, or the bath. Use other herbs in the form of essential oils. (See pages 203–205 for more on essential oils and their use in aromatherapy.) Many recipes for sachets and potpourri use both dried herbs and essential oils to produce a visually beautiful and fragrant end product.

You need to add fixatives to potpourri and sachets to hold their combined fragrances and make them last longer. Examples of commonly used fixatives are orris root, myrrh, benzoin, oak moss, reindeer moss, clary sage, sandalwood, patchouli, and frankincense.

# Dream Pillow

*The key ingredient in this dream pillow is hops, which have been used for centuries as a mild sedative. Hops, combined with sweet-smelling herbs and lemon oil, ensure that this pillow is both calming and "a dream" to make. Give your favorite restless sleeper a gift of a dream pillow along with extra "stuffing" and a recipe card with directions for refilling the pillow.*

## What You Need

### for Dream Pillow

- ¼ yard muslin fabric
- 2 ounces dried hops
- 1 ounce dried costmary leaves
- 1 ounce dried sweet woodruff leaves
- Lemon oil
- ¼ yard decorative fabric, such as calico
- Straight pins
- Sewing needle and thread

### for Sachet

- Scrap fabric
- ½ cup dried lavender flowers
- ½ cup dried rose petals
- 1 tsp benzoin powder
- Lavender oil
- Lace fabric (optional)
- Matching or coordinated satin ribbon
- Ribbon roses
- Sewing needle and thread
- Rubber band
- Pinking shears
- Glue gun and glue sticks

## Dream Pillow

**1.** Cut two 8×11-inch squares from the muslin fabric. Place one muslin square on top of the other and pin together around the edges.

**2.** Sew ½-inch seams along the two long sides and one short side of the fabric, leaving the second short side open. Turn the seams to the inside.

**3.** Place hops, costmary, and sweet woodruff in a stainless steel or glass bowl and mix together. Add a few drops of lemon oil and stir well.

**4.** Stuff the muslin pillow case with the herb mixture. Keep the pillow flat because you will place it in your bed pillow and you don't want it to make a lump. Turn the raw edges under, pin the opening shut, and slip stitch along the open end to enclose the contents of the pillow securely.

**5.** Cut two 9×12-inch squares of decorator fabric. Place one square on top of the other with the right sides together. Repeat step 2.

**6.** Slide the muslin pillow inside the decorator fabric sleeve. Turn the raw edges under, pin the opening shut, and slip stitch along the open end to enclose the muslin pillow.

**7.** When the pillow loses its scent, undo the slip stitching on both the inner and outer pillows. Remove the old contents, add a fresh herb mixture, and restitch the openings.

## Square Sachet

**1.** Cut desired size squares or rectangles from scrap fabric. Turn so right sides are together, and sew ¼-inch seams along three sides as in step 2 of the Dream Pillow. Turn seams to the inside.

**2.** In a stainless steel or glass bowl, mix together the lavender flowers, rose petals, benzoin, and lavender oil.

**3.** With a small spoon, fill the sachet with the lavender mixture.

**4.** Turn under the raw edges, pin, and slip stitch the open end shut.

## Sack-Style Sachet

**1.** Cut a circle 8 inches in diameter from the scrap fabric. If you have an open lace fabric scrap, cut a circle out of the fabric just slightly larger than the decorator fabric circle.

**2.** Lay the lace circle on a flat surface, right side down. Place the decorator fabric circle on top of it, right side down. Spoon a small amount of the sachet mixture into the center of the fabric.

**3.** Gather the fabric up to form a sack, and place a rubber band around the top to hold it closed. Cut the top of the fabric with pinking shears to neaten the raw edge of the fabric.

**4.** Cut a length of ribbon long enough to tie around the top of the sachet and make a bow. Tie the ribbon, hiding the rubber band underneath. Make a bow, and use the glue gun to affix a ribbon rose as a finishing touch.

# Quarter Hour Herb Wreath

*These small wreaths take only about 15 minutes to make once you learn the technique used. Making them is a perfect way to end an afternoon spent working in your garden—they are your just reward! These tiny inspirations also make quick, easy, inexpensive gifts for guests or to give at holiday time. Whether plain or dressed up with dried flowers, they are sure to please.*

## What You Need

- 12 inches of 18-gauge wire
- Floral tape
- 26-gauge florist wire, 1 paddle
- 15–20 small bunches each of fresh artemisia and dwarf catnip or herbs of your choice
- Ruler
- Wire cutters or pruners
- Glue gun and glue sticks

1. Form the 18-gauge wire into a circle about 3½ inches in diameter. Wrap the ends of the wire around the circular form so no ends protrude.

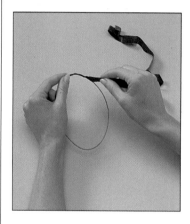

2. Pull out about a 12-inch length of floral tape from the roll. Floral tape becomes sticky as it is stretched, which keeps the herbs from slipping out of place as you attach them. Stretch out one end of the tape and wrap it around the wire form. Continue to wrap in this fashion until all the wire is covered.

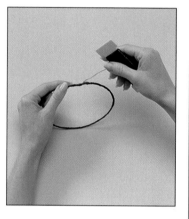

3. Attach the 26-gauge florist wire to the form by twisting the loose end around the taped form several times. Leave about 6 inches of wire between the form and the wire paddle.

4. Make a small bundle with your first herb. Keep the foliage in a tight bunch, and make sure your bunches are full but not bulky. You will need three to five stems of herbs for each bunch. Neatly trim off any excess stem with wire cutters. Bunches should be no longer than 3 to 4 inches when trimmed.

5. To attach the bunch, place it on the form near the florist wire and hold it there with your thumb. Keep the bunches to the inside of the form so the wire does not show through the finished wreath. Bring the florist wire around the bunch. Wire the bunch near the top of the stem, close to the foliage but not on it. Wrap the wire around two or three times to secure the bunch. Do not cut the florist wire until you have finished the wreath.

**6.** Form the next bunch of herbs. When you place the remaining bunches, work around the wreath in one direction. Be sure to place the second bunch just close enough to the first bunch to hide its stems. If you place the bunches too close together, you make more work for yourself and the wreath will look bulky. Continue making and adding the herb bunches.

**7.** To attach the final bunch and complete the wreath, lift the foliage of the first bunch and tuck the stems of the last bunch underneath. If a gap remains, hot glue a small piece of the herb into the gap to fill it.

**8.** Turn the wreath over and cut the florist wire, leaving a 6-inch tail attached. Create a loop to hang the wreath by tucking the loose end of the wire under a wire on the form about 2 inches away. Wrap the end of the wire around the loop you've just formed to secure it.

**9.** If you wish to decorate your wreath, hot glue small dried flowers or herb flowers into place. Dry flat in a warm place for about one week.

# Balsam Herb Bead Necklace

*This necklace, based on beads crafted from costmary leaves (which smell like balsam when dried), makes a beautiful and unique gift for yourself or for a friend. This creation is a twist on an age-old tradition—making rosary beads from rose petals. The gentle scent is released from the beads each time you wear your necklace. Keep a cotton ball dabbed with the scent oil in the jar in which you store your necklace to renew the fragrance during storage.*

## What You Need
(for about 60 beads)

- 150 fresh costmary leaves
- Fragrance oil of your choice
- 1 cup ground myrrh
- Vegetable oil
- Small spoon
- Straight pins
- A plastic foam tray or clean meat tray
- Dental floss
- Additional decorative beads
- Beading needle
- A clean glass jar with a lid
- Cotton ball
- Needle threader
- Necklace clasp

1. Remove the stems from the costmary leaves. Cut or slice them into pieces and place in a small saucepan. Just cover the leaves with water. Place on low heat and simmer until the water is gone. Just cover with water again and repeat this step.

2. Process the costmary in a food processor or blender until the mixture becomes a paste. Add a bit of water to process.

3. Return the costmary to the saucepan and heat on low until only the paste is left. This dries the paste and makes it easier to roll.

4. Transfer the mixture to a small ceramic or glass bowl. Add about 20 drops of fragrance oil to give the mixture a pleasant scent. Add myrrh 1 tablespoon at a time, until the mixture becomes one entire mass. From this point on you must work as quickly as possible.

5. Lightly oil the palms of your hands with vegetable oil. The oil helps keep the mixture from sticking to your hands and gives sheen to the beads. With the spoon, remove a small amount of the mixture and roll it in the palms of your hands to form a pea-sized bead.

6. Place a straight pin through the center of the bead and stick the pin into the plastic foam tray. So the bead doesn't flatten on the bottom, don't let it touch the tray. Continue rolling beads until you've used all the mixture. Wash and re-oil your hands as needed.

7. Place the tray of beads in a warm, dry spot. The beads may take three to five days to dry thoroughly.

8. Use a needle threader to thread the floss through the beading needle. String the balsam beads with standard beads, creating your own design. Add a necklace clasp if you wish.

9. Store the necklace in a jar when not in use. Moisten a cotton ball with the fragrance oil, and glue it to the lid of the jar to help the beads retain their fragrance.

# Herb-Dyed Easter Eggs

*A beautiful accent for your Easter table, these eggs are also a great way to introduce children to the world of herbs.*
*They'll watch wide-eyed as the colored eggs emerge from under the plant material. Use hard-boiled or*
*blown-out eggs, but note: Herb-dyed eggs are to be admired but not eaten!*

## What You Need

- White hen's eggs
- Onion skins, whole (yields burnt orange to russet)
- Dandelion flowers, whole (yields bright yellow)
- 2 tsp powdered turmeric (yields deep gold)
- Red cabbage, sliced fine (yields blue)
- 4 Tbsp elderberries, whole (yields gray)
- Sage branches, cut into large pieces (yields soft greenish-gray)
- Hat pin
- Paper towels
- Waxed paper
- White enamel spray paint
- Natural sponge

1. Hard-boil or blow out the eggs. To blow out an egg, pierce one end with a hat pin, then enlarge the hole slightly. Carefully make a slightly larger hole in the opposite end. Place the pin as far into the hole as you can and move it from side to side vigorously to break up the egg white and yolk.

2. Shake the egg vigorously, taking care not to break it. Blow hard through the small hole, catching the egg contents in a bowl. When the egg is empty, run a little water into it, shake vigorously, and blow out again. Repeat until the inside seems clean.

3. To speckle your eggs, spray some paint on waxed paper. Dip the sponge lightly into the paint and apply to the undyed eggs in a haphazard fashion as you would if you were sponging a wall. Sponge one half of the egg, let it dry, then sponge the other half. If you do not want the speckled effect, just skip this step.

4. Line a saucepan with paper towels and place the eggs to be dyed in the pan. Cover the eggs with water. Place the dye material in the pan. If you use onion skins, red cabbage, sage, or dandelion flowers, fill the pot with plant material to achieve the best color. To avoid having to turn the eggs and risk breaking them, make sure the water and dye material cover the eggs.

5. Simmer the eggs for 20 minutes, then check for color

by gently removing the dye material. If the color is not sufficient, continue to simmer until you achieve the desired color. With the red cabbage, simmer the eggs for 30 minutes, then remove them from the stove and let them cool. As the eggs cool, the blue color will gradually develop.

# Herb & Woodland Swag

*A morning in the garden and a stroll through the woods provide all the materials you need to make a beautiful herb swag. Swags make the perfect accent above a doorway or window. Substitute floral or seasonal accents such as larkspur or pussy willows if you can't find feathers. Use your imagination and make each swag a unique creation.*

## What You Need

- Block of Sahara foam
- 16-gauge wire, 6 inches
- Floral pick
- Floral tape
- 3–4 large bunches of silver king artemisia
- 1 stalk dried sweet Annie
- 1 bunch assorted dried wild grasses
- 8 sensitive fern fronds
- 6 large feathers, collected, or store-bought pheasant feathers
- 1 dried echinacea center
- Glue gun and glue sticks

1. Cut the floral foam to 4×3×1½ inches.

2. Make a loop out of the 16-gauge wire, and attach the loop to a floral pick. Tape with floral tape. Position the floral pick in the center of the foam on the back.

3. Trim all the artemisia stems to about 18 inches. Clean up the artemisia stems: Take all lower leaves off; keep only the top flowering parts and the very top and best-looking leaves.

4. Now you are ready to start the swag. First, determine the size you wish the finished swag to be; with the stems starting at 18 inches, the swag will measure about 13 inches on each side from the foam to the tip. You'll trim the artemisia as you go because depending on where you place the stems, you'll need different lengths. Trim a stem of artemisia, and place it at an angle midway up

the side of the foam. Angling the stems is important—working in straight lines does not look good in floral work. It's also important to work with the natural flow of the material: Artemisia has wonderful flow, and each piece should flow down, following its natural arch to achieve the best appearance. Trim another stem and place it in the opposite side of the foam. Take a smaller (about 7-inch) flower top and center it in the top of the foam.

5. Study the flow of the piece. You should see that you must vary the length of the artemisia you use, and vary the angle to achieve the correct proportions. Continue trimming and adding pieces. It is easiest to work first on one side for a while, then the other, to make sure the sides remain even.

6. When the sides start to fill in, move to the top. Proportions are very important here. Make sure you maintain the natural flow of the piece. As the swag begins to fill in, you

will need to begin working on the face of the foam. Use short pieces here to achieve a shorter, fluffy look—some pieces can stick out toward you. Continue to place the short pieces on the face of the foam with the same angles you used on the sides.

**7.** Continue filling in the swag until no gaps remain, the swag has a natural arch, and the sides are even.

**8.** Silver king artemisia's one drawback as a background is that it's bland and has almost no color variation; therefore, it desperately needs contrast. In this swag, sweet Annie gives this contrast. Place the sweet Annie at intervals that allow the artemisia to show through. Use your glue gun to place shorter pieces. Just a small amount of glue on the ends will hold the pieces in place as long as the glue catches in the artemisia.

**9.** Finish the swag by adding the grass, fern fronds, and feathers in the same manner you placed the sweet Annie, gluing if necessary. Place the echinacea in the center of the foam.

# Herbal Aromatherapy Candle

*Make an aromatherapy candle to help deliver the powerful properties of essential oils and improve your well-being. Use only pure essential oils—never synthetic fragrance oils—for aromatherapy, and make your candle from 100% beeswax—the all-natural candle wax. A candle made with lavender, neroli, or ylang-ylang oil sets the mood for relaxation; a candle with peppermint, rose geranium, or rosemary provides an invigorating atmosphere.*

## What You Need

- 12-ounce frozen juice can or candle mold
- Medium flat braided wicking
- 1 pound of beeswax
- Essential oil of your choice
- Awl, ice pick, or other sharp object
- Pencil
- Scissors
- Candle mold sealer or masking tape
- 1-pound coffee can
- Candy thermometer
- 6-inch length of coat hanger wire

1. Find and mark the center of the juice can bottom. First measure across one way, and mark the center with a line. Next measure perpendicular to this line, marking the center again. With an awl or ice pick, pierce the bottom of the can where the two lines intersect.

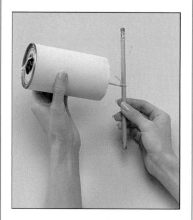

2. Run the wicking through the hole in the bottom of the mold. Tie the top end tightly around a pencil to prevent it from slipping back into the mold. Cut the wick on the bottom, leaving about 2 inches. Seal this hole with candle mold sealer or several layers of masking tape. If you use masking tape, it is a good idea to further seal the hole by dripping wax from another candle over the tape to prevent hot wax from leaking out the bottom.

3. Put the wax in the coffee can and the coffee can in the pan to create a double boiler. (Gently squeeze one side of the can to help you pour out the hot wax later.) Place the candy thermometer in the coffee can. Fill the saucepan with enough water to help melt the wax; heat over medium-low heat. Do not leave the wax unattended.

4. Heat the wax to 200°F. Turn off the heat. Stir in the essential oil.

5. Remove the coffee can from the saucepan. (Careful! It will be hot.) Gently pour the wax into the mold until the candle is the height you desire. Make sure the wick is centered in the mold, as this affects the way the candle burns. Wait a minute or two and then gently tap the mold with the handle of a knife. This releases any air bubbles that may be clinging to the inside of the mold.

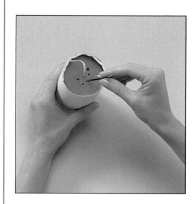

6. To speed the cooling process, place the mold in a bowl and slowly add cold water, taking care that the mold does not tip. After 10 to 15 minutes, you should top off the candle to prevent the formation of holes in the interior of the candle or a well in the bottom. To do so, pierce the wax all around the wick several times with the coat hanger

wire. Remelt the remaining wax and fill the holes, taking care not to pour wax above the original fill line.

**7.** Allow the candle to cool at least 12 hours. Remove the pencil and mold sealer, then remove the juice can. Beeswax doesn't unmold easily so you'll have to destroy the can—use scissors or a knife to make a small cut so you can tear the can. Trim the wick on the bottom, and trim the wick on the top to ½ inch. If the bottom of the candle is uneven, place a disposable pie plate on a warm burner, and work the candle over this surface until the bottom levels off. If you wish, decorate your candle with flowers; apply them with a little white glue.

# Old-Fashioned Pomander Balls

*In days gone by, pomander balls were made small enough to wear around the neck. Their purpose was to cover up the offending odors of everyday life and protect the wearer from disease. Our pomanders have a more pleasant purpose. They are wonderfully fragrant if hung in a closet or even in your car. They make ideal holiday gifts; just be sure to make them two months before the holidays so they have plenty of time to "cure."*

## What You Need

- 🌿 6 lemons, oranges, or limes
- 🌿 4 ounces each of powdered myrrh, cinnamon, clove, nutmeg, and ginger
- 🌿 Orange blossom oil (neroli) (optional) .
- 🌿 Plastic container with snap-on lid
- 🌿 Marker
- 🌿 6 ounces whole cloves
- 🌿 4 feet satin ribbon, ¼ inch wide
- 🌿 Assorted seed beads
- 🌿 Small dried flowers
- 🌿 Tapestry needle or similar sharp object
- 🌿 Widget or paring knife
- 🌿 Scissors

1. Starting at the stem end of the fruit, draw a line down both sides of the fruit with a marker. Go back to the starting point, and draw two more lines at right angles to the first ones. Cut away a strip of peel along these lines about ¼ inch wide. Cut through the skin of the fruit, but not through the zest. These ridges allow you to hang your pomander balls easily.

2. With the tapestry needle, pierce the peel of the fruit in each place you will insert a clove. Pierce ¼ of the fruit's peel, then insert a whole clove into each incision. Continue until you've covered the entire

surface of the fruit with cloves, except for where the peel has been cut away. Repeat steps 1 and 2 with each fruit.

3. In the plastic container, mix the powdered herbs, adding several drops of orange blossom oil if desired. Roll each pomander so the mixture clings to the entire surface. Place the fruit in the container of rolling

mixture and leave it in a warm place, with the lid slightly ajar.

4. In the next few weeks, check the pomanders daily. They will alternate from dry to wet, and you must adjust the lid accordingly. If the pomanders become very wet, set them out on a plate to dry. If too wet, the pomanders can get moldy; if mold develops

and progresses too far, your pomanders can be lost, so be sure to check them daily. Recoat with rolling mixture every other day or so. After a while, the pomanders shrink and become hard. This curing process usually takes about six weeks, but you must be the judge of when the pomanders are ready. Brush them off carefully before decorating.

**5.** To decorate a pomander, lay a length of satin ribbon around the pomander along one of the ridges, cross the ribbon at the bottom, and bring it up the length of the opposite ridge. Tie a knot at the top. Leave enough ribbon at the end to make a hanging loop by knotting the ribbon again. Cut the ribbon above the knot. Decorate with ribbon tails, bows, beads, and dried or satin flowers. The pomander pictured has a string of coordinated beads (about 8 inches long), gathered up and sewn to the ribbon on the underside of the pomander.

**6.** Pomanders never die! In fact, the pomander in the photo is about 10 years old! To renew their scent, place them back in the rolling mixture for a few weeks or dab them with fragrance oil.

# Tussy Mussies

*Tussy mussies are a lovely, old-fashioned way to display and give away fresh herbs.*

## What You Need

🌿 Fresh flowers, such as rose or tansy
🌿 Fresh herbs
🌿 Oasis holder

**1.** Insert the flower into the center of the oasis holder. Add small pieces of herbs around the center, rotating as you work, until the arrangement is 2 to 4 inches wide.

**2.** If you do not want to use an oasis holder, wrap the stems of a few flowers and herbs together in floral tape, then place the bouquet inside a decorative paper doily, a ring of wilt-resistant leaves such as ivy, or a lace circle. Add a small ribbon bow, if you want more color.

# Herbal Flower Pot Arrangement

*The simple flower pot arrangement is a staple in French countryside decor. The unpretentious materials used and the ease of making these arrangements appeal to busy gardeners. This arrangement makes a casual centerpiece for the lunch table or an attractive addition to a desktop. Experiment with other herbs and other types of containers for unlimited decorating possibilities.*

## What You Need

- Block of Sahara foam
- 3½-inch terra cotta pot, old or new
- 24–36 single stems of dried nigella transformer
- 6–12 stem bunches of dried lavender flowers
- 18 floral picks, 4 inches
- 6–12 stem bunches of dried rue seed heads
- Sheet moss
- 6 multi-flowered echinacea stems, dried
- Twist ties
- Glue gun and glue sticks

1. Trim the block of foam, tapering one end so it fits snugly in the pot. Cut off any excess foam above the rim.

2. To begin the arrangement, place the nigella transformer into the foam at the rear of the pot, slightly fanning them out to each side. The stems should protrude from the top of the rim about 8 to 9 inches in the center and lean back slightly. You need only place the stems about ½ inch into the foam to hold them firmly. If too much space shows between the stems, tie a twist tie about halfway down the stems to help hold them together.

3. Take apart the lavender bunches. Create new bunches, keeping the flower heads even at the top of each bunch. You need at least six bunches, and each bunch should have six to ten lavender stems. Trim the excess stem from each form, and attach each bunch to a floral pick. Place the pick into the foam, so the lavender covers the bare stems of the nigella.

4. Repeat step 3 with the rue seed heads.

5. Cut the sheet moss to fit the top of your pot and glue it in place. Use extra sheet moss to hide the twist tie.

6. Cut echinacea heads to varying lengths and position them to hide the rue stems. You may have to glue some right to the top of the pot; others will be able to stick in the foam. Continue until you've covered all the stems.

7. If you wish, you can decorate the pot with paint or a simple ribbon.

# Pressed Herb and Flower Picture

*Evoke the elegance and romance of the Victorian era with a beautiful pressed flower picture made with herbs from your garden.
The picture shown features handmade herbal paper, but you may choose to mount yours on other types of paper or
fabric. Capture a moment in time: Press flowers as a keepsake of your garden, or in remembrance of a favorite vacation
spot or a special occasion such as a wedding.*

## What You Need

- 🌿 Fresh herb foliage and flowers, garden flowers
- 🌿 Old telephone book or a small flower press
- 🌿 Construction paper or newspaper
- 🌿 Attractive paper or card stock
- 🌿 White glue
- 🌿 Picture frame
- 🌿 Tweezers
- 🌿 Toothpicks

1. Pick flowers and foliage on a dry day. Pick more than you think you will need, as not all those you press will turn out as well as you would like. If you use a phone book, leave at least 15 pages between each layer of plant material.

2. It can take up to a week for the flowers to dry properly. When you retrieve the pressed flowers, have tweezers handy as some of them can be quite fragile. Also have a box for storage handy if you plan to press a lot of flowers.

3. Practice the gluing technique with some expendable flowers before attempting a large project. Mount flowers on clean, dry paper. It takes only a tiny amount of glue on a toothpick to hold a flower in place.

4. You can work in a traditional pressed flower pattern as we have, or try your hand at a geometric pattern, which has a more modern look. Use tweezers to place flowers on a clean sheet of paper. Arrange your pattern of flowers first, so you can plan your design. Then simply transfer your design to a second piece of paper, gluing the herbs as you go. Start with flowers that lie under others; glue overlapping flowers last. Allow glue to dry thoroughly, and frame.

# Living Herbal Wreath

*This live wreath is made possible with a moist, foam wreath ring used by florists. The beauty of this elegant wreath comes from the variety of plants used. Change the wreath design according to the season by using fresh-cut herbs from your garden. This wreath makes an especially beautiful centerpiece for your table!*

## What You Need

🌿 Oasis fresh wreath form (contains floral foam for fresh flowers)

🌿 ½ bushel fresh herb foliage; pick many varieties. Our wreath contains sage, purple sage, mint, lamb's ears, santolina, germander, lemon balm, echinacea flowers, hyssop flowers, golden oregano, and *Artemisia stellerana.*

🌿 Fresh flowers

🌿 Pruners or wire cutters

1. Soak the wreath form in cold water for at least one hour. Remove it and allow the excess water to drip out.

2. As you work, trim the herb stems to the desired length; in most cases that will be 3 to 4 inches. Working the inner surface first, begin placing the foliage in the foam. Always position at least 3 or 4 stems of the same herb together or they will become lost in the overall picture. Face all foliage in the same direction and at an angle. Occasionally it is okay to place a piece straight into the foam.

3. Work this wreath in the following pattern: Place sage at intervals along the inner surface and then the top. Then select another herb and work it in right next to the sage in all the same places. Place another herb and so on. This technique gives continuity to both the wreath and your working order, and the wreath will appear to have no segmented areas.

4. After you cover the inner and top surfaces, proceed with the outside of the wreath. When all the foliage is in place, add a few seasonal flowers for a spectacular finishing touch.

5. By the time you finish the wreath, some of the foliage may look a bit tired. To perk it up, mist the wreath with a spray bottle of water, and refrigerate for a few hours. The wreath will need water from time to time, but do not keep it too wet. Mist it, then place it in the refrigerator at night to prolong its life.

# Herbal Wreath

*Completed herbal wreaths are as varied as the greens used to make them. Use a single species or a mixture of herbs.*
*Some combinations will look delicate and airy, others dense and handsome. Add other dried materials such as baby's breath*
*and statice, too. Hang the wreath or use it to surround a punch bowl or a candlestick base.*

## What You Need

🌿 Fresh or partially dried foliage and dried flowers
🌿 Florist wire or twine
🌿 Wire wreath base
🌿 Hand pruners

1. Use hand pruners to cut herb branches into 5-inch pieces.

2. Use a spool of florist wire or twine to attach the plant materials to the wire base. Lay a bundle of two or three herb

pieces on top of the wire base, then wrap the twine firmly for three or four turns around both the base and the herb stems, starting halfway down the stems and spiralling down toward the cut ends. Lay another bundle on top of the first herb's stems to cover them, and continue spiral wrapping until you fill the form.

3. Gently lift the first bundle of the circle to squeeze the last one or two bundles in. Flatten the lifted bundle back over the final ones by gently massaging it in place with your hand. Add pieces to thin or narrow spots, and thin or trim with pruning shears where the greenery is too dense or straggling.

4. Leave the wreath lying flat until the herbs are completely dried to prevent the wreath from becoming misshapen with further drying.

# Summer Garden Potpourri

*Potpourri brings your garden's bouquet into your home. Place this colorful potpourri in any room in a variety of containers such as antique bowls, crystal, baskets, and decorative jars; add it to sachets; or place it in cellophane bags tied with ribbon to give as gifts. This is a lightly scented potpourri; if you prefer it stronger, double the amount of essential oils.*

## What You Need

- ⅛ cup orris root powder
- 1 tsp whole cloves
- 3 cinnamon sticks, 6 inches, broken
- 3 drops lime essential oil
- 3 drops orange essential oil
- 9 drops rose geranium essential oil
- 1 cup dried yellow rose petals
- 1 cup dried pink rose petals
- 1 cup uva ursi leaves
- ½ cup bay leaves
- ¼ cup dried orange peel
- ⅓ cup lavender flowers
- 3 to 4 pressed assorted flowers (optional)
- 3 to 4 whole dried assorted rosebuds
- Airtight container or plastic storage bag

1. Mix first three ingredients in a glass or ceramic bowl. Add oils and mix.

2. Add remaining ingredients except for whole rosebuds and pressed flowers. Mix thoroughly.

3. Place mixture in an airtight container and leave for four to six weeks in a dark place to cure. Stir mixture every couple of days to blend and distribute ingredients well.

4. Transfer potpourri to a decorative container. Add whole dried rosebuds and pressed flowers to decorate. When the fragrance diminishes, you can revitalize the scent by placing the potpourri into a storage bag. Add a few drops of essential oils to some cotton balls, place the cotton balls inside the bag of potpourri, and seal. Leave cotton balls in the bag for two to three days.

**Hint:** It's easy to create your own potpourri with the scents you find most pleasing. Assemble dried herbs, citrus peels, spices, dried flowers, and essential oils. Use larger amounts of those with more delicate scents and smaller quantities of those with stronger scents. When the blend suits you, mix in 1 tablespoon chopped orris root to each cup of mixture to fix the scent.

# Herb Pinwheel Wreath

*A classic wreath of fragrant dried herbs placed pinwheel fashion creates a design of delicate beauty. The use of a variety of herbs adds delightful color and scent to this wreath, which will enhance any room.*

## What You Need

- 10-inch straw wreath
- Spanish moss, about ½ pound
- Floral pins
- Gray carpet thread
- German statice, about 30 clusters, 6 inches
- 12-inch chenille stem
- 60 steel floral picks
- Pliers
- Artemisia, about 30 clusters, 7 to 8 inches
- Tacky glue
- 1 package dried pennyroyal
- 1 bunch dried sweet Annie
- 1 bunch dried heather
- 10–12 cinnamon sticks, about 6 inches
- 1 bunch tansy
- 1 package dried globe amaranth, purple
- Dried bay leaves
- Statice sinuata, purple
- Straw flowers, burgundy
- Burgundy and mauve raffia
- Surface sealer

1. Lay the straw wreath in a bed of Spanish moss. Bring moss around wreath to cover it, and secure with floral pins. Wrap the gray carpet thread around the wreath to hold the moss in place.

2. Make a chenille hanger. Bend the chenille stem evenly into a U. Twist the U end into a 1- or 2-inch oval loop. Positioning the loop at the top, wrap and twist the ends around the wreath tightly.

3. Lay the stem of a small cluster of German statice on the prongs of a steel floral pick. Bend the prongs around the stems with pliers. Make 30 picks. Place the statice into

the wreath, distributing the clusters evenly. Direct all materials in the same direction. Repeat for clusters of artemisia.

4. Dip stems of all other plants into tacky glue and place into wreath. Place pennyroyal, sweet Annie, heather, and cinnamon sticks first. Then place tansy, globe amaranth, bay leaves, statice sinuata, and straw flowers.

5. Shred three or four strands of both burgundy and mauve raffia with a straight pin. Form shredded raffia into a bow, and tie in the center with another strand of raffia. Slip floral pin through the center of the raffia strand, dip the end of the pin into glue, and push it into the bottom of the wreath. Spray wreath with surface sealer to protect dried materials from shattering.

# Potpourri Heart Wreath

*Fragrant fabric hearts trimmed with lace, ribbons, and flowers decorate a lace-covered wreath base.
This versatile wreath is embellished with a lovely silk flower nosegay and a loopy lace bow. Remove the hearts and give
them as afternoon bridge favors or to guests as bridal shower favors. Make an extra set of hearts and give the
wreath to the bride-to-be for her new home.*

## What You Need

- Flat foam wreath, 12×1½×1 inch
- 5 yards French blue moire ribbon
- Craft glue
- Scissors
- 8 yards eggshell lace ribbon, 3 inches wide
- 28-gauge white-covered wire
- Wire cutters
- Stapler and staples
- Tracing paper and pencil
- ¼ yard small pink and blue floral print fabric
- Needle and thread
- Potpourri
- 3 yards eggshell lace, ½ inch wide
- 8 round head pearl corsage pins, 2 inches long
- Small silk flower cluster, about 5 inches in diameter
- Green floral tape
- ⅛ inch satin ribbon: 3 yards French blue and 1¼ yards rose mauve
- 8 small pink silk flowers

1. Wrap wreath with moire ribbon; secure ends of ribbon with glue. Wrap 3 yards of lace ribbon over moire ribbon. Secure ends with glue.

2. To make wreath hanger, bend wire into U. Twist the U end into a 1-inch oval loop. Bend the cut ends at right angles to the loop and push them into the wreath until the loop is flush with the wreath. Secure to the wreath with hot glue placed on the twisted end of the hanger.

3. Using 2 yards of lace ribbon, make ½-inch pleats approximately an inch apart; staple. Attach pleated ribbon to back edge of wreath with glue.

4. Use remaining lace ribbon to make six-loop bow (about 9 inches wide, with 8-inch streamers). Do not add a center loop to this bow. Glue the bow to the wreath.

5. Trace the heart pattern onto tracing paper with a pencil, and cut out. Double fabric, and use heart as a pattern piece. Cut out 8 hearts.

6. With wrong sides together, stitch around heart ½ inch from edge; leave 2 inches unstitched. Fill hearts with 1½ to 2 tablespoons of potpourri. Stitch heart closed and trim edges ¼ inch from stitching. Glue lace ruffle on top of the stitching on front side of the heart. Make 8 hearts.

7. Place a corsage pin through the center of each heart and pin to wreath.

8. Tape the stems of the flower cluster together with floral tape. Using 1¼ yards each of French blue and rose-mauve satin ribbon together, make a 16-loop bow (4 inches wide, with 4- to 5-inch streamers). Wire bow to stem of flower cluster. Glue cluster to center of bow on wreath.

9. Make 8 small shoestring bows from the blue satin ribbon. Glue a small pink flower onto the center of each bow. Glue a bow to each heart.

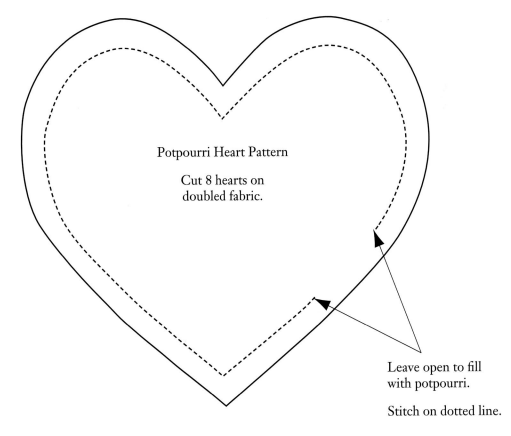

Potpourri Heart Pattern

Cut 8 hearts on doubled fabric.

Leave open to fill with potpourri.

Stitch on dotted line.

# Chapter Seven

# The Beauty of Herbs

**C**leopatra had Egypt, but she didn't have Max Factor. The Queen of the Nile maintained her legendary beauty by using herbs. So did Napoleon's Empress Josephine. For centuries, women and men alike have made cosmetic use of the aromatic and healthful essences derived from herbs.

The Greeks, who considered the human form an *object d'art*, knew well the rejuvenating secrets of unguents and oils. And in bath houses throughout the imperial city, Romans sought herbal soaks, rubs, and rinses to keep them looking fine and feeling fit. Today we don't have to rely on herbal beautifiers. The manufacture of cosmetics is a multibillion-dollar industry. Yet in this high-tech, high-stress world of ours, more and more people are turning to herb-based—and often homemade—perfumes, baths, soaps, powders, and lotions.

Why are so many of us using beauty products made with herbs? First, cosmetics are expensive. Second, most contain chemicals that may cause rashes and allergies in people with sensitive skin. Third, many cosmetic companies test chemical products on laboratory animals before putting them on the market for human use, a practice considered abhorrent by people concerned about the ethical treatment of animals. Finally, herbal cosmetics are now quite easy to obtain. With the current enthusiasm for natural

*An herb harvest such as this yields many of the herbs you can use in beauty products.*

products, many specialty shops and health products stores offer a broad variety of herbal cosmetics.

But if you want to be certain of what you're putting on your skin, or if you simply wish to feel more connected to the Earth, you can grow your own herbs and make your own lotions, creams, and powders. And homemade herbal cosmetics make inexpensive and innovative gifts for friends.

Unless you have a very large garden to provide a generous supply of herbs, as well as the equipment necessary for distilling herbal oils, you'll need to buy at least some of the ingredients to make your own cosmetics. Your local health supply store probably stocks most of what you need: scented waters, essential oils, powdered orris, and other ingredients.

## Benefits of Herbal Cosmetics

Herbs are natural and most of them are good for you. Unlike synthetic chemicals, herbs work in harmony with the body's natural forces and contain nutrients your skin and hair need to thrive. Many boast antiseptic and antibacterial properties, so not only can you cleanse and pamper your skin, you can heal it at the same time.

Which herbs are best to use in cosmetics? It depends on your skin and hair type. If you have normal skin—and very few of us do—your complexion is soft and translucent and requires little more than a good cleansing to keep it healthy. If your skin is oily, you should use herbs that decrease oil production. Taut, dry skin needs moisturizing herbs and mild cleansers to prevent further drying. Most people have combination skin—some parts are oily and other parts are dry. If you fall into that category, use different herb products on each type of skin or choose herbs that are good for most skin types such as lavender, geranium, and rose.

## Aromatherapy

Many of the cosmetics you'll want to make contain essential herbal oils—the aromatic, fragrant substances in plants and the basis of a growing cosmetic and healing technique known as aromatherapy.

*The source of an herb's aroma is its essential oil.*

Aromatherapy is the practice of using fragrant plants as medicine. Different natural aromas have different effects on our physiology and our emotional state—inhaling various aromas can promote relaxation, increase mental awareness, or improve sleep, for example. The body also benefits from herbal oils absorbed through massages, baths, or preparations rubbed on the skin.

Although aromatherapy may seem new to us, it's been around for at least 5,000 years. The Egyptians prized scented oils, and the Bible is full of references to anointing herbs used by Hebrew kings and queens. You've already experienced aromatherapy even if you didn't call it by that name. Perhaps the smell of fresh-baked bread conjures up the image of your beloved grandmother's kitchen. Or the smell of new-mown hay makes you recall the wonderful summers you spent on your uncle's farm when you were a child. These smells, and the images they produce, affect your mood and your state of mind—they can even affect your health.

The source of an herb's aroma is its naturally occurring essential oil. You can purchase essential oils for use in aromatherapy. Distilled from many pounds of plant material, these oils are very concentrated. (In some cases it takes more than one ton of plant material to distill an ounce of essential oil!) Essential oils should always be used with caution, and in very small doses, as they can elicit strong reactions from those who inhale them or use them on their skin. If you use them topically, be sure to dilute them in an almond or vegetable oil.

You can use essential oils medicinally in a variety of ways. They are typically dispensed by placing a small amount of the oil into another liquid. An essential oil such as eucalyptus added to a pot of steaming water becomes a natural vaporizer for a stuffy nose, sinus infection, or chest cold. Added to a liniment or massage oil and applied topically, essential oils can treat sore muscles, infections, and inflammation. Rubbed into the temples or brushed through the hair, essential oils can relieve headaches; added to bath water, they can promote relaxation.

Other ways to achieve the effects of aromatherapy are to add essential oils to potpourri or place a few drops on a cotton ball and tuck it into your pillow or in a dresser drawer. You can also add essential oils to the rinse cycle of your washing machine. You can wear essential oils as you would perfume (diluted, of course!), or place a few drops in a potpourri cooker, on a light bulb or light ring, or in a special aromatherapy diffuser that disperses the aromas without using heat.

## Essential Oils for Facials

For a soothing facial steam, mix oils and sprinkle on the surface of a bowl of hot water. Or make a lotion by adding ingredients to vegetable oil. Store in a dark bottle in a cool, dry area that receives little or no light.

| Normal Skin | Dry Skin | Oily Skin |
|---|---|---|
| 6 drops geranium | 7 drops geranium | 12 drops lemon |
| 3 drops jasmine | 4 drops rose | 8 drops cypress |
| 16 drops lavender | 14 drops sandalwood | 5 drops juniper |

## Healing Benefits of Essential Oils for Skin Care and Aromatherapy

| Herb | Uses |
| --- | --- |
| Basil | Oily skin, stress, fatigue, depression, migraines |
| Caraway | Bruises, rough skin |
| Chamomile | Sensitive, puffy, inflamed skin, rashes, enlarged capillaries, insomnia, depression |
| Eucalyptus | Oily skin, acne, infections, fatigue |
| Fennel | Bruises, fatigue |
| Geranium | Acne, wrinkles, eczema, inflammation, burns, infection, anxiety, depression |
| Jasmine | Dry, sensitive, mature skin, insomnia, anxiety, depression |
| Juniper | Acne, eczema, dandruff, fatigue, anxiety |
| Lavender | Wrinkles, burns, inflammation, infections, rashes, stretch marks, depression, nervousness, insomnia |
| Lemon | Oily skin, infections, depression |
| Lemon Grass | Oily skin, infections |
| Marjoram | Bruises, burns, inflammation, infections, irritability |
| Myrrh | Mature, chapped, or dry skin, eczema, itching, bruises, wounds, varicose veins, infection, fatigue |
| Peppermint | Dry skin, itching, fatigue, headaches, nervous disorders |
| Rose | Mature skin, burns, wrinkles, infections, headache, insomnia, depression |
| Rosemary | Dry, mature skin, dandruff, mental fatigue |
| Sage | Oily skin, acne, excessive perspiration, nervousness, grief |
| Sandalwood | Acne, dry skin, rashes, inflammation, insomnia, nervous tension |
| Tea Tree | Acne, rash, infections |
| Thyme | Infections |

True essential oils are distilled from herbal flowers and leaves. Because this process is difficult and time-consuming, essential oils can be expensive, but many health food, nutrition, and specialty stores carry essential oils in small glass bottles at a reasonable price. Oils such as peppermint, orange, or cinnamon are quite inexpensive. You'll pay more for precious flower oils such as rose and jasmine; however, you need to use only a couple of drops at a time to benefit from the preparation's healing properties. And because you use such tiny quantities, your initial investment is likely to last many years.

There are many advantages to using essential oils. They are easily incorporated into any sort of base creams, lotions, ointments, gels, toilet waters, and perfumes. Their scents are strong and appealing. And the skin readily absorbs their healing gifts.

The use of essential oils topically requires great care: Many essential oils such as thyme, peppermint, and cinnamon can irritate and even burn the skin. While other essential oils, such as tea tree and lavender, tend to be less irritating, as a general rule, always dilute essential oils with almond or a vegetable oil, and use them cautiously on the skin. Be extra careful when using essential oils with children, highly allergic individuals, and those with sensitive skin.

Be aware that "perfume" and "fragrance" oils are not the same as essential oils. Essential oils are natural plant constituents that have been extracted from the plant. They are aromatic, oily liquids. Perfume and fragrance oils are synthetic and are not derived from plants. Sometimes perfume and fragrance oils are labeled as "essential oils"; try to buy essential oils from a reputable source that will verify that plants are the source of the oils. Never use perfume oils internally. Use essential oils internally only under the guidance of an experienced herbalist or naturopathic physician.

## Herbal Complexion Products

There's no end to the list of cosmetic preparations you can make from herbs. Virtually any product you can buy in an expensive boutique you can make yourself. These include creams, lotions, aftershaves, deodorants, dusting powders, and even toothpastes.

*Herbs are used in a variety of cosmetic products.*

Most cosmetics take little time to make. The only drawback is that many homemade herbal cosmetic preparations don't store well because they don't contain chemical preservatives. So prepare small batches of skin-care products; store in dark jars or in the refrigerator. You can expect the cosmetics you make yourself to last several months.

## Lemon Cleansing Cream

This soothing cream refreshes and cleans your skin thoroughly. It's especially good for eliminating excess oils and smoothing wrinkles. Plus, the lemon gives it antiseptic qualities.

*1 Tbsp beeswax*
*3 Tbsp vegetable oil*
*1 Tbsp witch hazel (purchase at a pharmacy)*
*1 Tbsp lemon juice*
*$\frac{1}{8}$ tsp borax*
*6 drops lemon essential oil*

Over low heat, gently melt beeswax in vegetable oil. Beat for five minutes until mixture has a creamy, smooth consistency. In a

| Herbs for Facials | | |
|---|---|---|
| Chamomile | Scented Geranium | Rosemary |
| Hyssop | Peppermint | Sage |
| Lavender | Rose | |

separate pot, gently warm witch hazel and lemon juice; stir in borax until dissolved and add to cream. Beat steadily. After the cream has cooled, stir in the lemon oil. Spoon into clean jars, label, and date. Store in a cool place.

## Astringent Facial Scrub

*$\frac{1}{8}$ cup astringent herbs, such as sage, yarrow, or chamomile, ground fine*
*$\frac{1}{4}$ cup oatmeal, ground fine, or cornmeal*
*Cider vinegar*

This cleansing preparation is great for oily skin. And you've probably got the ingredients in your kitchen cabinet. Combine herbs and meal, then add enough vinegar to make a paste. Scrub your face with this mixture and rinse with cool water.

| Essential Oils for Skin Care | | |
|---|---|---|
| **Normal Skin** | **Oily Skin** | **Dry Skin** |
| Geranium | Basil | Jasmine |
| Lavender | Cypress | Peppermint |
| | Eucalyptus | Rose |
| | Lemon | Rosemary |
| | Lemon Grass | Sandalwood |
| | Sage | |

*One of the most popular herbs for use in cosmetic products is chamomile. Chamomile infusions make excellent skin cleansers, and creams and lotions made with this herb treat irritated skin.*

## Cleansing Facial Steam

To open your pores and give your skin a deep cleaning, add 1 heaping tablespoon of fresh or dried fragrant herbs to a quart of steaming water in a warmed bowl. Close your eyes and place your face over the bowl (not too close, or the steam could burn your skin). Cover your head and the bowl with a bath towel. Allow the vapors to cleanse your face for five to ten minutes total—raise your head away from the steam every few minutes for a few-second break. At the end of the treatment, splash your face with lukewarm water, then with cool water. If you have dry skin, apply a cream or moisturizer. You may also use cotton balls to apply an astringent lotion if your skin is especially oily.

## Lotions

If winter whips your hands red and raw, keep a supply of this soothing, nourishing lotion on hand. It acts as a softener and emollient.

## Hand Healing Lotion

*2 Tbsp cocoa butter*
*¼ cup sweet almond oil*
*1 tsp beeswax*
*3 Tbsp strong infusion of chamomile flowers*

Heat the cocoa butter, oil, and beeswax until the wax melts. Warm the herb infusion. Put the oil mixture in a blender, turn on low, and slowly add the infusion until well blended.

## Aftershave Lotion

If shaving irritates your skin, try this lotion on your face or any-where you shave. It's styptic (stops bleeding from razor nicks), astringent, and stimulating.

*½ cup fresh or dried sage leaves*
*¼ cup fresh or dried yarrow flowers*
*¼ cup fresh or dried lavender flowers*
*Grain or rubbing alcohol*
*15 drops peppermint oil (optional, if you like the smell of menthol)*

Place herb leaves and flowers in a quart jar. Fill the rest of the jar with grain or rubbing alcohol, making sure the alcohol covers the herbs. Allow to sit for two weeks. Give it a shake once a day. Then strain, and dilute with water to desired strength.

If your skin is dry, add 1 Tbsp of glycerine.

## Powders

Body powders are easily made by adding powdered, sifted herbs and/or a few drops of your favorite essential oils to ½ pound corn-starch. If you use essential oils, add 8 drops, a drop at a time, to the cornstarch. Mix thoroughly to distribute the oil throughout the powder base.

## Herbs for Powders

Cloves     Coriander     Sandalwood
Lavender

## Herbal Deodorant

This powder won't stop you from perspiring, but it will keep you feeling cool and confident. If you have sensitive skin, test the powder on your wrist before applying it to your underarms.

*½ tsp cloves*
*1 tsp myrrh*
*1 Tbsp coriander seeds*
*1 tsp cassia*
*2 Tbsp lavender flowers*
*1 tsp thyme*

Grind and mix ingredients. Pat under arms as you would with a deodorant.

## Herbal Perfumes

To make a pleasant perfumed toilet water, add a few drops of essential oil—lavender, rose, orange, and lemon are good choices—to an ounce of grain alcohol. Shake every day for one week. Keep your herbal perfume in a small, tightly stoppered bottle.

## Herbal Hair Care

Did you know that the shampoo you buy is basically a detergent? Treat yourself to a natural herbal wash that will nourish your hair and leave it healthy and shining. Rosemary is a wonderful herb to bring out highlights in brunettes; chamomile leaves make blonde hair glow. And sage reputedly restores gray hair to its natural color.

## Basic Shampoo

In a blender, barely cover a soap-producing herb such as soapwort leaves with water. Strain and use as a shampoo base to which you may add an infusion of herbs or a few drops of essential oils. The proportion is 3 parts of soapwort infusion to 1 part herbal infusion.

## Quick Shampoo

If you're in a hurry and don't have the herbs or the time to prepare a soapwort infusion, add 2 tablespoons of a strong herbal decoction or 4 drops of essential oil to a cup of gentle or baby shampoo.

## Herbal Rinses

After you've shampooed your hair, give it added luster by conditioning with an herbal rinse. To make a rinse, add 3 tablespoons of dried or fresh herbs to a pint of boiling water. Steep for half an hour, strain and cool. Add ¼ cup apple cider vinegar if you wish to use a vinegar tincture.

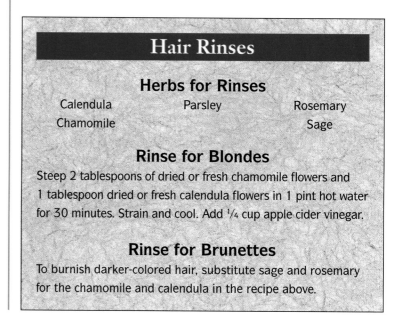

## Hair Rinses

### Herbs for Rinses

Calendula     Parsley     Rosemary
Chamomile            Sage

### Rinse for Blondes

Steep 2 tablespoons of dried or fresh chamomile flowers and 1 tablespoon dried or fresh calendula flowers in 1 pint hot water for 30 minutes. Strain and cool. Add ¼ cup apple cider vinegar.

### Rinse for Brunettes

To burnish darker-colored hair, substitute sage and rosemary for the chamomile and calendula in the recipe above.

## Herbal Baths

What could be more pleasant—and luxurious—than a soothing soak in an herbal bath? When you bathe with herbs, your skin absorbs their essential oils. Not only are you clean when you step out of the tub, you feel energized and ready to take on the world.

A simple method of preparing an herbal bath is to gather several sprigs of one or more fresh or dried herbs and place them under the hot water tap as you fill up the tub. To avoid getting bits of leaves and flowers in the water, place the sprigs inside a fine-meshed drawstring bag or cheesecloth pouch and hang it under the tap or allow it to float while the tub fills. After the tub is filled, squeeze the bag to get out all the herbal extracts. Discard the herbs and allow the bag to dry before using it again.

Another approach is to add 1 or 2 drops of essential oil to the tub water. Remember that herbal oils are highly concentrated, so a little goes a long way. Avoid using oils such as peppermint, clove, and cinnamon. These hot oils can burn sensitive skin.

You can also make your own herbal bath salts. Mix 1 cup table or sea salt with ¼ teaspoon essential oil such as lavender or rosemary. Mix well and store in an airtight container. Use a handful per bath.

### Herbs for Baths

**All-Purpose Bath Herbs**

Basil
Calendula
Chamomile
Fennel
Geraniums, scented
Ginger (a hot herb, so use carefully)
Lavender
Lovage
Marjoram
Mint
Parsley
Rosemary
Sage
Southernwood
Thyme

**Herbal Baths for Restful Sleep**

Chamomile
Hops
Lavender
Valerian

## Herbal Oral Care

For strong, healthy teeth and gums, try an herbal toothpaste or mouthwash. It'll leave your mouth feeling clean and refreshed.

### Herbal Toothpaste

*1 Tbsp baking soda*
*1 drop peppermint oil*
*1 tsp powdered sage*
*Water*

Baking soda is an excellent tooth cleaner and whitener. Peppermint is antiseptic and refreshes your breath. And sage is one of the best herbs for oral health. Mix and add just enough water to form a paste.

### Herbal Mouthwash

*2½ cups distilled water*
*1 tsp fresh mint leaves*
*1 tsp rosemary leaves*
*1 tsp anise seed*
*1 tsp myrrh*

Rosemary is a strong antiseptic, and mint imparts a sweet smell to breath. Infuse herbs for 20 minutes in hot water. Strain and use as a gargle. To preserve your mouthwash, add 1 teaspoon tincture of myrrh, a strong antibacterial herb.

### Herbs for Oral Care

| | | |
|---|---|---|
| Cloves | Parsley | Rosemary |
| Lavender | Peppermint | Sage |

# Herb Resources

## Starts and Seeds

**Abundant Life Seed Foundation**
P.O. Box 772
Port Townsend, WA 98368

**Elixir Farm**
General Delivery
Brixey, MO 65618

**Fungi Perfecti**
P.O. 7634
Olympia, WA 98507

**Gardens of the Blue Ridge**
P.O. Box 10
Pineola, NC 28862

**Logee's Greenhouses**
141 North Street, Dept. IP
Danielson, CT 06239

**Missouri Wildflowers Nursery**
9814 Pleasant Hill Road
Jefferson City, MO 65109

**Native Gardens**
5737 Fisher Lane
Greenback, TN 37742

**Nature's Cathedral**
1995 78th Street
Blairstown, IA 52209

**Nichols' Garden Nursery**
1190 North Pacific Highway
Albany, OR 97321

**Prairie Moon Nursery**
P.O. Box 306
Westfield, WI 53964

**Seeds of Change**
P.O. Box 15700
Sante Fe, NM 87506

**Taylor's Herb Gardens**
1535 Lone Oak Road
Vista, CA 92084

**Thompson and Morgan, Inc.**
P.O. Box 1308
Jackson, NJ 08527

**Woodlanders, Inc.**
1128 Colleton Avenue
Aiken, SC 29801

## Publications

**American Herb Association Newsletter**
Kathi Keville
P.O. Box 1673
Nevada City, CA 95959
*Twenty-page newsletter that covers the latest studies, books, videos, CDs, web sites, news releases, and legal concerns about medicinal herbs.*

**HerbalGram**
Mark Blumenthal, Editor
P.O. Box 201660
Austin, TX 78720-1660
*Magazine that focuses on medicinal herbs.*

**The Herb Companion**
Linda Ligon, Editor
201 East Fourth Street
Loveland, CO 80537
*Glossy newsstand magazine that covers growing and using herbs.*

**Herb Growing and Marketing Network**
The Herbal Connection
P.O. Box 245
Silver Springs, PA 17575
*Publishes a 36-page networking newsletter and the* Herbal Green Pages, *a list of more than 3,000 herb resources.*

**The Herb Quarterly**
Linda Sparrowe, Editor
P.O. Box 689
San Anselmo, CA 94960
*Magazine on using herbs in crafts, cooking, and in medicines.*

**Herbs and Health**
Jan Knight, Editor
201 East Fourth Street
Loveland, CO 80537
*Glossy newsstand magazine that covers the use of medicinal herbs.*

**Potpourri from Herbal Acres**
Phyllis V. Shaudy, Editor
Pine Row Publications, Box 42A
Washington Crossing, PA 18977
*Twenty-page newsletter on herbal crafts.*

## Education Programs and Retailers

The AHA Directory of Herb Education lists herb schools, classes, and correspondence courses in North America. Updated every other year: $3.50 post paid to AHA, P.O. Box 1673, Nevada City, CA, 95959.

The AHA Directory of Herb Mail Order Sources lists products sold by mail. Updated every other year: $4 post paid to previous address.

## Associations

**American Association of Naturopathic Physicians**
2366 Eastlake Avenue East
Suite 322
Seattle, WA 98102
*Professional organization which offers doctor referrals and lists of authorities in botanical medicine.*

**American Botanical Council**
P.O. Box 201660
Austin, TX 78720-1660
*Publishes HerbalGram and sponsors expeditions to rain forests.*

**American Herbalist Guild**
Box 1683
Soquel, CA 95073
*Professional organization for medical herbalists and students that offers a newsletter and annual herb seminar.*

**American Herb Association (AHA)**
P.O. Box 1673
Nevada City, CA 95959
*Herbalist organization; it offers directories and a newsletter.*

**Herb Research Foundation**
1007 Pearl Street, Suite 200
Boulder, CO 80302
*Dispenses information about medicinal herbs.*